◆ All New Edition ◆

Englefield & Arnold Publishing

The All New

Passing

The Ohio Ninth Grade Proficiency Test

◆

**Test-Taking and Problem Solving Skills Specifically
Designed to Help You Pass The Ohio Ninth Grade Proficiency Test**

◆

Learn Strategies and Techniques Including:

- MASTERING THE OHIO LEARNING OUTCOMES
- HOW TO REDUCE TEST ANXIETY AND INCREASE PERFORMANCE
- HOW TO SCORE MORE POINTS
- TEST-TAKING AND PROBLEM-SOLVING SKILLS
- PRACTICE ON SIMULATED PROFICIENCY TEST ITEMS

Written by:
Kevin D. Arnold, Ph.D
Charlie Doyle-Warren, Ph.D.
Rosemary A. Garmann
Susan Hennessy
Deborah Tong

Illustrations by:
Cindy Kerr

Graphic Designs by:
Cindi Englefield Arnold

Passing The Ohio Ninth Grade Proficiency Test

Published by:
Englefield and Arnold, Inc., P.O. Box 341348, 6344 Nicholas Drive, Columbus, Ohio 43234-1348
Printed by: McNaughton & Gunn, Inc.

03 02   20 19 18 17 16 15 14

ISBN 1-884183-06-9

Distributed in the United States by Englefield and Arnold, Inc.
and Partners Distributing Company

For sales inquiries and special prices for bulk quantities, write to the address above or call Englefield and Arnold Publishing at (614) 764-1211 or 877-PASSING (727-7464) toll free. Our email address is eapub@eapublishing.com. You may also place your order from our web page: www.eapublishing.com

Englefield & Arnold Publishing

Specializing In Proficiency Test Preparation Materials

Acknowledgments

E & A Publishing acknowledges the following people for their efforts in making this material available for Ohio's students, teachers, and parents.

Layout and Editing Assistant: **Judi L. Jemson**   Proofreading and Editing: **Angela Mesarchik**

And, Vanessa Hetrick, Johnathon Feczko, The students of St. Michaels, Sister Judith Maver, Norbert Garmann, Carrisa Lipaj, Lauren Lipaj, Michael Lipaj, F.W. Englefield, III, and Michael Jokerst.

Kevin D. Arnold, Ph.D. is a graduate of Galion (Ohio) High School, Grace College (Indiana, B.S.), and The Ohio State University (M.A., Ph.D.). He earned his doctorate in psychology in 1983, and served as a faculty member, researcher, and administrator in The Ohio State University's College of Education until the early 1990s, when he went into private practice. He earned his psychology license in 1991, completing a two year post-doctoral training experience under the wise supervision and mentoring of Dr. Thomas M. Stephens. Dr. Arnold has since received a basic and two advanced certificates in Cognitive-Behavioral Therapy, one under the supervision of Mark Gilson, Ph.D., another under the supervision of Arthur Freeman, Ed.D., and the third under the supervision of Jeffrey Young, Ph.D. In 1995, he helped to form the Center for Cognitive and Behavioral Therapy of Greater Columbus and North Central Ohio (Mt. Vernon), serving as the Center's Director. He presently lives in southern Delaware County with his wife and three stepchildren. Dr. Arnold is the contributing writer of the Test-taking Strategies and Test Anxiety chapters of this book.

Charlie Doyle-Warren is an experienced teacher, writer, curriculum developer and assessment specialist. He has a Masters in Taxonomy and Evolutionary Biology from State University of New York. His Doctorate is in Science Education (Adolescent Education, and Minority Education) from The Ohio State University. He has taught Science for ten years in upstate New York in grades 4 ,5, 6, 7, 8, 10, and 12, He worked with the ERIC Clearinghouse for Science, Mathematics, and Environmental Education where he authored more than 5000 abstracts, syntheses, and documents. Charlie was a main author on the Ohio Science Model, and is a national reviewer of curriculum and curriculum frameworks. He has assisted in dozens of local curriculum guides and courses of study. Charlie guided the content articulation for the Ohio Science proficiency test. He was author of Scholastic Science Place Assessment Collection. Charlie is now the Coordinator of Science, Mathematics and Technology for the Forest Hills Local Schools in the Cincinnati area. Charlie Doyle-Warren is the contributing writer for the Science chapter of this book.

Deborah Tong is a free-lance writer and editor. She has taught and tutored both English and Writing at the middle and upper school levels. Her background in education and writing includes experience as a teacher, museum education coordinator, copywriter, and published author. Her honors and awards include an Educational Press Award for a youth magazine article. Deborah graduated from Middlebury College, and has lived in New England, California, North Carolina, and Ohio. Deborah lives in Gahanna with her husband, Kyle, and their two children.

Kyle Tong Majored in History at Bowdoin College, and received his M.Ed. from Springfield College. Kyle has taught history at the middle and upper school levels for fourteen years. He has taught a wide variety of History classes, including American, European, Chinese, Japanese, and South African History, as well as Comparative Religion, Comparative Government, and United States Government and Politics. Kyle enjoys traveling, and has used his travel experiences to develop new class materials. He is currently the Curriculum Coordinator, a History teacher, and Varsity Soccer coach at The Columbus Academy. He lives in Gahanna with his wife and two children.

Acknowledgments

Susan Hennessy lives in Canton, Ohio with her husband, Daniel; her three children Kimberly, 20, Colleen, 18, and Kathleen, 12, and their tri-colored collie. Her career began in Pittsburgh teaching seventh, ninth, and tenth grade English and twelfth grade Creative Writing. While raising a family, her substitute teaching provided the opportunity to experience all grade levels from preschool through high school. Since 1991, Susan has been teaching seventh and eighth grade English and literature at St. Michael School in Canton. She also coaches St. Michael's Power of the Pen teams which compete in writing competitions. Susan is a graduate of St. Francis College, Loretto, PA. She has earned graduate credits from Penn State University, Ashland University, and Drake University just to name a few--being a teacher means continuously learning. When summer arrives, she and her husband can be found fast walking around the neighborhood, playing a round of golf, or concentrating on a hand of bridge. All other time is spent cheering her own children or students toward success. Susan is the contributing writer of the Writing chapter of this book.

Rosemary Garmann is a graduate of Marian College (B.A.) and University of Notre Dame (M.S. in Mathematics). She also has completed postgraduate study in mathematics and education at the University of Cincinnati, Xavier University, University of Akron, and Butler University. She is currently a mathematics consultant at the Hamilton County Educational Service Center. Formerly, she was a mathematics supervisor, building administrator, and mathematics teacher in Cincinnati City Schools; as well as classroom teacher at the elementary and middle school levels outside the Cincinnati area. Rosemary resides in west Cincinnati with her husband, daughter, and two miniature poodles. Her hobbies include: playing piano, musical performances, and flower gardening. Rosemary is the contributing writer of the Mathematics chapter of this book.

About the Illustrator:

Cindy Kerr was born and raised in America's Midwest. She attended Wilmington College. She graduated from The Ohio State University with a Bachelor of Arts degree in Education in 1975. She has taught art to elementary school children and travelled America with her husband's medical training. She is the program coordinator for The Arts Castle, of the Delaware County Cultural Arts Center. She is trying to remain sane and creative while raising five children and a dog in Powell, near Columbus, Ohio. Cindy's talent is evident with her beautiful illustrations found throughout this book.

About the Graphic Designer:

Cindi Englefield Arnold lives north of Columbus, Ohio with her husband and three children. She has a B.S. degree in Business Administration with a Marketing major from The Ohio State University. She has received a certificate from The University of Chicago for the completion of The Business of Publishing's intensive seminar. She is also a member of the Publishers Marketing Association. Her love of art when combined with the technology of computers has allowed her hands on training into the business of publishing and the art of graphic design. Cindi's line graphics are found throughout this book.

Table of Contents

Table of Contents

Test-Taking Strategies

Ninth Grade Proficiency Test: Introduction to Test-Taking Strategies

Introduction

The Ohio Ninth Grade Proficiency Test has made most eighth and ninth grade students nervous. Many of you probably think that the Proficiency Test measures how brilliant you are. This is simply not true. There are plenty of students who aren't straight A students but who pass anyway. The Proficiency Test does not tell you if you are an OK person. So, take it easy and stay calm. Let the test-taking tips in this book, along with the information in the chapters that follow, show you how to dramatically improve your chances of passing. Use what is in this book, pass the test, and finish high school with a smile on your face.

About the Strategies to "Show What You Know"

The test-taking and problem-solving strategies that are taught in this book are designed specifically to deal with the Ohio Ninth Grade Proficiency Test. The book uses an outline of information based on the Ohio Department of Education's "learning outcomes." The Ninth Grade Proficiency Test is based on those learning outcomes. Professionals who are experts on creating and taking tests designed the strategies you will be taught in this book. Specially selected teachers and other professionals wrote the chapters on Mathematics, Science, Citizenship, Reading, and Writing. This team of writers were able to use their unique knowledge to help you breakdown the proficiency test questions, and to understand the test questions as if you too were an expert on the Ninth Grade Proficiency Test. (You should feel like one when you are finished with this book!)

Our test taking skills will show you how to:
1. figure out the answers that look right, **but are wrong**,
2. use all the knowledge you have to be the best guesser you can be, if you have to guess.
3. be confident and calm when you take the test so you can do the best you can do.

It is very important to understand that taking a test is something you learn to do. When you were in elementary school, the tests you took in first and second grade were pretty simple. One of the reasons you took any kind of tests when you were that young was to teach you how to take a test. It's like learning the words to a new song on a CD. First you practice a few times, and after you sing it over and over, you can remember the words without even thinking about them. You learn how to sing the song.

Taking the proficiency test is just like learning that song, but you haven't really practiced very much on any proficiency tests. Of course, you probably had a chance to take the practice test for the State, and maybe you took the 4th or 6th Grade Proficiency Test. That would mean that you practiced taking proficiency tests a couple of times. You just haven't had enough chances to practice the skills in taking a proficiency test yet. This book will not only teach you the content of the learning outcomes, one by one; but it will also teach you the skills of taking a proficiency test.

We teach you those test taking skills first by going over them so that you understand what they are. Then we help you to learn all the important information that is a part of the learning outcomes. Finally, we teach you how to apply the information on practice test questions that are very much like the ones you'll see on the proficiency test. When you solve these practice questions, we show you how to use the test taking skills to apply what you know. We teach you how to get the most credit for your knowledge. We teach you to use the proficiency test as an opportunity to "SHOW WHAT YOU KNOW."

To learn how to take a Proficiency Test, you must think like a Proficiency Test author. The people who wrote the questions on the Proficiency Test had to follow certain rules so that their questions were picked for the test. Of course, they had to write questions that were fair, so the test isn't too hard. But they also wrote questions so that some of the answers will look right when they are really wrong. These "wrong" answers are called distracters, because they catch your attention and distract you from using all your knowledge to solve the problem in the question. So you must think like a test question writer, and try to imagine what kinds of distracter answers you would write. When you think like that, you can spot the distracters, and then you won't pick them so often, thus improving your score.

Another important thing to remember is that this book is not going to replace what you learned in school. The schools have done a good job in teaching you Science, Mathematics, Reading, Citizenship, and Writing. This book goes over the information that you already learned in school, and shows you which information is included in the learning outcomes. The book, in the next chapter, also teaches you how to calm down and be more confident on the Proficiency Test. Most importantly, though, is what this book teaches you about taking tests. There are three very important ingredients to passing a test--KNOWLEDGE, TEST-TAKING SKILLS, and CONFIDENCE (see below), and this book tries to teach you all three, but especially test-taking skills.

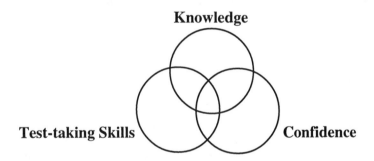

We want you to learn to use you knowledge to find wrong answers and rule them out. That helps you to find the right answers.

We want you to learn how to analyze the questions so that you figure out the problem that the writers of the Proficiency Test are asking you to solve.

We want you to get credit for what you do know even if you don't know the right answer to a question. That probably sounds a little strange, but take a moment to think about it. If you know that some of the answers can't be right, then you rule those out. If you have only one or two answers left, you have a pretty good chance of getting the question right, EVEN IF YOU DON'T KNOW THE INFORMATION ABOUT THE RIGHT ANSWER. So you get credit for that part of your knowledge that relates to the wrong answers

We want you to guess wisely. If you read a question and don't know the information you should, go over the answers to see if you know something about them. Rule out some of the answers, and when you have two or three left, you can guess wisely--use the power of knowing that you have a better chance of getting the question right now than before. NEVER LEAVE A QUESTION BLANK--GUESS WISELY .

Get ready to learn test taking skills. As the song says, "Yawl ready for this?"

Ruling Out Wrong Answers

Finding out which answer is right often is a process of deciding which answers are wrong. By ruling out some answers you can see which one is right. Below is an example.

You are an expert Ohio historian. No? Try this question.

Exercise:

Which U.S. Senator from Ohio was an astronaut in the 1960s?
Don't know? Try it as a multiple choice problem.

1. Which U.S. Senator was once an astronaut in the 1960s?

    A. Ronald Reagan
    B. John Glenn
    C. John Kasich
    D. Al Gore

Analysis:
You know it's not Al Gore, he's our Vice-President. So rule out answer choice "D". It can't be John Kasich, since you've heard about him being called a representative, and he's too young looking from the newspaper to have been an astronaut over 30 years ago. Rule out "C". What about Ronald Reagan? No, he was president, and an actor that you've seen in old movies. Rule out "A". It must be John Glenn.

Try another.

2. What Ohio town is famous for being in the center of the state?

    A. Toledo
    B. Cleveland
    C. Centerburg
    D. Cincinnati

Analysis:
Rule out the wrong answers. Which one do you pick? You see, even if you don't know the right answer, you know that Toledo is almost in Michigan, Cleveland is on Lake Erie, and Cincinnati is down south. It can only be "C".

You can see that by knowing something about the wrong answers, you get the question right. You may think that guessing is wrong to do. IT'S NOT. Getting a question wrong because you didn't use all that you know is wrong. You're not any worse off if you guess, so rule out wrong answers and go ahead and go for it--guess.

Always answer every question--even if you guess!
You have 1 out of 4 odds of getting a question right, even if you don't rule out any answers. That means that for every four questions you guess, after enough questions, you should get one question right for every four you guess on. Now imagine that you rule out one of the answers. That makes your chances 1 out of 3. If you rule out two answers, then the odds are 1 out of 2. Each time you rule out an answer and then go ahead and guess, you keep increasing the odds that you will get more and more of the questions right, even if you guess.

You are allowed to write on the test booklet. It's the only scrap paper you'll get. So don't try to remember which answers you've ruled out. Instead, draw a line through the answers you rule out. Just cross them out.

Finding Distracters
You should know that the average student who doesn't know much about test-taking skills will be misled pretty often by distracters. If you knew you could count on your friend, Bob Average, to pick the distracter most of the time, you'd be able to know not to pick his answers, since you would get them wrong too.

You see, some of the questions on the test are really "hard." Not hard because the questions ask about little known things, but hard because most students get them wrong. Sometimes it's possible that more kids miss a question than they would if they just guessed. Why? Because on some questions, the wrong answers are written to <u>look</u> right. You get tricked into picking them. Your job is to spot these distracters and avoid picking them. This doesn't mean that every answer that looks right is wrong! It means that you should be careful about just picking answers on hard problems without thinking through the answers first.

Don't waste your energy!
You get plenty of time on this test. Don't rush yourself and spend all your energy trying to race the other students. Also, don't get stuck in a rut on one question, going over it again and again. Just rule out the wrong answers and go on. Otherwise you'll waste important strength.

Don't trust yourself to not make a simple mistake like marking the wrong answer on the answer sheet. Make a big mark on the test booklet next to the answer you pick, put a finger on it, look over to the answer sheet and find that letter, then put your pencil in the circle for that answer. Be that careful. There is no sense in missing any question because you weren't careful.

Additional Information

➠ You will have a maximum of 2 1/2 hours to complete each section of the test.

➠ The State Department of Education found during the field testing of the Ninth Grade Proficiency Test that students performed poorly on questions from certain learning outcomes. We have marked these learning outcomes with a "✍". Pay very close attention to those learning outcomes. The field test results showed other learning outcomes that student performance was very high. We marked these learning outcomes with a "✓." Make sure that you review these too. These questions should be where you can pick up "easy" points on the test.

➠ Use a number "2" lead pencil. Don't use mechanical pencils on this test. If you have a pencil that says "1996 Olympics," that's great but don't use the pencil on the proficiency test. It might not be a number "2". If it isn't and you miss a question because the machine that read your answer sheet could make out your mark because of your pencil, then you've missed a question that you really got right. That's bad. JUST SAY NO TO PENCILS THAT DON'T SAY NUMBER "2."

Key:
> ✍ = Student performance was LOW during field testing.
> ✓ = Student performance was HIGH during field testing.

Analyzing the questions

You should read the whole question. Often you will want to read through the question quickly, rushing to the answers to find the correct one. Sometimes you will want to read part of a question because it is underlined or set off from the rest of the question. The Proficiency Test will probably give you some questions where formulas are set up in the middle of questions, and you may want to go to the formula and try to solve it for the correct answer.

✓ Do not rush through the question. Read all of it.

Reason 1:
Reading the whole question will slow you down and keep you from rushing through the test because your fear has increased.

Reason 2:
Reading the whole question gives you valuable information that you may need to answer the question correctly.

For example, try this problem:

3. Michael is a fourteen year old boy who lives in Lewis Center, Ohio. He likes to fish, and once caught a seven pound catfish in the Ohio River. He also caught a three pound bass in Alum Creek Reservoir, and a three pound sheephead in Lake Erie. His largest fish was a yellow fin tuna in Florida. How old is Michael?

If you're like most people, you started thinking about the ever-changing size of fish that Michael had caught, believing that the question had to do with the size of the fish. If you didn't read the whole problem you'd be caught by surprise when you looked at the answers. You'd be expecting answers about the pounds of fish, when the answers were in "years since Michael had been born." If you were to ignore all of the unnecessary information, your job would have been a lot simpler. In fact, take a look at the problem if we cross out what we don't need to know to solve the problem:

3. Michael is a fourteen year old ~~boy who lives in Lewis Center, Ohio. He likes to fish, and once caught a seven pound catfish in the Ohio River. He also caught a three pound bass in Alum Creek Reservoir, and a three pound sheephead in Lake Erie. His largest fish was a yellow fin tuna in Florida.~~ How old is Michael?

The answer's really obvious now isn't it? Of course this example's a little too easy to be real. But it shows that when you focus on the REAL QUESTION, the answer comes much easier.

Another example:

4. Carissa talks 22 minutes on the phone with Cortney and twice as long with Adrian, both right after school. She talks 30 minutes with Rachel but only after 9:00 p.m. She also uses the phone line one hour per day to be on the Internet, unless she only reads her e-mail. Then she is on the Internet only 45 minutes. The Internet costs $20 per month without any hourly charges.

    How long does Carissa talk after 9:00 p.m.?

    Here are your answer choices:

    A. 22 minutes
    B. 30 minutes
    C. 44 minutes
    D. 45 minutes

If you rush through the problem you won't be sure what information to use and you will not be able to answer the question. Instead, you'll probably get frustrated, decide it is a trick question, and guess.

Instead of this becoming so stressed and start telling yourself that the test is trying to trick you, read the whole question aloud.

"Carissa talks 22 minutes on the phone with Cortney and twice as long with Adrian, both right after school. She talks 30 minutes with Rachel but only after 9:00 p.m. She also uses the phone line one hour per day to be on the Internet, unless she only reads her e-mail. Then she is on the Internet only 45 minutes. The Internet costs $20 per month without any hourly charges. "

Now, that took less than 30 seconds. You have plenty of time on the real test to read each question. And, you now know that the amount of time Carissa is on the phone after 9:00 p.m. is what is needed to solve the problem. You also know that the question wants to know the amount of time she talks, not is on-line on the Internet.

Finding the Real Question.
Now that you have read the whole question, you can figure out what the Proficiency Test is really asking. We call that the Real Question! Figuring out the Real Question is much like other types of problem solving methods you use every day. Think of the following situation.

> Lauren and Nick have been fighting lately, and you just found out they broke up. You've wanted to date Nick for about one year. Later, Tom, Nick's friend, asks you if you are going to the movie on Friday, just happening to mention that Nick and he are going. You say yes, and Tom asks if you're going to the 7:30 showing of the movie.

If this were the situation, you might think, "It sounds like the Real Question isn't "Am I going to the 7:30 showing,' but the Real Question is, "Do you want to meet Nick at the movies and maybe start going out with him?" You have just figured out a Real Question.

Try this technique out on the sample question.

> 5. You receive an allowance of $5.00 per week. If you do the laundry, you earn an extra $5.00 per week. If you cut the grass, you get and extra $3.00 per week. When you took care of your younger brother after school, you earned $12.00 for four hours of baby-sitting. Last week you baby-sat four hours. How much can you earn extra if you cut the grass and baby-sit two hours next week?

What is the Real Question here? Let's work through the steps together.

Step 1: Cross out unimportant words.
In the real-life example of Lauren and Nick, was it <u>really</u> all that important that Tom was Nick's friend? No. What was important was that Tom, Nick's friend, wanted to know if you were going to the same show as him, and Tom acted like Nick was hoping that you'd be there. Just like real life, there are words in the questions on the Proficiency Test that aren't important. Cross them out with your pencil (you are permitted to mark on the test booklets). Lets try crossing out unimportant information in this example.

> 5. ~~You receive an allowance of $5.00 per week. If you do the laundry, you earn an extra $5.00 per week~~. If you cut the grass, you get and extra $3.00 per week. ~~When you took care of your younger brother after school,~~ you earned $12.00 for four hours of baby-sitting. ~~Last week you baby-sat four hours.~~ How much can you earn extra if you cut the grass and baby-sit two hours next week?

The only important facts are CUT GRASS = $3.00, Baby-sit = $3.00 per hour ($12 ÷ 4 hr = $3 per hour), TOTAL BABY-SITTING TIME = 2 HOURS.

Step 2: The Real Question
The Real Question can be restated like this: "What is ($3.00 X 2) + 3.00?"

There are two important things to remember. First, it is likely that many of the questions will have more words in them than those that are relevant to the Real Question. You will need to cross out these words so they don't distract you. Second, there are no trick questions on the test. Sure, there are some hard questions, but if you use the E & A techniques, answer the Real Question, and have at least some knowledge about the answer, you should do just fine.

Analyzing the Answers

Why are all those answers there on a multiple choice test? There is a reason. Many of the test answers on the Proficiency Test are there because they represent answers that are common mistakes easily made by you when calculating an answer. These answers look right because they were so easy to come to, but they are really wrong. Let's consider the sample item again.

5. You receive an allowance of $5.00 per week. If you do the laundry, you earn an extra $5.00 per week. If you cut the grass, you get and extra $3.00 per week. When you took care of your younger brother after school, you earned $12.00 for four hours of baby-sitting. Last week you baby-sat four hours. How much can you earn extra if you cut the grass and baby-sit two hours next week?

    A. $8.00
    B. $9.00
    C. $15.00
    D. $27.00

Analysis:
Answer D is the answer you would get if you tried to solve the problem and didn't read the whole question carefully. You might confuse the amount you earned for 4 hours as the amount you earned per hour. If you did make that mistake, you would have multiplied 2 times 12, arriving at 24. Then adding 24 to 3 would have produced 27, which is answer D. The wrong answers are often there because they represent easy to make mistakes.

It is comforting to see the answer you came up with printed on the page. You immediately think: It must be right, my answer's there on the page. WRONG! Many of the wrong answers on the Proficiency Test are selected so that if you make a common mistake you'll get an answer that will be on the page. The lesson to learn is to use the techniques found in this books and something called rating the answers.

Rating the Answers.

Step 1: Read <u>all</u> the answers.

Step 2: Rate each one with a +, /, or −.

Sometimes one answer can be better than the other answers, but all might seem a little bit right. This can really happen when the questions are about a reading passage or an historical document. To use the rating system, mark a "+" by answer choices that your pretty sure are correct; put a "/" by answers you're not sure about; and put a "-" by answer choices you know are wrong. Be sure to decide why you rated some answers low before answering the question. If you have only one "+" answer, mark that one. If you have more than one "+" answer, re-think what you've done because two answers can't be right, then guess which is best, mark it, and move on to the next question. Let's try rating the answers.

5. You receive an allowance of $5.00 per week. If you do the laundry, you earn an extra $5.00 per week. If you cut the grass, you get and extra $3.00 per week. When you took care of your younger brother after school, you earned $12.00 for four hours of baby-sitting. Last week you baby-sat four hours. How much can you earn extra if you cut the grass and baby-sit two hours next week?

− A. $8.00   (No--this is the sum of either the allowance or the laundry plus cutting the grass).

+ B. $9.00   (Yes--This is the sum of three 9s, one for cutting the grass and two for each of the two hours of baby-sitting).

− C. $15.00   (No--This is the sum of what you would get for 4 hours of baby-sitting plus cutting the grass).

− D. $27.00   (No--This is the sum of 2 times $12 plus $3.00 for cutting the grass).

Step 3: Put your finger on the answer you select as correct.
When you go to mark the answer, be sure you know that the answer you chose from the test booklet is the one you are marking on your answer sheet. This process has several steps. You select the answer, you put a mark next to it, you find the corresponding "bubble" on the answer sheet, and then you mark the answer.

Step 4: Be sure that the question number on the test booklet is the same as the one on the answer sheet when you make your mark. There are horror stories of people, including those with years of training like lawyers or doctors, getting to the last question on a test and realizing that they are answering question number 200, but the answer blank is 199. Avoid this frightening experience and check the question number with the answer sheet EACH TIME YOU MARK AN ANSWER. It may save you time and stress if you mark your answers in the margin of the test booklet, then transfer them over to your bubble sheet once you've reached the end of a page.

A Final Tip on Questions and Answers.

If you're really dedicated, you can learn to understand test questions and answers more fully by making up some questions and answers yourself. Use the information on the different topics we cover in the different sections of this book. Create some of your own questions, making sure to add "extra" words to some of the stories in the questions. Then make up answers that are there because they are the answers you would get if you made easy to make mistakes. For example, if you make up a question for reading, and the topic is knowing what a word means from its context, then make some of the answers other meanings for the word, but ones that are not consistent with the context. Each time you write up the answers, write down why the wrong answers are wrong, and why the right answer is correct. Then later, say in a couple of days, answer several of these questions. Read all the answers, and if you get the wrong answer, be sure to understand the common or easy-to-make mistake that you made. This method is a great study tool, helps you understand how to work with the questions, and will reduce your fear of the test. If you want to use flashcards, "Pass In A Flash" are 100 flashcards already made up, with all the questions set-up just like the proficiency test. On the back are the explanations of each answer, including why the wrong answers are wrong and how you may have picked each wrong answer. There is an order form in the back of this book of all the proficiency test preparation materials.

Test Anxiety

Reduce Your Fear of Taking the Test

Understanding Test Fear

What is fear?

Fear of anything, the proficiency test included, is a reaction to a situation or event that we *believe* to be dangerous to us. Usually, you will experience fear (or anxiety) when you 1) come into contact with situations you find dangerous and 2) can not avoid these situations and then must deal with them. For example, if you must go to school and present a paper in class, and you believe you will do a bad job, you will probably start to feel fearful each time you think about it or are reminded of it. So, if you're scared that you won't do well on a class presentation, you will be frightened until you complete the paper and begin to believe you are prepared to get up in front of the class. But even then, you will still feel a little scared when you're waiting to give the speech. This is NORMAL. Everybody, including well trained professional speakers, feel a little scared sometimes before they speak.

You usually know you are afraid if your body feels scared. Sometimes you start to think about being scared before your body tells you you're afraid, but in the end, it is almost always your body that reacts to whatever is frightening you. According to psychologists, fear is usually felt in our bodies as increased heart beating (your heart "pounds"), more rapid breathing, sweating, tightened muscles, and dry mouth. Sometimes you pace the floor, can't sleep, get diarrhea, or go to the bathroom more than usual. Your body does this because it is programmed to get ready for any event that is threatening enough to scare you, in case you need to either run away or fight. Often, when you become aware of your body reacting this way, you begin to think about how scared you are, and it sometimes makes you even more frightened.

It is important to understand that this reaction is normal. It is to be expected if something frightens you. If you play football, you know that you must get "psyched" up for the game in such a way that your body is ready to go. If you have ever been faced with a mean dog or a fight, you can see how your body reacts and why it reacts this way.

Can a small amount of fear be good?
It is just as important to understand that your body reacts this way when your mind thinks something is threatening, even if the threat is not truly there. The idea of giving a speech in class may seem threatening, especially if you think that you'll get a bad grade or others will make fun of you. These ideas may or may not be true, but the way you believe will affect how your body reacts.

This is a good thing! Why, you ask? Because the same fear that makes us ready to run or fight is also the feeling that gets us motivated to do our best. When a basketball player gets ready to make the game's winning foul shot, he or she must have enough motivation to try and do his or her best, but not so much that he or she chokes (that is, he or she becomes distracted by the fear). So, thoughts turn to the basket, two deep breaths are taken, and concentration on the shot is used to turn the fear into something useful: motivation.

You can see that the Proficiency Test is an event that should cause some concern. Enough that you are motivated to study and prepare, but not so much that you "choke" before or during the test. If you feel a little scared, say to yourself "This is OK. It's normal. In fact, it's helpful." When you say this to yourself, you are thinking of the anxiety as normal and accepting it. It seems strange to some teenagers that accepting anxiety actually makes them less nervous, but for most students, that is exactly what happens.

Exercise:
Fill out the Test Anxiety Exercise Sheet #1.
➠ Practice thinking that being a little frightened is OK.
➠ List times when being a little scared got you "psyched" up.

Test Anxiety Exercise Sheet #1

List of Times When Being a Little Scared Got Me "Psyched Up"		
Describe Situations In Which You Became Scared	**How Scared You Were (Rate from 1 to 10)**	**How "Psyched" You Were (Rate from 1 to 10)**

What is Test Anxiety?

Test anxiety is a combination of at least three different things. First, you can feel fear in your body, so anxiety is physical. Second, you can see anxiety in what you do, so nervousness causes actions. Third, fear can be heard in the things you say to yourself, so anxiety causes certain thoughts.

How your body feels when you are anxious

Anxiety can be felt in your body in many different ways. Below is a description of some of the ways that different parts of your body feel when you become anxious.

heart	pounding, beating much harder that usual
breathing	very quick, sometimes hyperventilating, short of breath
muscles	very tense, feeling sore and achy
stomach	butterflies, upset, vomiting
mouth	becoming dry
vision	hard to focus, vision can be blurry
head	headaches, sometimes the feeling of a rubber band around forehead
hands, feet	numbness, tingling, shaking
throat	closes up, swallowing is hard
digestive system	constipation, diarrhea, urinating all the time

As you can see, your body has many different ways to react when you are too nervous. It reacts this way because of a very old part of our genetic makeup. When humans lived three thousand years ago, we had to be able to fight or run away from something if it was threatening to us. Our bodies reacted automatically so that we didn't end up dead by the time we thought about whatever was going on. Today, most people don't run into dangerous animals so there isn't much need for the automatic reactions of our bodies. Unfortunately, our bodies still react this way, even if the threat (like a proficiency test) isn't going to physically harm us. Your body react the same way to a threatening proficiency test as it does to something that attacks you. Unfortunately, the physical reactions don't do you much good on the proficiency test—in fact, you can be hurt by these reactions if you don't calm yourself back down, because they can get in the way of your studying and your ability to think clearly on the test.

What you do when you're anxious

When you learn to be afraid of tests, you begin to act in fairly predictable ways. You will usually try to avoid the thing that makes you nervous. You'll see yourself delaying your study time, watching TV, or making phone calls. When the test time arrives, you might get up late, be late for school, or, if it is really bad, you'll skip school. You do something called procrastination, which is putting things off because they make you nervous. If you are an "avoider," you are letting the anxiety make you do things that will hurt your performance on the proficiency test.

How you think when you're anxious

When students become anxious about tests, they begin to have thoughts that can make them even more anxious. These thoughts can appear very rapidly, seeming to you as if they are automatic ideas that come to you whether you want them to or not. Often times these thoughts feel so real that you forget that they are just ideas, and you begin to believe that your thoughts are actually true. When that happens, you begin to react emotionally to the thoughts. That is how ideas can lead to anxiety.

In the last 15 years, psychologists have learned much about these thoughts. For example, there are certain types of thoughts that seem to affect how we feel. Below is a list of the types of thoughts that can often lead to anxiety. When you find yourself feeling anxious about the proficiency test, check out your thinking to see if you having any of these kinds of thoughts.

Black and white thinking—Thoughts that describe everything as all bad or all good.

Mind reading—Thinking you know what other people think about you.

Catastrophizing—Predicting a terrible thing will happen, making things so bad in the future that they are beyond repair.

Jumping to conclusions—Drawing a conclusion when you don't really have enough information to reach the conclusion.

Future predicting—Deciding you know what will happen next without any good reason to make the prediction.

Discounting—Deciding that things are not important when they really are important.

Should statements—Second guessing yourself by thinking that you "shoulda" done something else, and then only focusing on what you wish you had done instead of what you will do differently now.

Beating Anxiety on The Proficiency Test

The remainder of this chapter will help you handle your anxiety by giving you ways to deal with your body's reactions, your fearful actions, and your automatic thoughts. Be sure that you do the exercises, all of them. Each exercise is designed to help you learn how to handle anxiety from the Proficiency Test.

Keeping Your Body From Fighting Against You

When your body becomes anxious while you are studying for the Proficiency Test, or when you are actually taking it, you need to relax it. There are two ways to do this: learning to calm down the body itself, and stopping yourself from paying too much attention to your body. Let's work on calming the body down first.

Relaxing your body

You are about to learn how to relax your body in three ways: focused breathing, focused attention, and muscle relaxation. Even though all three are useful, you may find that one of them is better for you than the others. If so, then use that method to relax and don't waste your time on the other ones. The most important thing about relaxing is that it works for you, and **you practice it every day.**

First, you will learn how to focus on your breathing. You might remember that one of the things that happens when your body reacts to anxiety is that you breath too rapidly. We will use your breathing to control the anxiety. Read these instructions, and then follow them. First, sit back in a soft chair, put a pillow behind your head to support your neck, and then close your eyes. While your eyes are closed, begin to breath slowly and in a steady rhythm. Now begin to pay attention to your breath as it comes in, noticing how cool it feels inside your nostrils. Notice too, how the breath is warm as it passes out. Say to yourself, "Cool air in, warm air out, RELAX." Do that for about two minutes. Once that is done, begin to focus on the feeling of your chest expanding when you breath in, and contracting when you breath out. Say to yourself, "Expand, contract, RELAX." Do that for about two minutes. Once you're done, rate yourself on Test Anxiety Exercise Sheet #2 to describe how relaxed you became from the focussed breathing.

Second, you will learn how to focus your attention. Sit back in your chair, with the pillow to support your neck. Now, begin to concentrate as much as you can on something. Some people use images of the beach or a cool pond. Other people say the same word over and over again, or they recite poetry. Yet others work out complex problems such as reciting the multiplication tables to themselves. Whatever it is that you use, make sure that the idea helps you to concentrate as much as you can. Do the concentration exercise for about ten minutes, then rate yourself on Test Anxiety Exercise Sheet #2 to describe how relaxed you became from focusing your attention.

Third, you will learn how to relax your muscles. Sit back in your chair with your neck supported. Now begin to focus on the following muscles, one at a time, for about 30 seconds each, and keep saying to yourself the word RELAX. While you focus on each muscle area, allow the tension in those muscles to drain out, and allow the muscles to become heavy and warm. They should feel like they are drooping. Try this order: Feet, Lower Legs, Upper Legs, Stomach, Chest, Lower Back, Upper Back, Shoulders, Upper Arms, Lower Arms, Hands, Neck, Jaw, Face Muscles, Eyes, Forehead. As with the other exercises, rate yourself on Test Anxiety Exercise Sheet #2 to describe how relaxed you became from your attempts to relax your muscles.

Finally, once you've learned to relax, begin your relaxation exercises by taking a deep breath, hold it for five to ten seconds, say to yourself RELAX, and then let yourself relax your body. This will create a "signal breath," or a cue to help your body relax later. When you are taking the proficiency test, you may not be able to do the focused breathing, the focused attention, or the muscle relaxation, so it is important to have a cue to bring on some relaxation. By using a "signal breath," you are teaching your body to relax in response to the breath. You can use the "signal breath" during the test if you find your body becoming anxious. Now practice using a signal breath and record your exercises just as you did with the other three methods for relaxing on Test Anxiety Exercise Sheet #2. Most importantly, practice your relaxation exercises every day.

Paying less attention to your body
Some students have developed a keen sense of what their body is doing from one minute to the next. When they become anxious, they begin to notice the early signs of a headache, of diarrhea, or of soreness in their muscles. By paying so much attention to their bodies, they are distracted from studying for the proficiency test. They also begin to get nervous about what their bodies are doing, and then they get even more anxious from over attending to their bodies. If you find that you are one of those who pays so much attention to his/her body that you become anxious because you worry about what your body might do, then you may want to learn how to distract your attention. First, try shifting your attention to something more important, like the material in the Math chapter of this book. If that doesn't work, then try something called Thought Stopping. When you notice that you are paying too much attention to your body, then smack a book or your hand on a table (not too hard, you wouldn't want to break the table or you hand) and say, at the same time, STOP. The loud noise and the word stop should interfere with your attention to your body. If it works, then practice just saying the word STOP out loud for a few times, and then say it just in your head. Using the word STOP in your head can usually help you to bring an end to the attention you are paying to your body. If that is not helpful, try the rubber band technique. Take a rubber band (a thin one) and lightly snap it on your wrist when you find yourself focused on your body's physical reactions to the proficiency test. Don't do it too hard, you don't want to leave welts. The physical sensation of the snapped rubber band will distract you. If it helps, practice this several times to begin to reduce the attention you pay to your tense neck or your upset stomach.

If you try these techniques and they produce the opposite effect (they make you more physically nervous), stop them and make an appointment with a psychologist. If you have a history of trying to hurt yourself, then you should not use the rubber band technique. If none of these strategies work at all and you feel you need to learn to control your body while you study for the proficiency test, then contact a local psychologist who does "Relaxation Therapy."

Test Anxiety Exercise Sheet #2

Relaxing Your Body	
Directions: Rate how relaxed you are after each exercise on a scale of 1 to 10. One is tense, 10 is extremely relaxed.	
Exercises: (date each time you do an exercise)	**Relaxation Rate (1 to 10)**
Focused Breathing:	
Date:_____	Rate:_____
Date:_____	Rate:_____
Date:_____	Rate:_____
Date:_____	Rate:_____
Date:_____	Rate:_____
Date:_____	Rate:_____
Focused Attention:	
Date:_____	Rate:_____
Date:_____	Rate:_____
Date:_____	Rate:_____
Date:_____	Rate:_____
Date:_____	Rate:_____
Date:_____	Rate:_____
Muscle Relaxation:	
Date:_____	Rate:_____
Date:_____	Rate:_____
Date:_____	Rate:_____
Date:_____	Rate:_____
Date:_____	Rate:_____
Date:_____	Rate:_____
Signal Breath:	
Date:_____	Rate:_____
Date:_____	Rate:_____
Date:_____	Rate:_____
Date:_____	Rate:_____
Date:_____	Rate:_____
Date:_____	Rate:_____

Controlling Your Anxious Actions

Avoidance

Sometimes acting scared is almost automatic. You don't even seem to think about the thing making you scared, it just seems to have a power of its own. You learned to be scared of tests, if you are frightened of them, just like you learned not to touch something hot. When you touched something hot, you learned that it really hurt. Some young children who were mildly burned by hot water will go through some very scary nights of taking baths before they learn that not all hot water is going to burn them. Before they learn that lesson, they get REALLY SCARED. It's the same with tests. Ever since you've been a student in school, the importance of tests has been very clear. For some of you, this is more true than for others. Some of you have had worse experiences with tests. Maybe your friends made fun of you for doing poorly, or maybe someone important to you always got mad at you when you didn't do as well as *they* thought you should. Perhaps you studied hard in a particular class (like science) and found that it didn't matter that you'd studied, you still didn't do well on the test. These experiences will teach you that tests are scary. It's not a lot different that the "hot water fear." So, just as you probably tried to stay away from the water in the tub after you were burned, you learned to avoid tests when you were "burned" by an exam or quiz.

One really effective way of learning not to be scared in situations like these is to repeatedly expose yourself to the frightening thing (in your case, the proficiency test), but a little bit at a time. Each time, make the little bit bigger, until you are facing the whole thing. Let's apply this idea to the proficiency test. The test has five parts: Reading, Writing, Math, Science, and Citizenship. Each part has some questions in it. The things you have to deal with when taking the test are 1) the questions and 2) the *actual* experience of taking the test. A great way to act less anxious is to practice taking test questions, a few at first, but eventually practicing whole sets of forty or fifty. It's a lot like immunization shots, you take a little of what is supposed to make you sick so your body will build up a defense to the germs.

Another way to reduce your fears is to get familiar with the actual experience of taking the proficiency test. Some of this is accomplished by practicing test questions, but there is another part: the test taking situation. You will be taking the proficiency test in the school room. If you study and practice the test questions in a similar room, you are exposed to surroundings that are much like the actual experience of taking the proficiency test. As the newness of this situation wears off, so will the fear that is associated with the novelty of taking a proficiency test.

Exercise:
On the next page fill out Test Anxiety Exercise Sheet #3.
➡ Develop an "immunization" plan for practicing the test questions.

Test Anxiety Exercise Sheet #3

Test Anxiety Immunization Program for The Proficiency Test Virus				

In the form below, design your own "immunization" plan for increasing your "psychological" immune system's defenses against the newly discovered Proficiency Test Virus. Be sure to follow this plan in order to have the best chance of not getting "sick" this Proficiency Test Flu Season. Indicate the number of practice items and the test they are from under the Shots column. Indicate the place where you'll be "immunized" and when, then initial that date when you've taken "the shots."

	Place	Date		Initials /verification
Shot #1			Test Area: _____ # of Items in "Shot": _____	
Shot #2			Test Area: _____ # of Items in "Shot": _____	
Shot #3			Test Area: _____ # of Items in "Shot": _____	
Shot #4			Test Area: _____ # of Items in "Shot": _____	
Shot #5			Test Area: _____ # of Items in "Shot": _____	
Shot #6			Test Area: _____ # of Items in "Shot": _____	
Shot #7			Test Area: _____ # of Items in "Shot": _____	

Getting technical for a minute.

It is sometimes good to know a few technical words that help explain why we get scared. Whenever we must perform, we get more scared if we are less capable. Taking the proficiency test is certainly a performance situation. The technical terms for this idea are mastery (what we know and how well we can do things) and anxiety. As mastery increases, anxiety (fear) decreases. Now you know the mastery-anxiety function. If you like graphs, here is how it would look on a graph:

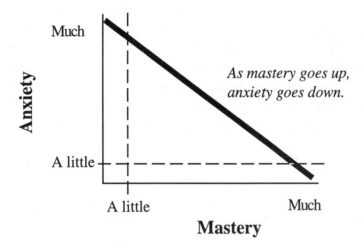

Breaking the anxiety-avoidance cycle.

If you believe that you know very little, whether this is true or not, you will likely be scared. If you are scared enough, you will deny being scared and act like the test is not a big deal. This happens because of an anxiety-avoidance cycle.

Here's how it works.

1. Your fear of the test, and what you believe you don't know, reduces your energy, and makes you less able to a) prepare for the test and b) think clearly about the proficiency test.

2. As your energy level goes down, you begin feeling more frightened. You begin to believe that you are all alone and there is no way out.

3. You then begin to believe that you will do very poorly on the Proficiency Test, and also begin to think that you are a poor student.

4. As your ability to think clearly goes down, you start to believe that there are other reasons for not passing the proficiency test. Maybe "it's the schools fault." Maybe if you are not studying, then it's because "I couldn't study," not because "I didn't want to study." It is almost like you decide not to pass, so you don't study to avoid thinking about the test and to give yourself a reason to fail. Your mind starts to ignore any "evidence" that you can pass. It only sees reasons why you can't pass. Your mind puts a "naval blockade" around your beliefs and only lets in things that will be sure to continue your belief that you can't pass. Failing the proficiency test because you didn't study really means that you decided not to pass, but you will try to give yourself a

reason to say you couldn't pass. So, you don't prepare for the proficiency test in order to give yourself an excuse for not passing. But the reality is that you avoided studying.

5. At some point, you realize that your avoidance is wrong, but now all that time has passed. With too little time to study, you begin to panic more, so the fear level goes up and the cycle begins all over again.

So long as you believe the material covered on the test is one big and scary creature, you will be plagued by this cycle. The key is to break down the material to be studied into smaller parts, and identify each one as a unique (one of a kind) body of information. For the Ohio Ninth Grade Proficiency Test, the topics you need to study can be seen in the material provided to you in the rest of this book. The State of Ohio has provided the specific areas that need to be learned for the test. Your school can help you with organizing this information, or you can call us for individual tutoring.

Once you have organized *the things* to be studied, set up *a method* for studying. Remember, try to study in a place a lot like the one where you'll be taking the test. For example, go to the library, find the quiet study section, and sit where other people are working. Decide to use specific techniques for hard to remember ideas. A good strategy is to use colored index cards, or "Pass In A Flash" flash cards. If, for example, you find that you keep missing certain practice questions in citizenship and science, use blue cards for citizenship and white ones for science. Put the study material on the cards and use them as flash cards. Remember, a great way to use the cards is to write questions about the hard material on the front of the cards and put the answers on the back. That way, you are learning the material as answers to questions, which is the way you will need to know it on the proficiency test. As you learn the material better, you'll see the number of cards in your deck get smaller. The smaller the deck of cards, the more you know. The smaller the deck, the less you have to be frightened about.

Once you've organized how you'll study and where you'll study, you will now need to schedule your time to study. Think of this as a job. The pay is great: a high school diploma and the freedom from worrying about the proficiency test ever again. Say to yourself "I'm going to make this a once in a lifetime experience." Put together your Proficiency Test Study Schedule and stick to it. Set aside time each day to study, and make sure the time is *not* when you're dead tired. When you study, pace yourself. Don't study for hours: the fatigue will stop your ability to study well. Instead of cramming, study for about 1/2 hour and then take a five to ten minute break. Go for a short walk. Get a drink of water and use the restroom. Splash water on your face. Eat a small snack. Then go back to studying. When you are studying, use a watch or clock to keep track of your progress through the material. As you finish each area you're studying, take note of the time and think about how you really did cover all that information in that small amount of time. Now the studying won't look so impossible.

After you have developed your study calendar, talk with your parents and teachers. Ask them to help you with questions you have when you're studying, and let them know that importance of your studying when planning family activities. For you, preparing for the test is a job, and you don't want to miss work. You want to work and get that pay check (the diploma and passing the Ohio Ninth Grade Proficiency Test).

Exercises:

On the next two pages fill out Text Anxiety Exercise Sheet #4 and #5.

➠ Write a letter to your family explaining your need to study when you've scheduled yourself to study, and tell them that you'll need to concentrate during those times. Use Exercise Sheet #4 for the letter to your family.

➠ Set up your study calendar using Exercise Sheet #5.

Test Anxiety Exercise Sheet #4

A Letter To My Family About My Study Schedule

Dear Family:

I will be studying for the Ninth Grade Proficiency Test. I have made out a schedule. My schedule will be from   to   . Here are the reasons I'll need to have you work with me on the time I'll need to study:

I would like to have your help in rescheduling the following chores so that I can stick to my schedule:

Finally, here are some other things that you could help me with so I can study for the test:

Sincerely,

Test Anxiety Exercise Sheet #5

The "Show What You Know" Calendar – Prepare to PASS

Month:

Sunday	Monday	Tuesday	Wednesday	Thursday	Friday	Saturday
Time: Subject:	Time: Subject:	Time: Subject:	Time: Subject:	Time: Subject:	Time: Subject:	Time; Subject:
Time: Subject:	Time: Subject:	Time: Subject:	Time: Subject:	Time: Subject:	Time: Subject:	Time; Subject:
Time: Subject:	Time: Subject:	Time: Subject:	Time: Subject:	Time: Subject:	Time: Subject:	Time; Subject:
Time: Subject:	Time: Subject:	Time: Subject:	Time: Subject:	Time: Subject:	Time: Subject:	Time; Subject:
Time: Subject:	Time: Subject:	Time: Subject:	Time: Subject:	Time: Subject:	Time: Subject:	Time; Subject:

How We Think Can Affect How We Feel

Developing a positive attitude.
There are lots of ways to convince ourselves that the Proficiency Test is the worst thing that will happen to us during high school. This is not true, but during the time before the test, it is easy to believe it. Below are some common ideas about the Proficiency Test that are not true, but easy to think. Let's call these Useless Thoughts (UTs):

✓ I am the only one scared of the test. [Black and White Thinking]

✓ My mother and father will be so disappointed in me if I fail. [Mind Reading]

✓ The test is too hard to pass. [Black and White Thinking]

✓ If I fail, my life is ruined. [Catastrophizing]

✓ If I am this scared now, I'll never get the answers right. [Jumping to Conclusions]

✓ The school didn't get me ready, so I probably will fail. [Future Predicting]

✓ My teacher is really expecting me to pass, so if I don't he (she) won't like me anymore. [Mind Reading]

✓ The test isn't really important. They'll probably get rid of it before I graduate anyway. Nobody else takes it seriously either. [Discounting]

✓ I can always take it again later, so why try this time. I'll just practice on this one. [Discounting]

Now let's develop some other ways to think about the test that you can use to replace the UTs. You can do this pretty easily by developing ideas that use experiences from your past. For example, if you think that you are the only one who is this upset about the test, you might think about how many of your classmates have talked about their nervous feelings just before taking a test. You've probably even talked with some of your friends about the Proficiency Test and found out that they are "up tight" about the test as well. Try to think up replacement thoughts to substitute for the UTs listed above.

Exercise:
On the next two pages fill out the Test Anxiety Exercise Sheet #6.
➠ Create your own replacement thoughts for the UTs.

Test Anxiety Exercise Sheet #6

Getting Rid of the UTs

Directions: After each UT (useless thought), you are given one example of a replacement thought that will likely reduce your fear of the Proficiency Test. Make up another replacement thought in the blanks.

Useless Thought	Replacement Thought
√ I am the only one scared of the test.	Everyone who wants to pass the test is somewhat concerned. _____ _____
√ My mother and father will be so disappointed in me if I fail.	My parents will understand how hard the test is. _____ _____
√ The test is too hard to pass.	At least 50% of all freshman in Ohio pass the test the first time they take it. So can I. _____ _____
√ If I fail, my life is ruined.	I've made it through harder things than the test in my life and I'm still OK. _____ _____
√ If I am this scared now, I'll never get the answers right.	I've been able to control my fear in the past and I still did pretty well then. _____ _____
√ The school didn't get me ready, so I probably will fail.	The school taught me what I need to know to be a freshman, so they must have taught me enough to pass the test. _____ _____

Test Anxiety Exercise Sheet #6 Continued

Getting Rid of the UTs	
Useless Thought	Replacement Thought
√ My teacher is really expecting me to pass, so if I don't he (she) won't like me any more.	I'm the one taking the test so my feelings are the ones that count. I'll like myself no matter what. _____ _____
√ The test isn't really important. They'll probably get rid of it before I graduate anyway. Nobody else takes it seriously either.	I will take this test seriously so I can pass it the first time. I know at least a few people, probably more if I think about it, that are studying for it too. _____ _____
√ I can always take it again later, so why try this time. I'll just practice on this one.	I'm going to take this test just once in my life if I have anything to do about it. _____ _____

Showing what you know.

The fact that you are taking the test should tell you that you are "proficient" enough to be a ninth grader in your school. Of course, you may have forgotten some of the information you'll need for the Proficiency Test, but you can study and relearn that material. The bottom line is that you have passed the "entrance" requirement for the test: you have been promoted into ninth grade.

If this is true, then you must change your thinking to believe that the test, instead of being a nasty trick to keep you from graduating, is a great chance to show what you already know. On a test like the proficiency test, even knowing that some of the answers are wrong counts if you can use that knowledge to get closer to the right answer—EVEN IF YOU DON'T KNOW WHAT THE RIGHT ANSWER IS! So you should start believing that you are a good student, able to relearn whatever you have forgotten, and that you are capable of showing all that you know because the State of Ohio has provided you with an opportunity to prove how much you have learned. You can call that opportunity the proficiency test.

Exercise:
On the next page fill out the Test Anxiety Exercise Sheet #7.
➠ Make a list of reasons you would tell others to show that you are qualified to take the test.

Test Anxiety Exercise Sheet #7

A List of Reasons Why I'm Qualified to Take the Test
1.
2.
3.
4.
5.
6.
7.
8.
9.
10.

You are not the test.

Many of the scary thoughts you have about the test come from a belief that how you do on the test is a statement about you as an individual. It is not. This test is just another task you must complete before graduating with a diploma. You have to take courses in Math, Sciencey, History and English before you graduate too. You have to pass the tests in these classes to complete high school. The proficiency test is just another hurdle you must jump in order to get to the finish line. How you do on the test tells you NOTHING about you as a person. It tells you only how well you can apply knowledge in this testing situation. Even the people who developed the test would admit that your score on the test is not likely to be your "true" score on the test, because there are so many things that can influence you when you take it. So, while doing well on the test is important, you are still the same OK person you were before the test, no matter how you do on it.

Exercise:

On the next page fill out Test Anxiety Exercise Sheet #8.

➠ Make a list of things you know about the test, then a list that describes you. Write down all the ways you and the test are different on Exercise Sheet #8. Then think about how you are not the same as what your score will be on the test.

Test Anxiety Exercise Sheet #8

The "I am not the test" Comparison Sheet		
Description of the Test	Description of Me	How I am Different from the Test

You are the one taking the test.

It is very tempting for teachers and parents to judge how well they have done their jobs by how well *you* do in *your* life. This is normal. However, sometimes parents and teachers can get stressed by events that *you* will go through as if they are going through the events themselves. When this happens, it is also easy for you to get nervous. Most of you have thought: "If my teacher (or mom) is so 'freaked out' by the test, it must be really awful. I guess I should be scared too." DON'T! The Ohio Ninth Grade Proficiency Test is being taken by you, not your teachers or parents. What they think about the test is important to all of us, but if *they* get scared, *you* don't have to. They are not taking the test, and while they may feel like they are being judged by how well you do, they are not the ones whose diploma depends on the test. It's good that you care about how they feel, but remember, you're taking the proficiency test, so **your** feelings are what's important while preparing and taking the test.

Exercise:

➠ Close your eyes and try to imagine a crowd of people including yourself, your parents, and your teachers. See them all frightened. Now see yourself not scared, walking out of the crowd. Try it right now!

The test is real, but it is only a test.

Almost everyone will try to think that the test is not really important. Some people will say that it doesn't matter, others will say that it will go away in a while. A word that often is used in describing this attitude is denial. We deny that the test is important. After all, if it isn't important, then we don't have to be scared of it. If it isn't important, we don't have to do well, study, or try hard. Just saying these things should give you a clue about how destructive such thinking can be. It takes away the healthy part of the fear that motivates you to do well. It also sets you up to fail, unless you are the test whiz of the world. Instead of thinking this way, see the test for what it is. The Proficiency Test is an important test, but it is only a test. It is necessary to pass it, and it will not go away. No matter how many times you click your heals together and say "There's no place like home," you will still have to pass the test. Come to think of it, Dorothy faced the scary forest and the wicked witch, passed both tests with hard work and a little nervousness, and then got to go home.

Exercise:

On the next page fill out Test Anxiety Exercise Sheet #9.

➠ Make a list of things people could say to try to convince you that the test is not important. Now list out reasons why it is.

Test Anxiety Exercise Sheet #9

| **Five Reasons Why the Test is Important** ||
Why others say the test is not important.	Why the test is important to me.
1.	
2.	
3.	
4.	
5.	

Take the test just once in your life.

Have you ever seen a tennis match? The players try to win every point. They have to, because by the end of the match, they won't win if they don't have enough points. That is the way you should think about the test. If you fail it now, eventually you'll run out of chances. Why not concentrate on winning the "match" now?

The kind of thinking that makes you believe you can afford to fail the test now is like your body running away from danger. Let's consider the way your mind might be working. First, you begin to believe the test is a big, scary monster. The monster can either be faced or run away from. If you begin to prepare for the test and think about it, you will have to face the "TEST MONSTER." If you believe the monster is going to beat you or is too big to fight, then you would be crazy to face it. You then run away. You say to yourself, "I don't need to face it today. I'll wait until I am bigger and stronger.

Then I'll face it." Of course, this only works if at some point your mind quits running and begins to face the "TEST MONSTER." If you are going to need to face it eventually, you should think straight about two things:

1. You can pass the test, once you have mastered the knowledge and test taking problem solving skills required, and

2. You will face the test this year, whether you want to or not, unless you move away or quit school. If you want a diploma, you will need to face the test each time the school administers it.

The test is not a monster, but just another challenge in your academic career as a student. You will be required to take it, even if you pretend that this time isn't important. But it is.

Exercise:
Fill out Test Anxiety Exercise Sheet #10 below.

➡ Try writing a letter to someone telling them about five things you were scared of, but that turned out OK in the end.

Test Anxiety Exercise Sheet #10

A Letter About Being Afraid of Things That Really Turned Out Okay
Directions: Write a letter to your best friend and list five things that you worried about, but when each one happened, things turned out much better than you thought they would. Describe how you felt each of the five times, both when you were worrying and when you realized that things turned out Ok.
Dear   ;   I wanted to write you about five things that I worried about in the past that really turned out OK. They were . . .   Your best friend,

Using your imagination.

Sometimes it is helpful to put something as "unreal" or abstract as the proficiency test into more "real" terms. For example, most of you are familiar with stories about dragons and evil knights. When you think about the test, imagine it to be an opposing knight in a far away castle. Each day you must rise, the carrier of knowledge (Ninth Grade knowledge), and face a new obstacle to reach the enemy knight (the proficiency test). Maybe you can see a picture of him/her, with Ohio Ninth Grade Proficiency Test written across his/her armor. Each morning you get up, face whatever obstacles are before you (studying, reviewing practice items) and move forward toward the castle and the opposing knight. Each day, you can see the castle a little closer. Finally, the day of the test, you rise and see the knight before you. He/She looks you over, and realizes that you are so well prepared, so motivated but not frightened, that instead of challenging you, he/she extends his/her hand to you. He/She has decided to yield to your superior ability. In the same way, your learning the knowledge and the test taking/problems solving skills will make the Ohio Ninth Grade Proficiency Test yield to your superior abilities. You too will pass the test and enter the castle of graduation.

Exercise:

Fill out Test Anxiety Exercise Sheet #11.

➠ Write a one page story about winning a contest in which you are the hero.

Test Anxiety Exercise Sheet #11

A Story in Which I Prepare Well and Become a Hero

Directions: Write a story in which you face a difficult and challenging task. Write about how you prepared long and hard, becoming stronger each day. End the story by overcoming the task and becoming the hero because of your hard work and newly developed skills. When you are done with the story, think about how it feels to be a hero and so strong. Try to remember that feeling, and relive it when you become nervous about the test. Begin writing here and continue on the next page.

Test Anxiety Exercise Sheet #11 Continued

A Story in Which I Prepare Well and Become a Hero

Handling Fear During the Test

Breaking the test into small parts

Just imagine, the State of Ohio has said "No student should fail a test as a result of working or reading slowly." (Ohio's Statewide Testing Program: Rules for High School Proficiency Testing, May, 1990, p. 6) You will have a maximum of 2 1/2 hours to complete each section of the test. So there is no rush to finish quickly and no advantage to being done early. For you to reduce your fears during the test, use the same techniques you used in studying: break the test down into smaller amounts. Decide to do a small number of questions every fifteen minutes. If you are given one hour to take the math test, then breakup the test into four parts, with 10 questions in each 15 minute block. When you finish the 10 questions, take a minute to relax. Realize that you have finished that section. Think about the fact that you actually are getting the test done.

Below is a table to help you convert the four multiple-choice tests into a certain number of questions in 15 minute sections. Remember, if you start to fall behind, no problem, just ask for more time to finish the test and keep plugging away.

Test	Number of Questions	Questions per 15 minutes
Citizenship	50	12 to 13
Math	40	10
Reading	40	10
Science	45	11 to 12

Another thing to remember while taking the test is that the hardest questions on each test are mixed in with the easy ones. Every so often you will be trying to answer a question that is written so that most people miss it. It is alright to miss one every once in a while. A little earlier today, you discovered that sometimes you believe things that aren't true, but seem to be true. The notion that you must get all the answers right to be a good student is not true. How good would a test be that lets lots of students get all the questions right? Not very good. This test is a very good test, and it has some very hard problems on it. So decide right now that every once in a while you'll be trying to answer one you don't know. Use the techniques taught in this book and answer it, then move on.

One last piece of advice on staying calm in the test. You have now been taught that your body starts to tell you that you are afraid: your heart will speed up, etc. You also now know that if you are really scared, your ability to think clearly decreases. With this knowledge, you can now recognize that you're beginning to become frightened, and you can calm yourself down. A real tell-tale sign is catching yourself thinking things like "This question doesn't matter. I'll guess at it." When this starts to happen, slow down and do what every good basketball player does at the foul line, take a couple of deep breaths and relax. Think about your winning the respect and friendship of the knight in the castle, and realize that this test is a great chance to "Show What You Know."

Good Luck!

Writing

Ninth Grade Proficiency Test: Writing

Introduction: What is the writing proficiency test?

The ninth grade writing proficiency tests your ability to respond to two writing prompts. A writing "prompt" is the topic that you are being asked to write about. It includes the style you are to use, directions for your writing and possible suggestions for your focus. You do not have a choice of prompts; you must answer both of them. We will include twenty writing prompts for practice. You will have to produce writing which is expository, descriptive or narrative in style. An expository essay explains in much the same way you might explain your reasons for arriving home after curfew. A descriptive essay is a form of writing you have been using since primary grades. Remember on the first day back to school when your teacher asked you to describe your summer vacation; this was a descriptive paragraph. Narrative writing tells a story. It includes plot, setting, characters and often times dialogue. Letter writing has also been used for the proficiency writing test. This includes both business letters and friendly lettters. Remember to put these in the proper letter-writing form. Your general knowledge and life experiences will be the basis for answering all of these prompts.

The state has developed a number of learning outcomes for passing the writing proficiency. Each piece of original writing :

1. Conveys a message related to the prompt.
2. Includes supporting ideas or examples.
3. Follows a logical order.
4. Conveys a sense of completeness
5. Exhibits a word choice appropriate to the audience, the purpose, and the subject.
6. Includes clear language.
7. Contains complete sentences and may contain purposeful fragments.
8. Exhibits subject-verb agreement.
9. Contains standard forms of verbs and nouns.
10. Exhibits appropriate punctuation.
11. Exhibits appropriate capitalization.
12. Contains correct spelling.
13. Is legible.

How will my writing be scored?

Each written response will be scored independently by two readers. The scores for the two samples will be added together. If the student fails, an analytical scoring on each sample will be done, and the results will be combined and reported. Analytical scores will not be done for students who pass. The analytical scoring will categorize the learning outcomes in this manner:

- content and organization (outcomes 1 - 4 listed above)
- language (outcomes 5 - 6 listed above)
- writing conventions (outcomes 7 - 13 listed above)

Each paper will be scored holistically (as a whole) based on the following four point scale ("4" being the highest and "0" being the lowest).

SCORE:

4 – The writing focuses on the topic with ample supporting ideas or examples and has a logical structure. The paper conveys a sense of completeness or wholeness. The writing demonstrates a mature command of language, including precision in word choice. With rare exceptions, sentences are complete except when fragments are used purposefully. Subject/verb agreement and verb and noun forms are generally correct. With few exceptions, the paper follows the conventions of punctuation, capitalization, and spelling.

3 – The writing is generally related to the topic with adequate supporting ideas or examples, although some lapses may occur. The paper exhibits some sense of completeness or wholeness. Word choice is generally adequate and precise. Most sentences are complete. There may be occasional errors in subject/verb agreement and in standard forms of verbs and nouns but not enough to impede communication. The conventions of punctuation, capitalization, and spelling are generally followed.

2 – The writing demonstrates an awareness of the topic but may include extraneous or loosely related material. Some supporting ideas or examples are included but are not developed. An organizational pattern has been attempted. The paper may lack a sense of completeness or wholeness. Vocabulary is adequate but limited, predictable, and occasionally vague. Readability is limited by errors in sentence structure, subject/verb agreement, and verb and noun forms. Knowledge of the conventions of punctuation and capitalization is demonstrated. With few exceptions, commonly used words are spelled correctly.

1 – The writing is only slightly related to the topic, offering few supporting ideas or examples. The writing exhibits little or no evidence of an organizational pattern. Development of ideas is erratic, inadequate, or illogical. Limited or inappropriate vocabulary obscures meaning. Gross errors in sentence structure and usage impede communications. Frequent and blatant errors occur in basic punctuation and capitalization, and commonly used words are frequently misspelled.

0 – Non-scorable. A paper may be considered non-scorable for any of the following reasons:
-illegible
-not enough text
-flagrant disregard of the topic

What other information do I need to know while taking the test?

Here is some additional information that will be helpful for you to know when taking the writing proficiency test.

• Ample space will be provided for prewriting activities on the answer document. Prewriting is a valuable tool to help you plan the body of your essay or narrative. Suggested prewriting activities will appear later in the chapter.
• Sorry, you will not be able to use a dictionary or thesaurus for the writing test.
• Either a pen or a pencil is permitted, but no other writing implement.
• You are allowed to erase or cross out without penalty. Remember to do so neatly.
• Either printing or cursive writing is acceptable, but it must be legible.
• A maximum of two and one-half hours is the alloted time frame for completing the writing test. You may finish writing before the time is up ,but make sure you have completely answered the prompt.

What should be in your writing piece?

A. Introductory Paragraph - Introductory or purpose setting paragraphs will begin your essay, narrative or letter. Beginning an essay can be done in a variety of ways:
• telling a story to attract your reader's attention
• giving a quote which relates to your prompt
• asking a question
• providing general background about your subject

No matter which method you choose, keep in mind that expressing your purpose in clear and simple terms is what is needed. Following are samples of each of the suggested beginnings.

Telling a story to attract your reader's attention can bring about an effective beginning by arousing the reader's curiosity as illustrated below:

As soon as she opened the door, she knew something was wrong. Her mom and dad sat silently on the floor next to the phone. Its receiver was lying sideways next to her mom's slippered foot.

A quote from a famous person helps set the opening for next beginning to the introductory paragraph:

"Ask not what your country can do for you, but what you can do for your country."
These were the words of John Fitzgerald Kennedy, our thirty-fifth president . . . He is the person I most admire and hope to be like.

Occasionally, **a short, precise question** is an effective means of introducing a subject.

Who is the best shortstop in the major leagues? Omar Vizquel of the Cleveland Indians wins this award hands down. . .

Giving a general background enables you to state the purpose of your essay and fill in your reader at the same time.

The one place I've lived that I find desirable is Hollywood Beach, Florida. Hollywood Beach is a small city about fifteen miles outside of Fort Lauderdale on the east coast of Florida. This is a very convenient location because you can fly into the Fort Lauderdale airport and drive to Hollywood Beach from there.

B. Body of the paper

The body of your paper will consist of a minimum of three paragraphs. These paragraphs will contain ample supporting details presented in logical order. A favorite question from students whenever they are asked to write an essay is, "How long does it have to be?" Make it a general rule of thumb that each time you practice a writing prompt it will be at least a page and a half long. Your maximum success will be achieved by developing each paragraph fully and not worrying about the number of sentences which that requires.

Let's continue with the story that began, "As soon as she opened the door..."

Her dad looked at her and nodded for her to come in; his narrow face looked like stone, and his eyes glazed over. The only sounds in the quiet room were from her crying mother, but those sounds were muffled, because she was crying into her husband's shoulder.

"Come sit down, Ashley," her dad said.

Ashley silently walked past the unmade bed, growing more pale and frightened with every step. She sat down near her mother.

"Ashley," whispered her mother, "there's been a. . .a. . ." she stopped for a minute and started to shake, like she was in her own private earthquake. Her face was red and tear-stained, and her hair was messy. She bravely tried to continue, "an. . .an. .an.," she burst into tears.

"An accident," Ashely's father finished. "Your uncle was in a serious car accident today. Early this morning a drunk driver broad-sided him. . ." His voice trailed off, and he became choked-up.

A single tear rolled down Ashely's right cheek, and she couldn't bring herself to ask, "Is he dead?" It just seemed too final. She had seen him just yesterday. Joyful Uncle Tom, now either in the hospital or what she dreaded most, dead.

It didn't seem fair. Tom had been the nicest person. He had always helped his family and strangers in need. He was the head of every "help the homeless" committee and was known by everyone in the community. Just thinking about him made the flow of tears turn to a flood.

She gathered up all of her courage and asked softly, "Is he dead?"

Ashley's mother looked up and said, "Yes." Her voice was faint, and Ashley could barely hear her.

"It's not fair! It's just not fair!" Ashley's voice was loud but filled with sorrow. She clung to her parents as if they were all she had to keep her from falling off a high cliff.

We'll save the ending paragrahs for our next section. Let's focus on some aspects of a narrative story which were used by this writer:

• setting (the bedroom)
• characters (mom, dad, Ashley)
• logical sequence of events
• dialogue (note how the writer began a new paragraph each time a different person spoke)
• descriptive phrases
• similes for comparisons

Expository writing requires that the body of the essay follows a logical sequence which clearly explains the subject of your paper. Let's continue with the second writer's view of Hollywood Beach, Florida.

The first thing that makes this place attractive is the condo that we stay in. My uncle owns the condo, so we get the same one every year. The condo is three stories high. The first floor has a bedroom, two bathrooms and a storage closet where we keep the bikes. The second floor has a kitchen, a family room and dining room. The top floor has a bedroom, a fold-out couch, and a bathroom. Every floor, except for the first, has a balcony over-looking the ocean. From there you can see the many cruise ships leaving Port Kennedy as they pass by. The condo is right on the beach, so you don't have to walk that far to the ocean. The only thing that stands in the way of the condo and the beach is the boardwalk.

The boardwalk is a two-way street that is lined with small shops and the Oceanview Mall. The Oceanview Mall is a food court, mall, movie theater, and hotel all-in-one. Among the other shops along the boardwalk are various surf shops and miniature golf courses.

The next great thing about Hollywood Beach is its beaches. Very few people know about this place, so they are untouched. They have clear water and great shelling; a combination that is rarely found along the Floridian Peninsula. You're able to see various types of fish and coral in the water by the condo. At about four o'clock, a sandbar rises about fifty yards off shore. This can be as shallow as six to twelve inches in some places.

The sand is soft at the top of the beach and hard at the bottom, providing an excellent terrain for biking. Biking is permissible anyhwere and widely encouraged.

Here are some observations we can make from the expository writing sample:
- transitional words (first, next) to help organize material logically
- substantial amount of information to adequately answer the prompt, "Explain why this is a desirable place to live."
- writing out all references to numbers under ninety-nine
- subject/verb agreement even when the subject and verb are split.
  For example: *The next best thing about Hollywood is its beaches.*
- prepositional phrases to vary sentence beginnings.
  For example: *Among the other shops...*
- personal pronouns having antecedents.
  For example: *"They have clear water and great shelling."* Who are "they"?
  Corrected : *These beaches have clear water and great shelling.*

C. Concluding Paragraphs
The last paragraph in your essay, narrative or letter sums up what you have written. This can be accomplished simply in two or three sentences and in several different ways. Let's return to our narrative and see how the writer concluded her story.

They were all silent, sharing the same thoughts. She knew something was wrong when she opened the door.

Here are some observations we can make about the above conclusion:
- summed up the characters' feelings
- cleverly repeated the opening sentence

The expository writer took a simple direct approach:

Hollywood Beach is a great place to go and relax every year. That is why I find it a fun and "desirable" place to live, no matter how brief the stay may be.

Here is the observation we can make about the expository writers conclusion:
- It restated the purpose of writing this essay

How long should writing be?

Whenever you practice writing, you are usually using standard-sized tablet paper that is eight and one half inches by eleven inches. When practicing, start by writing one page and eventually work yourself up to two pages as you continue practicing throughout the year. This will help you write enough when you get to the actual proficiency test, because the pages in the booklet you will write in are sized a bit differently than your paper. One way to make sure you write enough is to add details that are needed, explanations that are requested, all information that is expected, or a sufficient number of events to make the story complete.

What are prewriting activities?

Prewriting activities are methods for organizing your ideas without writing them out. They will play a crucial role by providing you with an ample amount of information you can use to write your paper. The best part about "prewriting acitivities" is they only take a few minutes to do.

Webbing or Mapping graphic organizer

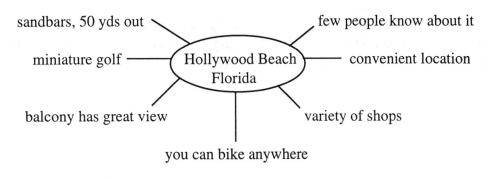

Webbing or Mapping your ideas about a subject is a good way to prepare and organize your ideas before you begin writing. In the Writing Web, the main topic of the story is inside the circle and each branche represents different thoughts or ideas about the topic. You may use all of the branches in your writing or only choose a few of your ideas.

Chain of events graphic organizer:

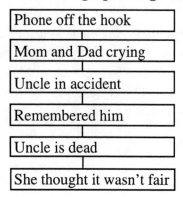

The graphic organizer above illustrates how you can organize the events in a story. This is an effective way to organize your thoughts before you begin to write. This is a good example of how the writing selection used earlier may have looked during the prewriting stage of his/her story.

Venn Diagram graphic organizer:

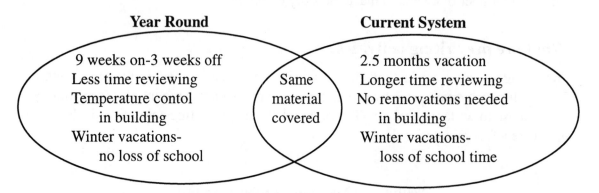

Venn diagrams are excellent tools for comparing and contrasting any topic. This particular diagram is comparing and contrasting the pros and cons of year-round school system and the traditional "summers off" system.

What are the learning outcomes?

The learning outcomes are developed by a committee consisting primarily of Ohio educators and adopted in 1988 by the State Board of Eduction. The learning outcomes make up the content and design of the writing test. Below we have listed them

A. Content
1. Conveys a message related to the prompt. This means you must understand what you are being asked to write about. Reading the prompt through at least twice will help you get a clear understanding of what the content of the writing must be.

Writing Activity:

1. Below is a paragraph with unrelated sentences. In the space provided, rewrite the paragraph eliminating those ideas which are not necessary.

   The most desirable place I have ever lived was Pittsburgh, Pa. Our house was in a very friendly neighborhood. The neighbor next door had a beautiful collie. This dog was always barking. We had a split-level house on a corner lot. Split-level houses are O.K., but two stories are the best. There were lots of kids so whenever you wanted to play baseball or street hockey, you could. One time my team was behind a point with two minutes to go; I batted the puck towards the net and scored. What a victory! There were plenty of those above-ground swimming pools. During the summer, we often played 'Marco Polo' in the water. I never was very good at playing water games. At night a whole gang of us would wait until dark and play "Capture the Flag." Because every house had three or four kids, there were plenty of birthday parties to attend. I'll never forget Matthew's sixth birthday party. His parents had arranged for a pony to come and take the guests for a ride. I'd rather go somewhere for a party than stay at home. It started to pour, and Matthew never did get his turn. Boy did he cry!

Rewrite here.

_____

_____

_____

_____

_____

_____

_____

_____

_____

_____

_____

_____

_____

_____

_____

_____

_____

Sample Rewrite:

The most desirable place I have ever lived was Pittsburgh, Pa. Our house was in a very friendly neighborhood. We had a split-level house on a corner lot. There were lots of kids so whenever you wanted to play baseball or street hockey, you could. There were plenty of those above-ground swimming pools. During the summer, we often played "Marco Polo" in the water. At night, a whole gang of us would wait until dark and play "Capture the Flag". Because every house had three or four kids there were always plenty of birthday parties to attend. I'll never forget Matthew's sixth birthday party. His parents had arranged for a pony to come and take the guests for a ride. It started to rain and Mattthew never did get a turn. Boy did he cry!

2. Includes supporting ideas or examples. As you are writing think of extra information you can add that supports the things you are writing about.

Writing Activity:

2. Rewrite the following paragraph by adding details to the setting, giving the characters names and/or occupations, explaining the reason for the room looking like it does, and by describing what was on the computer screen. Be sure to supply specific details and add prepositional phrases to improve this writing. Finish this with a surprise ending.

    It was a cold winter day. Two people entered the building. Down the hall, a door was ajar. The people entered the room and found papers scattered all over the floor. Drawers were open and chairs upset. A computer screen displayed information. Steam arose from a coffee cup on the desk. A window above the counter was open. There were muffled sounds coming from a closet.

Rewrite here.

_____

_____

_____

_____

_____

_____

_____

_____

_____

_____

_____

Sample Rewrite:
There are many ways you can write this. Check the instructions to see if you have done everything you were asked to do.

3. Follow a logical order. You could organize your ideas into a logical order by using a writing web or graphic organizer. If the writing is obviously out of order or does not follow a logical path of ideas, you could lose points.

Writing Activity:

3. Rewrite the following paragraph which describes a trip to Disney World. Include transitional words (next, first, last, dates).

> The family left for Disney World early Saturday morning. On Monday the first thing on the agenda was Epcot Center. There wasn't enough time to see all the attractions in all of the countries at Epcot, but the night laser light show was terrific. Sunday was spent driving the remainder of the distance from Savannah, Georgia to Orlando. How excited they were to see their hotel at Walt Disney World. The third day of vacation was devoted to the Magic Kingdom. Tuesday was enjoyed at MGM Studios, studying the special effects and watching them put together cartoon clips for their up and coming movies. Space Mountain and Thunder Canyon were the favorite rides of day three. On the last day, they relaxed by cooling off on the waterslides and gliding along on the lazy river. On Thursday, they returned to Epcot Center to complete their world tour of countries.

Rewrite here.

_____

_____

_____

_____

_____

_____

_____

_____

_____

_____

_____

_____

_____

_____

_____

_____

_____

Sample Rewrite:

The family left for Disney World early Saturday morning. Sunday was spent driving the remainder of the distance from Savannah, Georgia, to Orlando. How excited they were to see their hotel at Walt Disney World. On Monday, the first thing on the agenda was Epcot Center. There wasn't enough time to see all the attractions in all of the countries at Epcot, but the night laser light show was terrific. Tuesday was enjoyed at MGM Studios, studying the special effects and watching them put together cartoon clips for their up and coming movies. The third day of vacation was devoted to the Magic Kingdom. Space Mountain and Thunder Canyon were the favorite rides of day three. On Thursday, they returned to Epcot Center to complete their tour of the countries. On the last day, they relaxed by cooling off on the waterslides and gliding down the lazy river.

4. Conveys a sense of completeness. Avoid abrupt endings. When put in the correct order, the paragraph in the preceeding section ends very abruptly. *"On the last day, they relaxed by cooling off on the waterslides and gliding along on the lazy river."*

Writing Activity:

4. Below, add a sentence or two to sum up their week's activities at Disney World and put closure on the vacation.

_____

_____

_____

_____

_____

_____

_____

Sample Response:
Your answers can vary. Make sure you summarized and made an ending to the vacation story.

B. Language

5. Exhibits a word choice appropriate to the audience, the purpose and the subject. The persons who will read your writing are educated adults. They are not your friend on your basketball team. Locker room talk or profanity will cause you to lose points. Don't use slang words that are unfamiliar to the reader. This is not the time to try a new word that you have never tried before. You might use it incorrectly and it won't make sense to the reader.

Writing Activity:

5. Write a more appropriate way of expressing the following ideas:

a. That sucks! Let's concentrate on the baseball game._____

_____

b. That man is a selfish, inconsiderate, greedy idiot._____

_____

c. Then after that, they shot all the reindeer and ate them for their Christmas meal._____

_____

d. How dumb can you be? I mean, you have to be a jerk. _____

_____

Sample Responses:
a. *That's terrible. Let's concentrate on the baseball game.*
b. *That man is selfish and inconsiderate.*
c. *(The entire subject matter may be inappropriate).*
d. *How annoying. Surely, you don't mean that!*

6. Includes clear language. Write so that you will be clearly understood by the reader. Many times you can correct an unclear sentence by rewriting as you read.

Writing Activity:

6. Rewrite and correct the following sentences, eliminating any misunderstandings for the reader.

a. On the desk the boy placed his textbook._____

_____

b. The lady stole the picture with the briefcase from the wall._____

_____

c. The cat stared out the window sitting on the ledge._____

_____

d. The athlete started to very quickly run the last lap._____

_____

e. Accidentally, the small child tripped over the carpet with the bookbag._____

_____

Sample Responses:
a. *The boy placed his textbook on the desk.*
b. *The lady with the briefcase stole the picture from the wall.*
c. *Sitting on the ledge, the cat stared out the window.*
d. *The athlete started to run the last lap very quickly.*
e. *Accidentally, the small child with the bookbag tripped over the carpet.*

C. Writing Conventions

7. Contains complete sentences and may contain purposeful fragments. Your sentences must be complete. If you use a fragment, it must be used to make a point or for a reason. If your sentences have too many commas or seem too long, make them into two shorter sentences that say the same thing.

Writing Activity:

7. Determine whether each of the following sentences is a fragment, complete sentence or run-on. Correct if necessary.

a. The ball off the outfield wall._____

_____

b. Several dancers appeared on the stage the ballerinas were first up._____

_____

_____

c. Bright yellow lights blinded us._____

_____

d. We went to the football game they decided to go shopping._____

_____

e. A large crowd assembled for the concert._____

_____

f. Because we had a good idea._____

_____

g. Albert Bell hit a double Kenny Lofton eeked out a single and Jim Thome struck out._____

_____

h. If Spelling is a problem._____

_____

i. What a fabulous game!_____

_____

j. Isn't this the craziest weather you've ever seen!_____

_____

Sample responses:
a. Fragment
b. Run-on
c. Complete sentence
d. Run-on
e. Complete sentence
f. Fragment
g. Run-on.
h. Fragment
i. Purposeful fragment
j. Complete sentence

8. Exhibits subject/verb agreement. Make sure you have subject/verb agreement. Singular subjects go with singular verbs and Plural subjects go with plural verbs. You may practice correcting yourself by checking the incorrect sentences in the activity below.

Writing Activity:

8. The following sentences may not contain standard forms of subject/verb agreement. Correct the errors you find, or if it looks correct as is, mark it "correct".

   a. There is three children waiting for you.

   b. The fire marshall and the police chief is addressing the student body.

   c. He don't know the answers to this test.

   d. There's several reasons to complete this project.

   e. The coach gives the team a lecture before every game.

   f. Either pizza or two subs was ordered.

   g. Doesn't he look terrific?

h. Neither the girls nor the boy have a new bookbag.

i. News of the tragedy spreads quickly.

j. Romeo and Juliet were my favorite Shakespearean play.

k. The teams in the league was having a difficult time drafting players.

l. Ten dollars is the amount I received from my grandmother for Christmas.

Sample Corrections:
a. There are three small children waiting for you.
b. The fire marshall and the police chief are addressing the student body.
c. He doesn't know the answers to this test.
d. There are several reasons to complete this project.
e. Correct
f. Either pizza or two subs were ordered.
g. correct
h. Neither the girls nor the boy has a new bookbag.
i. Correct
j. Romeo and Juliet was my favorite Shakespearean play.
k. The teams in the league were having a difficult time drafting players.
l. Correct.

9. Contains standard forms of verbs, nouns and other words. You need to use the correct form of words in your sentences. Here are some incorrectly formed sentences. See if you can identify the incorrect form of verb, noun, or other word.

Writing Activity:

9. Circle the incorrect non-standard forms in these sentences and write the correct form underneath each sentence.

a. Their are to many questions to answer.

b. They're never enough hours in a day.

c. Can you except that consequence?

d. Please rise the window before you leave.

e. Give me too good reasons for being late.

f. The new curfew will have a big affect on us.

g. The team won the game and celebrates.

h. Janet should have went with Carla to the movies.

i. The Olympian had ran for two hours.

j. They should of called before coming.

Sample Corrections:
a. There are too many questions to answer.
b. There are never enough hours in the day.
c. Can you accept that consequence?
d. Please raise the window before you leave.
e. Give me two good reasons for being late.
f. The new curfew will have a big effect on us.
g. The teams won the game and celebrated.
h. Janet should have gone with Carla to the movies.
i. The Olympian had run for two hours.
j. They should have called before coming.

10. Exhibits appropriate punctuation. Look for correct punctuation when editing your writing. Practice editing for punctuation on the sentences below.

Writing Activity:

10. Correct the puctuation in the following sentences.

a. For the trip we packed the following items; a blanket: pillow, sleeping bag: canteen silverware and tent.

b. After a long summer vacation we anxiously awaited the start of school.

c. The Declaration of Independence was signed July 4 1776 in Philadelphia

d. Please come to visit: we'd love to have you?

e. Very truly yours

f. Send your reply to Cleveland Ohio 44118

g. Was'nt that a great surprise

h. I expect Sam said to have a new car soon

i. My favorite TV show is Seinfeld.

j. The poem The Raven was written by Edgar Allen Poe.

Sample Corrections:

a. For the trip we packed the following items: a blanket, pillow, sleeping bag, canteen, silverware, and tent.
b. After a long summer vacation, we anxiously awaited the start of school
c. The Declaration of Indepenence was signed July 4, 1776, in Philadelpia.
d. Please come to visit: we'd love to have you.
e. Very truly yours,
f. Send your reply to Cleveland, Ohio 44118.
g. Wasn't that a great surprise?
h. "I expect," Sam said, "to have a new car soon."
i. My favorite TV show is Seinfeld.
j. The poem "The Raven" was written by Edgar Allen Poe.

11. Exhibits appropriate capitalization. The letter below has incorrect capitalization.

Writing Activity:

11. Make corrections in the following business letter.

---

november 27, 1996

seventeen Magazine
5600 Fifth avenue
new york, NY 10021

dear Editor:

    I ordered a shirt from the back of your magazine. The shirt was turquoise blue embossed with a pearl jam decal. The shirt was ordered on august 20 1996, but i have not received it yet. I would like to have it to wear to a Winter concert at ohio state. I enclosed a check for $22.95 from fifth third bank.

    I would appreciate your checking the whereabouts of my shirt. If you are unable to send this item by december 1, 1996, please let me know. I will have to buy a similar item which I saw at a store called the limited in city center in columbus. Also, please return my check if unable to ship the shirt.

sincerely,

Colleen Dayton

Sample Correction Letter is on the next page.

Sample Corrected Letter:

121 Timberwood Drive
Columbus , OH 43201

November 27, 1996

Seventeen Magazine
5600 Fifth Avenue
NewYork, NY 10021

Dear Editor:

I ordered a shirt from the back of your magazine. The shirt was turquoise blue embossed with a Pearl Jam decal. The shirt was ordered on August 20, 1996, but I have not received it yet. I would like to have it to wear to a winter concert a t Ohio State. I enclosed a check for $22.95 from the Fifth Third Bank.

I would appreciate your checking the whereabouts of my shirt. If you are unable to send this item by December 1, 1996, please let me know. I will have to buy a similar item which I saw at a store called The Limited in City Center in Columbus. Also please return my check if unable to ship the shirt.

Sincerely,

Colleen Dayton

12. Contains correct spelling. Make sure you use words that you already know how to spell. This is not the time to take a chance on new words.

13. Is legible. You are allowed to print or write in cursive. Use your personal best style of writing. You will be given enough room to skip a space between lines so that it is easier for the reader to read. This also makes it easy for you to go back and edit and correct your work. You may cross out words or erase, but please do it neatly.

A Final Note

One of the most effective methods of preparation for the writing proficiency is to see actual student writing samples on the overhead. This way, you can evaluate the strengths and weaknesses of these essays. After reviewing the paper, try to explain what you consider to be the good qualities about this writing. Always start with the positive aspects. Then look at the paper again and pick out the weaknesses. When evaluating the paper, divide the paper into the four categories which correspond with the learning outcomes:

Content	Organization	Language	Writing Conventions
#1	#2, 3, 4	#5, 6	#7 - 13

Then label each section either with an S=satisfactory or U=unsatisfactory. Award each category that you labeled "satisfactory" with one point. Each category labeled "unsatisfactory" receives nothing. A passing grade would be a 3. It is best to strive for a score of 4. Doing it this way will enable you to become acquainted with the state's scoring system.

Below is a Passing writing sample.

The one thing I need to change about myself is the condition of my bedroom. It is a mess! My parents are constatnly reminding me that it needs to be cleaned. When that doesn't bring about results, they yell. When they yell, I get angry.

It's difficult to walk into my room, because there are usually clothes scattered on the floor. Clothes can also be found lying on my bed or hanging on door knobs. Papers from the previous night's homework are thrown here and there. CD's are out of their cases, tapes are not in holders, and make-up covers the top of my bookcase. Even gum wrappers litter the scenery. Wet towels are heaped in the corner, and my bed is seldom made.

This situation is easily corrected. I know that I am basically lazy! If only I would hang up my clothes, fold those to be returned to the drawer, or put the dirty ones in the clothes hamper, my life would be less complicated. Yes, I am ashamed to say that I have an unused hamper right in my room. As for the papers on the floor, after finishing my homework, I should pack my backpack. That would solve two problems -- my room would be neater, and I wouldn't be so rushed in the morning. It would only take a few seconds of time to put the CD's, tapes, and make-up away. Gum wrappers belong in garbage cans , and my bed looks much neater made.

I always tease my parents and tell them that I like my room like that, but I really don't. Procrastination and laziness will no longer rule my life. I'll start tomorrow. I can drag myself away from the television for the ten minutes daily it will take to keep my room clean and keep my parents off my back.

Here is an example of a Failed Writing Sample.

> I need to change my tone of voice and my attitude. I am always getting in trouble and I don't get to go anyweres with my friends. The only thing I get to do at home is stay in my room amd maybe listen to my music. I am always getting in trouble because of my little brother. He starts the fight and I get yelled at. It's not fair.
>
> I will change my attitude and my tone of voice. I will try to think about my actions before I do get mad. I will not go after my brother even if he takes a swing at me.
>
> If I change both my tone of voice and my attitude my parents will get off my case and leave me alone and not punish me anymore.

Let's review the description for what a sample writing needs to be to receive the highest score of 4.

4 – The writing focuses on the topic with ample supporting ideas or examples and has a logical structure. The paper conveys a sense of completeness or wholeness. The writing demonstrates a mature command of language, including precision in word choice. With rare exceptions, sentences are complete except when fragments are used purposefully. Subject/verb agreement and verb and noun forms are generally correct. With few exceptions, the paper follows the conventions of punctuation, capitalization, and spelling.

Writing Practice Prompts

What You Need To Know:

This section of your book will give you twenty simulated writing proficiency test prompts to practice your writing skills. Use the space provided on each page to plan your writing. You may use outlines, writing webs, or graphic organizers to brainstorm, plan, and organize your thoughts and ideas before you begin writing. Use notebook paper to write on but remember to skip a space between lines so that it is easy to read and easy to do your editing. Have someone read your writing and give it a score based on the 1 – 4 scoring described previously in the writing chapter of this book. When you have completed all twenty practice prompts you should be prepared to PASS the writing proficiency test.

Writing Prompt #1: Expository

You have just won a large sum of money from a contest sponsored by your favorite radio station. It would be very easy to splurge and spend it foolishly. You are determined that this is not going to happen. Explain your plan of action. Be specific with how much money will be spent and how much will be saved.

Writing Prompt #2: Descriptive Writing

Your parents come home after being away for the weekend. You were left in charge of the house, your younger brother, two dogs, and a cat. The house is a disaster and your parents are furious. Briefly describe what the house looked like and how it got that way. Remember not to incriminate yourself in your description!

Writing Prompt #3: Narrative Writing

A day in the life of _____. You're put into another person's body. Write a story about this real or imaginary person. Who are you? What will you do? Where will you be?

Writing Prompt #4: Business Letter Writing

Often times as teens, you feel a sense of being put down or ignored by adults who work in stores, restaurants or service-related businesses. Write a letter to a store owner, president of a company or a restaurant manager. Describe the ill treatment you received at their place of business expressing your displeasure with the employee's behavior. Remember to write your complaint in proper business letter format.

Writing Prompt #5: Descriptive Writing

Travel back in time to your favorite era in history. You could be a pioneer during the Gold Rush, a farmer struggling through the Great Depression, an explorer during the sixteenth century, a passenger traveling the Underground Railroad, a nurse in Europe during World War II, etc. Describe your setting and the life you are leading.

Writing Prompt #6: Narrative Writing

Sports influence us in many different ways. Some of us participate on the football field, join a pick-up game of basketball, watch Olympians set new world records. Choose a sport, create a scene, and become the star. Write a narrative featuring yourself as the winning force.

Writing Prompt #7: Expository Writing

Your class trip is quickly approaching. You need to convince your parents to let you go. If you write all your reasons on paper, they make more sense. You decide that the best way to convince your parents is to read them what you have written. Organize all your reasons in order of importance, but saving your best one until last. Now write your essay.

Writing Prompt #8: Friendly Letter

You convinced your parents to let you go on the class trip, and you had a great time. Now write to your cousin who has the chance to go on the same trip. Relate your experiences in chronological order. Give descriptive accounts of three major highlights of the trip. Remember to use friendly letter format.

Writing Prompt #9: Descriptive Writing

Describe a fantasy vacation or fantasy trip you would like to take. Why do you want to go there? How will you get there? What activities do you have planned once you arrive? Describe the location and the type of accommodations you will have. Don't forget to include a description of the people who will be going with you.

Writing prompt #10: Expository Writing (Contrast and Compare)

You have attended two concerts this past weekend. The first concert was well worth the money you spent on the ticket. The second concert was very disappointing. Contrast and compare the two concerts. How do the groups differ? Did the audience influence your opinion? Others factors to consider are the location of the concert, the length of the performance, choice of songs and popularity of the group.

Writing Prompt #11: Business Letter

You have been scanning the want ads and notice an appropriate part-time job opportunity. It's perfect for earning that extra money you need. The hours will fit with your school schedule. Write a letter to the person whose name is in the ad, explaining your qualifications and reasons why you should be hired. Be convincing!

Writing Prompt #12: Descriptive Writing

Sometimes you can feel alone in a crowd of people, a car full of friends, a three-way conversation, or even by yourself. Describe a time when you felt lonely. Include any feelings which may help describe your situation for the reader.

Writing Prompt #13: Narrative Writing

Kept in the _____. Fill in the blank by writing a narrative based on this title. Make sure your story has character and plot development.

Writing Prompt #14: Expository Writing

Most teenagers have an opinion about the possibility of a new law which proposes to change the driving age to eighteen. Is this a fair proposition? State your opinion and defend it. Support your position with at least four in-depth arguments.

Writing Prompt #15: Expository Writing

We all have things we want to change about ourselves. Things like putting off home-work until the last minute, being tardy for school or classes, not eating the way we know we should, not getting enough sleep or exercise. Choose one aspect of your life that you want to change and explain how you would go about improving it. Convince your reader that this change would improve your life.

Writing Prompt #16: Expository Writing

Professional athletes in all sports are asking for and receiving huge salaries. Sometimes they make more money in one day for one game than most people earn in a year. What reaction do you have towards this inequity? Do these athletes deserve these salaries? Is any one person worth that much money?

Writing Prompt #17: Descriptive Writing

We all have ideas about how to raise children. It's easy as a teenager to see others' parents and wish they were your own. Create the perfect parents. Describe some of their disciplinary techniques, rules, consequences and rewards for raising children.

Writing Prompt #18: Descriptive Writing

Every school has a dress code policy. Whether you attend a public school or a private school, whether it be in the city or a rural farming area, your school probably sets up guide lines for appropriate appearance. Describe your school's dress code policy, including any hair, shoe and accessory restrictions that may apply. Do you agree or disagree with the regulations? Express your opinion and explain why.

Writing Prompt #19: Expository Writing (Contrast and Compare)

There has been some serious consideration given to the possibility of implementing the concept of year-round school. As a matter of fact, several schools in Ohio have already adopted the year-round system. An example of this plan could be nine weeks of school, a three week break and the whole month of July off. There are a multitude of pros and cons about this subject. Contrast and compare the traditional system with the year-round alternative. After you have discussed the facts, give your opinion and explain your preference.

Reading

Ninth Grade Proficiency Test: Reading

Introduction: Strands and Learning Outcomes

The Reading section of the Ninth-Grade Ohio Proficiency Test is designed to test your *overall understanding* of several reading passages. The test is based on a series of learning outcomes which define skills you will need for the 9th grade reading test. This introduction will discuss the test itself. The next section explains each learning outcome and gives you a chance to practice using your skills. Finally, the last section of this chapter contains several reading passages and 43 sample multiple-choice questions.

What You Need To Know
As you take the 9th grade reading test, you will demonstrate your abilities by:
• reading at a 9th grade level
• understanding the main ideas of a reading selection
• making inferences and interpretations from a reading selection
• expanding upon the information you find in a reading passage

About The Reading Test
The test covers the learning outcomes outlined in the next section of this chapter. Every learning outcome will be tested with at least one question. The test contains two basic elements:

1. **The Reading Passage.** Reading passages will be of different lengths. Some passages will be over 500 words. Reading passages may be fiction or non-fiction.

2. **The Questions.** All of the questions will be multiple-choice. A reading passage may have up to eight test questions. The reading test contains a total of 40 multiple-choice questions.

Things To Remember
• Most questions will refer to a reading passage, but some will not. These "stand alone" questions will explain that you do not refer to a reading passage to answer them.
• There is NO penalty for an incorrect answer. If you are not sure of an answer, it won't hurt your score if you guess. Answer every question on the test.

Test-Taking Strategies For Reading
The key to success on the proficiency test is to use what you know, whether you gained your knowledge in school, at home, or in the reading passage itself. If you meet a question you can't answer, or simply don't understand, don't panic! Use what you know to attack the question in a logical manner. Use your knowledge to eliminate answers you know are wrong.

For the reading test, use the following four steps:

1. Skim through the reading passage. Read the title of the selection, and the first and last sentences of each paragraph. Be sure you have a general understanding of the passage.
2. Read the questions for this reading selection, but do not read the answers yet. Do you know what each question is asking?
3. Read the reading selection. Mark places you think will help you to answer the questions.

4. Answer the questions:
  • Read the question.
  • Read *all* of the answers.
  • Cross out any answers you know are wrong.
  • If more than one answer remains:
    — be sure you know the meaning of the question.
    — quickly review the passage. Can you find the correct answer?
  • If you can't answer a question, make your *best* guess. There is NO penalty for an incorrect guess.

Test-Taking Tips:
• Use common sense. The correct answer will make sense. Don't over-analyze a question, just answer it.
• Watch the language. Be careful of words like "never" or "always." It is rare that life is absolute, so it will be rare for an absolute answer to be correct.
• Don't fall for "trick" answers. An answer might state a fact from the reading passage, but it may not answer the question. These answers can "look right" because they use facts and language from the text. Make sure your answer *is* right— it must answer the question asked.
• If you have trouble understanding a particular passage, slow down and read it more carefully. Make notes in the margin to help you remember key points. You have 2 1/2 hours to complete the reading test—plenty of time. Don't worry if you need to slow down a bit for one set of questions.
• If you are not able to eliminate any answers in a question, take a guess. Circle the question in your test booklet and move on. If you have time at the end of the test, return to this question and try it again. If you do not have time, your guess will be your answer— if it's right, great; if not, you will not be penalized.

The Questions
Every learning outcome will be tested with at least one question on the Proficiency Test. The approximate distribution of items/questions on the test is shown in the chart below.

Type of Reading Material	Outcomes	Percent of Items
Fictional		40%
Constructs Meaning	1a, 1b, 1c, 1d, 1e	
Extends Meaning	1f, 1g, 1h, 1i, 1j	
Nonfictional		40%
Constructs Meaning	2a, 2b, 2e	
Extends Meaning	2c, 2d, 2f, 2g, 2h, 2i, 2j	
Everyday/Functional	3a, 3b, 3c, 3d	20%

The Learning Outcomes

This section will provide you with a review of all the Ninth-Grade Reading Learning Outcomes and analyze simulated proficiency test questions. The purpose of this review is to get you familiar with the style, format and layout of the test and to walk you through the analysis so that you can increase your skills of finding the correct answer on the test.

Fiction

You will need to demonstrate your skills in the following types of questions:

A. the meaning of an unfamiliar word

A passage may contain an unfamiliar word. This word may be uncommon, or new to you. An unfamiliar word will be underlined within the passage, and you will be asked to decide what it means. You are *not* expected to know what the word means, but if you happen to know the meaning of the word, great! You will answer the question quickly and move on to the next one. Otherwise, you will want to find the meaning from clues in the sentence or in other sentences close by.

Examples:

1. The mayor agreed to build a park area for teenagers, if the gang members would agreeto <u>desist</u> from fighting.

   A. to discuss

   B. to stop

   C. to insist

   D. to continue

Analysis:
What word would you use to replace <u>desist</u>? If gang members are fighting, why would the mayor build a park for them? The mayor might want them to "stop" fighting. This matches answer "B." Plug the answer into the sentence. It makes sense. Answer "B" is correct.

2. As the witch waved her wand and muttered <u>imprecations</u>, the man shuddered in fear at what bad luck he might encounter.

   A. nonsense words

   B. song lyrics

   C. magic powder

   D. evil curses

Analysis:

What might a witch say, while waving her wand? "Chants," or "Magic spells" might fit. Answers "A," "B," and "D" are all possibilities using this method. Are there any clues in the sentence which might help? Why is the man fearful of bad luck? This clue narrows our choices to answer "D," "evil curses." Plug this answer into the sentence to make sure it makes sense. Answer "D" is correct.

Things To Remember

• Remove the underlined word from the sentence, and fill in your own word. What word makes sense? Be sure your word doesn't change the overall meaning of the sentence.

• Check the answers. Are any of the definitions similar to the word you chose?

• Plug the answer you select into the sentence. Does the sentence make sense?

• If you can't think of a similar word, try eliminating words you know are wrong.

• Look for clues to meaning in the sentence, or in sentences close by.

• Watch out for "trick" answers. Be careful of definitions that sound the same (rhyme), or are a different part of speech from the word underlined.

B. the meaning of a multiple-meaning word

Some words have more than one meaning. For this skill, you will be asked to decide which meaning is correct for the word in the reading selection.

Examples:

1. Home sales increased last month due to <u>lower</u> mortgage interest rates.

        A. on a level below another

        B. to reduce in value

        C. to bring down in respect; demean

        D. being below land of a higher elevation

Analysis:
In this sentence, "lower" is used as an adjective: it is describing the noun "mortgage."
Make sure your definition is for an adjective. Answers "B" and "C" can be eliminated,
since they define verbs ("to _____" fits a verb definition). Answer "D" can be
eliminated using context clues: the sentence has nothing to do with land elevation. That
leaves answer "A". Plug it into the sentence. does it make sense? Since mortgage rates
last month were "on a level below another" (probably the previous month's level), it
makes sense. Answer "A" is correct.

2. Susannah dropped her <u>form</u> in the bowl, and hoped her name would be
   drawn to win the television.

> A. the style or technique of an athlete
> B. a printed document with blank spaces to be filled in
> C. the shape of anything
> D. a long wooden bench

Analysis:
Susannah is dropping something into the bowl, so the definition will be that of a noun. All
of the definitions fit nouns (a _____, or the _____, often marks a noun definition).
We must try another method. Susannah seems to be entering a raffle, so she must be
putting something with her name on it in the bowl. Answer "B" fits this idea. Answers
"A", "C", and "D" mention ideas that would not work in this sentence. Answer "B" is
correct.

Things To Remember
• For multiple-meaning words, *all* of the answers will be a correct definition of the *word*,
  but only one answer will define the word *as it is used in the sentence.*
• Plug each answer into the sentence, in place of the underlined word. Cross out any
  words which do not make sense.
• Be sure that your definition fits the same part of speech as the underlined word. If the
  word is used as a noun, the definition should be that of a noun.

C. sequence of time, places, events, and ideas
You will need to be able to recognize the order of events in a reading passage. Questions
will list up to 4 events in different orders. You will select the answer which represents the
correct order of events in the reading selection.

Try the examples on the next page.

Examples:

Senior News

Graduation is approaching quickly— only one more week of school. The art department asks that all seniors submit baby photos by Monday for Thursday morning's slide show. Senior projects must be turned in to advisors by 5:00 p.m. Wednesday. Permission slips for the Friday field trip must be received no later than Wednesday at noon.

Locker keys, and any team uniforms must be handed in at graduation rehearsal. You will not receive your diploma unless these items have been returned, or the appropriate fine paid.

Principal Foster will pass out graduation tickets (4 per student) at rehearsal on Thursday. Please be at rehearsal by 4:00 p.m. A reception and dance will follow the rehearsal.

Seniors need to be at the auditorium by 10:00 a.m. on Saturday. Graduation will begin promptly at 11:00 a.m. Saturday. Congratulations on a wonderful year!

5. Graduation week is filled with deadlines and events. Select the answer that puts four of these deadlines and events in proper order.

   A. slide show, field trip permission slips due, graduation rehearsal, reception and dance

   B. baby photos due, senior projects due, field trip, graduation

   C. field trip permission slips due, senior projects due, field trip, graduation rehearsal

   D. field trip permission slips due, baby photos due, slide show, reception and dance

Analysis:
This is a complicated sequence of events and deadlines. Many of the events have two entries: a deadline and the event itself. Try making notes in the margin to determine the actual timetable. Your notes should look like this:

> *Monday.................................. baby photos due*
> *Wednesday: noon.................. field trip permission slips due*
> *5 p.m. .... senior projects due*
> *Thursday: morning................ slide show*
> *4 p.m. .... graduation rehearsal*
> *................. hand in keys and uniforms*
> *evening..................... reception and dance*

Friday.................................... field trip
Saturday: 10:00 a.m. .... seniors arrive at auditorium
11:00 a.m............... Graduation begins

Now you need to compare the answers to the order of events. With your list, you will quickly see that answer "B" is correct.

Things To Remember

• For a simple sequence chain, simply underline events in the text, and find the answer that matches.

• With a more complicated chain, such as the one above, try taking notes in the margin. Leave space between entries, and fill in the correct sequence. Next, match the correct order to the correct answer.

D. most-probable outcomes

These questions will ask you to make predictions, based on your reading. You will be asked to tell what is likely to happen in a particular situation.

Examples:

Marcos is taking Anita to the school play. He told her he would pick her up after his tennis match, which ends at 6:30 p.m. Marcos and Anita will then pick up Amy and Larry, at Amy's house. They plan to be seated in the theater in time for the play at 7:00 p.m. The distances, in time, for Marcos' evening are listed below.

tennis match to Anita's house . . . . 10 minutes
Anita's house to Amy's house . . . . 8 minutes
Amy's house to the school theater . . . . . 5 minutes

6. If Marcos' tennis match goes 10 minutes later than he expected, which prediction will be true:

A. Anita will be angry that Marcos is late.

B. The group will miss the opening curtain at the play.

C. The play will be wonderful, and worth the rush to get there.

D. Heavy traffic will cause the group to miss the entire play.

Analysis:
This problem is similar to a math word problem. You know that it will take Marcos 23 minutes to go from the tennis match to the theater. If the match ends at 6:30 p.m., this would put the group in the theater at 6:53, seven minutes before the play begins. If Marcos is 10 minutes late, they will be three minutes late to the play. All of the answers are possible. However, you can predict only one of them for sure. Based on the information from the passage, answer "B" is correct. Since they will be 3 minutes late, they will miss the opening curtain at the play.

Things To Remember

• Be sure to use information found in the reading selection to make your predictions. For instance, if asked what a character might do in a certain situation, use your knowledge of the character's personality and previous actions to make your predictions.

• Eliminate any answers you cannot support with information from the text.

• For nonfiction selections, you may use knowledge from outside of the reading selection. Just make sure your answer makes sense, and remember not to over-analyze a question.

E. the identification of questions that will demonstrate comprehension of the main idea and supporting details

Following a reading passage, you will be given a list of questions. You will decide which is the best question to ask to see if someone understands the main idea of the passage, or to see if they understand an important detail of the passage.

Example:

Education in America: 1830s

In 19th century rural New England, children were not required to go to school. Most children wanted to attend classes, however, because the alternative— working on the family farm— was much harder work.

At school, students learned basic skills: reading, memorization, writing, and arithmetic. All of these skills were needed for farming and shop-keeping. Few students would need anything beyond basic skills. Students would usually stay in school through the 6th grade. Few students attended school beyond 8th grade for a very practical reason; most teachers only had an eighth grade education.

Going to school in a farming society was considered a privilege, but not the only priority. Even school vacations were planned around the needs of the farm seasons. Families needed their children to help with farm work during busy seasons, such as spring planting and the fall harvest. Once the heavy work period had passed, school would resume.

7. If you want to know if someone understands the main idea of this selection, which of the following questions would be the best one to ask?

    A. Why were school vacations planned around the farm seasons?

    B. What was the minimum education level for a teacher?

    C. What skills did students learn in school?

    D. How did towns balance the need for education with the needs of a farming community?

Analysis:

What is the main idea of this passage? Your answer might be something like, "In the 1830s children wanted to get an education, but their parents still needed them to help with farming." What question might have this statement as its answer? How about, "How were children able to go to school, if their parents needed them for farming?" Now check the answer choices. Notice that all choices ask questions that can be answered from the reading passage. Re-read the original question: you are looking for a question that tells if someone understands the main idea of the selection. Answer "D" is correct: it matches your question above, and the answer to this question will show if a person understands the main idea of the passage.

Things To Remember

• Try to restate the main idea of a passage in one sentence. Have you covered the basic idea?

• Now consider: what question would have my sentence as an answer? The question you just thought of will be the right one to ask someone to see if they understand the selection. See if you can find a similar question in the answer choices.

• Try the same activity if you are asked to see if someone understands a specific detail.

NonFiction

You will need to demonstrate your skills in the following types of questions:

A. whether a statement is a fact or an opinion

You will be asked to select a statement which is a fact (or an opinion) from a selection of four statements.

Try the example on the next page.

Examples:

October 10: The school levy issue, item #44 on the November ballot, has this town in an uproar. The main question is whether residents are willing to pay additional 0.1% per year in property taxes. For the owner of a $150,000 house, this would amount to an additional annual property tax of $150.

Opponents of the legislation argue that property taxes are already high enough. Property taxes have increased each year for the past ten years. Some opponents question whether the older town residents, whose children are grown, should bear the burden of educating the children of younger residents.

Proponents of the tax levy say that this is a small price to pay for the education of our future leaders. Although property taxes have increased over the past few years, they argue, so have property values. Ben Staples, leader of the campaign for the levy, noted that all property owners in town historically have paid for all town services through taxes. "It is not an issue of the age of the taxpayer, but rather our willingness to maintain the strength of our community."

According to the latest school board budget proposal, if the levy is not passed, the school system will need to cut 10 full-time positions and 12 part-time positions. The cut positions would include music, language, computer, and physical education positions, among others. Also lost to cuts would be art supplies, sports uniforms, and the hot breakfast program.

1. Based on the information in the newspaper article, which of the following statements is an opinion?

   A. Taxpayers with grown children should not be taxed for school education.

   B. Without the levy, music, language, computer, and physical education programs will become smaller.

   C. Property taxes in town are at 0.1% of property value.

   D. Ben Staples leads the campaign for the school tax levy.

Analysis:
All of these statements are referred to in the passage. Three are fact-type, one is an opinion. The correct answer is "A:" this statement represents the ideas of the group opposing the tax levy. Answer "B" is a fact; the schools will cut teachers in these programs, so the programs will be smaller. The numbers in answer "C" are incorrect, so this statement is neither fact nor opinion. Ben Staples is the campaign leader for the levy, so answer "D" is also a fact.

Things To Remember
• Remember that facts and opinions can sound similar. Compare the following:

> *The mayor's insult to the press represents the worst*
> *political mistake of the year.*

> *The mayor said the local press is "the biggest group*
> *of liars this side of the Mississippi."*

The first sentence is an opinion, it represents the ideas of the writer. How does the writer know the insult is "the worst" mistake? What research supports this? Since no proof is cited, this is an opinion. Although the quote in the second sentence is the mayor's opinion, the entire sentence is fact. The sentence quotes an actual statement by the mayor, so it represents a factual event.

• Mark each answer choice as fact or opinion. If you are looking for the fact statement, and you have only one, this is your answer. If you have two (or more) possible answers, read them carefully. If they are facts, they can be proven. If opinions, they represent someone's ideas.

B. details that either support or do not support the main idea

You will be asked whether certain statements support (or don't support) the main idea of the reading passage.

Example:

May 25, 1996

Dear Editor,

Since I began my subscription to your newspaper, I have noticed that your coverage of women's sports is much weaker than the coverage of men's sports. This is true at the high school, college, and professional levels.

We moved to this town in August of last year, and our children (a son in 9th grade, and a daughter in 11th grade) began playing sports on their local high school's teams.

We do our best to attend all of their games. I have noticed that the crowds seem to be fairly equal for both men's and women's soccer, basketball, and softball/baseball. However, I have noticed that your photographers appear six times as often at the men's events, and they seem to attend the women's games only if the team is doing exceptionally well. In addition, your paper tends to cover men's sports in article form, and limit women's sports coverage to box scores. It is frustrating to find a story and photos about a men's soccer game, while the women's game, which was played *on the next field*, receives no coverage at all.

Must women athletes be tops in their league to receive press coverage? **Title IX**, which calls for equality in men's and women's sports, passed a generation ago. Will we need a legislative order to attain equality in press coverage as well?

I hope that you will prepare to provide better women's sports coverage for the upcoming summer Olympics, and continued local coverage for many years.

Sincerely,

Amy Coes

2. This letter to the editor claims that the local newspaper offers more coverage of men's sports than of women's sports. Which of the following statements from the letter can be used to support that idea?

   A. I have noticed that the crowds seem to be fairly equal for both men's and women's soccer, basketball, and softball/baseball.

   B. It is frustrating to find a story and photos about a men's soccer game, while the women's game, which was played *on the next field*, receives no coverage at all.

   C. We moved to this town in August of last year, and our children (a son in 9th grade, and a daughter in 11th grade) began playing sports on their local high school's teams.

   D. **Title IX**, which calls for equality in men's and women's sports, passed a generation ago.

Analysis:
*The question states the main idea: "the local newspaper offers more coverage of men's sports than of women's sports." You want to find the answer choice which supports this main idea. Answer "A" discusses the crowds at sports events. It doesn't mention newspaper coverage, so answer "A" should be crossed out. Answer "B" does mention newspaper coverage, and it compares the coverage of men's sports to the coverage of women's sports. Mark answer "B" as a probable answer. Answer "C" is incorrect because it doesn't mention newspaper coverage. Answer "D" discusses **Title IX**, but not newspaper coverage, so "D" is incorrect. Answer "B" is the correct answer.*

Things To Remember

• Be careful! All of the answer choices may contain quotes from the reading passage, so they might all seem correct. You want to find the answer which supports (or does not support, according to the question) the main idea.

• Read the main idea as stated in the question. Then read each answer choice. Does it support the main idea? Does it offer evidence or proof of the main idea?

• Remember, there is only one correct answer. Pick the choice which supports the main idea (or does not support, according to the question).

C. the author's purpose for writing the selection

You will need to determine a possible reason an author wrote a passage. Choices might include: to persuade, to entertain, to inform, and to instruct. The reason will not be stated within the passage; you will usually need to determine the reason on your own.

Example:

> Directions to the luncheon: Take Route 122 into town. At the second light, turn left onto May Street. Follow May Street for 3.2 miles, then turn right onto Massasoit Avenue. Go through two stop signs, then look for #305, the third house on the left.

3. What is the author's purpose for writing this selection?

   A. The author wants to inform the reader about a luncheon.
   B. The author is trying to persuade the reader to go to the luncheon.
   C. The author is instructing the reader by explaining how to get to the luncheon.
   D. The author is entertaining the reader.

Analysis:
Answer "A" is incorrect, because the selection does not announce the details of the luncheon. In fact, the selection assumes previous knowledge of the luncheon. Since the passage does not try to convince you to go to the luncheon, answer "B" is incorrect. Answer "C" is correct, because the passage gives instructions to get to the luncheon. Answer "D" is incorrect because the passage is not entertaining.

Things To Remember

- How does the selection affect you? Do you laugh (purpose=entertain), learn (purpose=instruct or inform), change your mind (purpose=persuade)?

- Check the answer choices. Do any match with your feelings about the passage?

- Be careful about the difference between inform and instruct. Inform means to give you information about something. Instruct means to help you learn how to do something specific.

D. the best summary for a specific audience

When you give a summary for a young child, it is different from one you would give for a teacher. This learning outcome requires that you recognize that the "best summary" can vary with the situation, and that you can choose the "best summary" if you are given a situation.

Example:

1. Imagine that your school soccer team won the state championship. Your grandfather, who knows little about soccer, wants to hear all about the game. Which of the summaries below would you tell your grandfather?

   A. It was a tough game, because the other team was really good. Also, the field was very wet, and it was cold and even snowing some of the time. In the first minute of the game, the other school scored a goal. That made us wake up fast! By half-time we were ahead 2-1. Part way through the second half, the game was tied. We played our best, and scored the winning goal with only 1 minute left in the game!

   B. Although the conditions were bad, we played really well. The opponent's forward scored a goal in the first minute. We tied with a great corner kick, and went ahead on a penalty kick. One of our play-ers got a yellow card, but luckily no-one got red-carded. Our next goal was a beautiful one—off the post. The other team tied, and then we won as Tony passed to Nick, who dribbled it past the goalie and into the goal.

   C. We won!

   D. It was great. The weather was cold, but we played well and won the game.

Analysis:
We know that the audience is your grandfather, that he knows little about soccer, but that he wants to know "all about the game." You will need a fairly complete, but not too technical, summary. Answer "A" is complete, highlights the main events, and includes "setting" information: the field, weather, and quality of the opposing team. This answer is correct, and it should satisfy your grandfather. Answer "B" is incorrect because it uses too many soccer terms, which your grandfather might not understand. Answer "C" is wrong because it is not complete. Answer "D" tells the main points, but does not tell enough about the game to satisfy the audience. The correct answer is "A."

Things To Remember

• Consider the audience. Do they know much about the subject? Are they interested in the subject? What is their age and vocabulary level?

• Why does your audience need the summary? Will they need complete, technical information for their purposes? Will a brief highlight be more appropriate?

E. the author's attitude toward a topic

You will need to be able to recognize an author's bias, slant, or view toward a topic. Is the author supporting a cause, or otherwise showing his/her feelings toward the subject?

Example:

Advancing Technology
by Lawrence Schimel

They took away my pens,
And all my pencils, too,
And gave me this computer—
Now, what am I to do?

They gave me this computer,
Despite complaints and gripes.
To live in this new high-tech world,
I guess it takes all type.

Refer the the passage above and answer the question on the next page.

1. Which of the following statements best describes the poet's view as presented in this poem?

    A. Computers are great for everyone.

    B. He is nervous about new technology.

    C. He dislikes his company because they don't allow pencils and pens.

    D. He believes computers are a waste of time.

Analysis:

Answer "A" is incorrect. The poet clearly questions "now what am I to do?" when he receives his computer. Answer "B" is a possibility. The poet seems to complain about the new technology, but seems willing to give it a try. We could conclude that he is nervous about the new technology. Answer "C" is incorrect, because the poem makes no mention of a company. Answer "D" is incorrect, because the poet seems willing to try his computer, although he seems a bit nervous. Answer "B" is correct.

Things To Remember

• Read all of the answer choices. Cross out any whose point is NOT made in the reading passage.

• Which of the remaining choices might show the author's view about the subject?

• Once you make a choice, be sure it describes the author's view, and be sure your decision can be supported with evidence from the reading selection.

Fiction <u>and</u> NonFiction

The following learning outcomes will be used with both fiction and nonfiction reading passages.

A. details (e.g. who, what, when, where, how, or problem/solution)

You will need to answer questions that refer to important details in the reading selection.

Try the example on the next page.

Example:

```
┌────────────────────────────────────────────────────────┐
│                  Building Directory                      │
│ First Floor                                              │
│ Angelica's Wedding Gowns _____     Suite 102   │
│ Special Events: Event Coordinators _____    Suite 128   │
│ The Main Thing: hair salon _____     Suite 142   │
│ Second Floor                                             │
│ Mortgage Title Associates _____    Suite 240   │
│ Staples, Snow, Varnum, & Jacobson: Attorneys at Law ___  Suite 201   │
│ Sweet and Sauer Real Estate _____    Suite 225   │
│ Third Floor                                              │
│ Major & Mineur Insurance Agents_____    Suite 310   │
│ Professional Tax Associates _____    Suite 332   │
│ Bookkeeping by Bess _____    Suite 355   │
└────────────────────────────────────────────────────────┘
```

1. If you needed to have a legal will drawn up, which office would you visit?

    A. Suite 355

    B. Suite 128

    C. Suite 201

    D. Suite 415

Analysis:

For a legal will, you will need a lawyer. Look through the building directory and see if you can find a lawyer or law firm. Notice "Staples, Snow, Varnum, & Jacobson: Attorneys at Law," on the second floor. Their office is Suite 201, so answer "C" is correct.

2. Of the following professions, which one is **NOT** found in this building?

    A. lawyer

    B. hairdresser

    C. book binder

    D. realtor

Analysis:

Read the directory carefully, looking for each profession. Cross out the answer for any profession you do find. The remaining answer will be correct. The building does contain offices for a lawyer (Staples, Snow, Varnum, & Jacobson: Attorneys at Law), a hairdresser (The Main Thing: hair salon), and a realtor (Sweet and Sauer Real Estate). There is no book binder, although you do have to be careful not to confuse this title with the bookkeeper (Bookkeeping by Bess). Answer "C" is correct.

Things To Remember
- Detail questions require you to read carefully. Read the question and determine the information you need to find.

- Be careful! Most answers will be within the reading selection but will not answer the question.

- Some questions will ask you to find something which is NOT in the reading selection. Be careful not to choose an answer in the passage, just because it looks familiar.

B. stated or implied main ideas

For some reading passages, the main idea will be stated directly within the text. For most passages, however, the main idea will be implied. You will need to figure out the main idea from your understanding of the passage.

Example:

The first time Ellen drove a car, she nearly killed her family.

Ellen had been flying airplanes for almost two years before she ever sat behind the wheel of an automobile. She was well used to the controls of a small plane: pull the wheel back to climb, lower the wheel to descend; turn slowly right or left to make a turn; when taxiing to the runway, steer the plane with the rudder pedals on the floor of the cockpit—use the right pedal to turn right, and the left pedal to turn left.

When she was about to begin driver's education at school, Ellen asked her mother if she could try driving the car. Reluctantly, her mother allowed her to drive down a lonely dirt road. Her mother would remain in the car to help Ellen, and her three sisters in the back seat were instructed to remain silent.

Ellen sat behind the wheel feeling nervous and excited. She pulled the seat forward and put her hands on the steering wheel. She put her right foot on the gas pedal, and her left foot on the brake—she would be ready for anything! Carefully, Ellen put the car in drive, and began depressing the gas pedal, millimeter by millimeter. Finally, the car began to move.

Once they had gone about half a mile, Ellen's mother suggested she try a turn. She pointed out a small driveway just ahead on the right. Ellen agreed, but was unsure when to begin her turn.
"Do I turn now? Now? Is it time yet?" Ellen asked.

"I'll tell you," her mother replied. "OK, start turning. Turn a little harder, Ellen. Ellen, you need to turn NOW!"

With that, the car flew past the drive like a shot out of a cannon. Within seconds, they were going 30 miles per hour, having missed the turn altogether. Ellen's mother was in shock, and her sisters were yelping in fear.

"Stop the car, Ellen," her mother squeaked. "What on earth happened?"

Ellen looked at her mother and grinned sheepishly. "Sorry, Mom. When you yelled "turn" I hit the right-hand pedal. We would have turned just fine if we were in a plane, but in the car I guess I hit the gas!"

3. Which of the following is the main idea of the selection?

    A. Ellen will be a dangerous driver.

    B. Ellen nearly killed her family.

    C. Car controls work differently from those on airplanes.

    D. Ellen has her pilot's license.

Analysis:
Since we cannot predict the future of Ellen's driving career, answer "A" is incorrect. Answer "B" is a true statement, but it is not the main idea of the story. Answer "D" is incorrect, because it is not stated in the text and it would not be the main idea. Answer "C" is correct: the event in this story happened because of the difference between the controls of an airplane and the controls of a car. Ellen was used to steering with her feet when on the ground in an airplane. She quickly discovered that she couldn't steer with her feet in a car.

Things To Remember
• Usually the main idea is not directly stated. Think: what is the author's main point?

• Read each answer carefully. Most will be true, but only one will be the main idea.

• Make sure your answer reflects the author's *main* point.

C. cause-and-effect relationships

You will need to be able to identify the causes and effects of an action or event in a reading passage. Sometimes these causes and effects will be stated, but sometimes they will be implied.

Try the example on the next page.

Example:

I've had many summer jobs. I've worked as a lifeguard at a pool, a waitress at a nice restaurant, and a server at an ice cream stand. For all of these jobs, I worked for someone else. For my other jobs, I was an "entrepreneur," I worked for myself. As an entrepreneur, I have done babysitting, car detailing, pet care, and garden maintenance.

At first, I was not too successful— one babysitting job a week does not make you rich. I worried that I had chosen the wrong path, and I considered taking a job at a local store. Fortunately, I mentioned my problem to several people. Everyone had suggestions for me. Once I put the best of these ideas to work, I was working every day!

My greatest success was my brochure. Since I didn't have much money, I typed up the brochure and drew the pictures. I described my services and prices. I collected quotes from my "clients," and I used them to show that I was a good worker. I had the brochure copied at the copy shop. I delivered brochures to every house in the neighborhood, and asked my clients to give them to their friends.

Within a week, I was booked for two weeks. Once I began working for more people, they told their friends and I had even more work. I went from a nearly unemployed entrepreneur to a successful business woman. All it took was a little creative advertising.

4. At first, the narrator was an unsuccessful entrepreneur because

A. she got bad recommendations from her former employers.

B. she was lazy.

C. her social life didn't allow her time to work.

D. she had not advertised her business.

Analysis:
Our basic question is what made the narrator unsuccessful. One way to do this is to decide what made her successful. *We can then conclude that the absence of this quality made her unsuccessful.*

Try the math format for both issues:
successful = creating brochure + distributing brochure + being a good worker
unsuccessful = _____ + _____ + _____

How can you fill in the blanks to find your answer? Try using the opposite of what made her successful:

unsuccessful = no brochure + no way to spread the word + being a good worker

Since she is a good worker in both cases, it seems to be the advertising issue that made the difference between failure and success. Is this idea supported within the reading passage? It is, so answer "D" is correct.

Things To Remember
- Cause and effect are closely related: the cause will create the effect. Make sure the question and your answer have this relationship.

- If you have trouble seeing the relationships, try writing the problem out in math form: *(rainy days + active dog = muddy house)* Use the parts you know to determine the answer.

D. the difference between statements based on fact and statements based on inference

Some ideas are directly stated in a reading passage. These statements are based on fact. Other ideas are based on inference: we conclude that the statement is correct based on information in the reading.

Example:

Budget: May 1996

Income
Tony..............................$625.00
Andrea............................875.00
Total..........................$1500.00

Expenses
Housing........................$725.00
Utilities..........................109.50
Telephone........................45.00
Groceries........................350.00
Entertainment...................50.00
Car Expenses....................50.00
Insurance.........................35.00
Misc. Bills.......................35.50
Savings...........................100.00
Total..........................$1500.00

5. Which of the following sentences is **NOT** directly stated but is an inference you could make from the selection?

    A. Tony and Andrea spend about $100 a week total on groceries and entertainment.

    B. Tony works part-time.

    C. For the month of May, the family's income matched their expenses.

    D. Tony and Andrea drive older cars, which cost less to insure.

Analysis:

You are looking for inferences here: a conclusion that is not directly stated but is supported with facts from the text. Answer "A" is a possibility, but will require some quick math to be sure. Circle "A" as a possible answer. Answer "B" is incorrect. Tony's income is less than Andrea's, but we have no evidence that this is because he works part-time. Answer "C" is true, but it is stated directly in the text, so it is not an inference. Answer "D" is incorrect because, like answer "B", it has no support within the reading selection. Now check Answer "A." Tony and Andrea spend $350 a month on groceries, and $50 a month on entertainment, for a total of $400. Since most months have 4 weeks, this amounts to about $100 a week. Answer "A" is correct.

Things To Remember

• Quickly eliminate answer choices which do not fit the question. For example, the question above asks for a statement which is NOT directly stated. You should cross out any statements which *are* directly stated.

• Check the remaining answer choices. If you are looking for inferences, be sure your choice can be supported by facts from the reading selection.

E. predictions about whether certain information is likely to be included in material

Based on a reading passage, you will need to make predictions about other material.

Try the example on the next page.

Example:

Curtistown, OH, October 10: Drive through Curtistown in May, and you will see a lovely small city with traditional homes and gardens. As election day approaches however, the town's front porches and flower gardens are overshadowed by a multitude of campaign signs. "Re-elect Cavenaugh for School Board," "Marumoto for Mayor," "Jacobson for State Congress."

It is the school board race which has this town eagerly awaiting election day. The school board has 3 seats available this November, and it is a very close race among 5 contenders. Recent polls show Takeda and Cavenaugh in the lead, with the other three candidates fighting for the third post.

Evelyn Cavenaugh has represented the town on the school board for the past three years. She is a vice-president at State Bank, and has two grown children. Cavenaugh was appointed to the board following the death of board member Jacob Reiss in 1993. Since the upcoming election will be Cavenaugh's first, she is making a great effort in her campaign. Cavenaugh's positions include: FOR lengthening the school day by 30 minutes, so that the school year can be shortened by 13 days; AGAINST increasing taxes to update elementary school science textbooks; FOR raising taxes to develop a daycare for children ages 2 to 4.

Mika Takeda has three children in the local elementary school. She is a partner in the law firm Marumoto, Takeda & Richardson. Takeda is running for school board with a bias towards elementary education. "If we neglect the younger children, we will fail to develop a strong base for their later education. Let's focus on building a strong education in the early grades, and work our way through the system. Our current method of fixing problems in "spots" is merely a bandage approach— we need to completely re-evaluate our educational values." Takeda has taken no stand on most current issues, since she feels the school system needs a total reevaluation…

6. If the reporter for this story were to interview candidates Cavenaugh and Takeda, which one of the questions below would s/he be sure to ask BOTH candidates?

   A. Why are you running for school board if your children are grown?

   B. What three issues are most crucial to our town's educational system?

   C. Why are you against updating elementary school science textbooks?

   D. What are some examples of our "bandage" approach to education?

Analysis:

Through careful reading of the passage, you know that Candidate Cavenaugh has declared at least some of her opinions on the issues, whereas Candidate Takeda has not declared her views. Answer "C" is incorrect, because it refers to a particular issue, and we know that Takeda is not willing to take a stand on particular issues. Answer "A" is incorrect, because only Cavenaugh's children are grown; Takeda's children are still in school. Answer "D" is incorrect, because only Takeda has taken a stand against the "bandage" approach; Cavenaugh feels it is OK to solve the small problems. Answer "B" is correct, because both candidates would be willing to comment on three issues each feels is most important to the education system. For Cavenaugh, these issues would probably be current proposals, while Takeda would most likely comment on broader problems of the school system.

Things To Remember

• To make predictions, you need to understand the author's point of view and the subject of the reading selection.

• You might be asked about various types of "other material," such as what information would the author include if making a speech, a journal entry, a letter, etc.

• Consider the audience, the author's point of view, and the subject matter when deciding on the correct answer choice.

Everyday/Functional Reading

A. directions of two or more steps

You will need to be able to follow directions which include two, three, four, or five steps. Some directions will be followed by pictures. You will select the picture showing the directions have been followed in the correct order. Other problems will ask you to follow the directions mentally.

Try the example on the next page.

Example:

Photo Contest! Enter Today!!

To enter the photo contest:

1. Submit an 8"x10" photo in one of these categories: action; children; landscape

2. On the reverse of the photo:
   a. write your name, address and phone number in the upper left corner
   b. write your social security number in the upper right corner
   c. note the category you are entering in the center
   d. sign your name in the lower right corner

---

1. Which of the pictures below represents a correct format for entering the photo contest?

A.
```
            Children

       Jeane Dover
       123 Main Street
       Leverman, Ohio 43234
       614-233-4504
                  Jeane Dover
```

B.
```
Jeane Dover              012-23-2202
123 Main Street
Leverman, Ohio 43234
614-233-4504
              Children

  Jeane Dover
```

C.
```
Jeane Dover              012-23-2202
123 Main Street
Leverman, Ohio 43234
614-233-4504

         Children
              Jeane Dover
```

D.
```
  Jeane Dover
  012-23-2202

              Children

  123 Main Street
  Leverman, Ohio 43234
  614-233-4504
```

Analysis:
Go through the directions step by step, and cross out incorrect answers on the way.
1. Submit an 8"x10" photo in one of these categories: action; children; landscape answers are correct on this point.
2. On the reverse of the photo:
   a. write your name, address and phone number in the upper left corner
      Cross out answer A and answer D.

b. write your social security number in the upper right corner
   Both B and C are correct on this point.
c. note the category you are entering in the center
   Both B and C are correct on this point.
d. sign your name in the lower right corner
   Cross out answer B. Answer "C" is correct.

Things To Remember

* Follow the directions slowly, comparing each step to the pictures in the answer choices. Cross out any which are wrong. The remaining choice will be correct.

* If you have a map, draw a line on the map as you follow the directions. Be sure to orient yourself as if you were the traveler. Turn your book around if necessary to determine left from right for the traveler.

B. the selection and use of appropriate reference sources and illustrative materials

You will need to know how to select the most appropriate reference source to find information. Resources might include: dictionary, encyclopedia, almanac, atlas, phone book, card catalog, periodical/newspaper, schedule, table of contents, and index. You should be familiar with the use of all of these resources, and know what types of information you can find in each one. You will also need to have various skills for using these resources: alphabetical order; skimming and scanning; reading charts, tables, diagrams, graphs, maps, labels, and signs.

Example:

2. Which of the following resources would be best to use to find contact information for your state's U.S. Senators?

   A. the local newspaper

   B. the telephone book

   C. a table of contents

   D. an encyclopedia

Analysis:
You need contact information for your state's Senators. Contact information would include the Senators' names, addresses, and phone numbers. This information is most quickly and easily found in the telephone book, so answer "B" is correct. You might find the information in the local newspaper as well (answer "A"), but it would probably involve searching several issues to locate the information.

Strategies:

- You need to know the information you are looking for, and possible locations for that information.

- Some questions might have two or more reasonable answers. You need to choose the *best* answer— where you are certain to find all of the information you need, quickly and easily.

C. the meaning of vocabulary words used on an application form

These questions will require you to interpret vocabulary commonly found on various types of application forms.

Example:

Application for Waiters/Waitresses at La Petite Auberge: French Restaurant

1. Name _____
2. Address _____
3. City, State, Zip _____
4. Phone _____

Please state your
5. Years of experience waiting tables _____
6. Former employers _____
   _____
   _____
7. Days and hours you are available to work _____
   _____
8. Signature _____

3. What is the meaning of the words on line 5 of the application?

A. the length of time you usually wait to get a table in a restaurant
B. the number of years you have been a waiter or waitress
C. the number of years you have been waiting to get a job
D. your experiences eating in restaurants

Analysis:

The application is for a job as a waiter or waitress at a restaurant. Line 5 reads, "Years of experience waiting tables." "Waiting tables," means working as a waiter or waitress in a restaurant, so line 5 is asking for the number of years of experience as a waiter or waitress. Answer "B" is correct.

Things To Remember

• Read the indicated application line carefully.

• Be aware of words that have multiple meanings. Which meaning is correct for the situation?

D. the use of propaganda

For this learning outcome, you will be required to recognize propaganda (a systematic promotion of ideas to further one's own cause or damage an opposing one, *Webster's New World Dictionary*). You will not need to identify the methods used for propaganda.

Example:

4. Which of the following statements contains propaganda?

   A. Women are a growing force in the business world; in Columbus, one-third of the businesses are owned by women.

   B. "We must fight against the enemy; they are all evil people who are trying to take over the world," said the General to his troops.

   C. Virus XYZ proved to be dangerous in lab tests: two-thirds of the rats injected with the virus died within three days.

   D. Salt Lake City, Utah is one of the fastest growing cities in the country.

Analysis:

Answer A: This statement is a fact. It does not try to promote or injure a particular cause. It is not propaganda.

Answer B: The General is appealing to the emotions (fear) of his troops. He is trying to promote his cause (to fight) and to injure the cause of the opponent (by calling them all evil). This statement is propaganda. Answer "B" is correct.

Answer C: This statement is fact: the virus is dangerous, at least to rats. No propaganda is used here.

Answer D: Again, this statement is pure fact. It does not promote or injure any cause.

Things To Remember
- Remember that propaganda is trying to convince you of something. It will often pull at your emotions.

- There is a fine line between propaganda and truth— that's what makes propaganda so dangerous.

- Choose an answer which tries to convince you, which pulls at your emotions, and which is promoting or trying to injure a particular cause.

Reading Practice Items

Reading Practice Items

Remember these basic strategies for tackling the reading practice items:

1. Skim through the reading passage. Read the title of the selection, and the first and last sentences of each paragraph. Be sure you have a general understanding of the passage.
2. Read the questions for this reading selection, but do not read the answers yet. Do you know what each question is asking?
3. Read the reading selection. Mark places you think will help you to answer the questions.
4. Answer the questions:
   - Read the question.
   - Read *all* of the answers.
   - Cross out any answers you know are wrong.
   - If more than one answer remains:
     — be sure you know the meaning of the question.
     — quickly review the passage. Can you find the correct answer?
   - If you can't answer a question, make your best guess. There is NO penalty for an incorrect guess.

The Antifisherman
by Ron Enderland

There are those who are born with an <u>innate</u> ability to catch fish. There are also those who, through long hours of practice, research, and studying of experts' techniques, have developed the ability to harvest the elusive creatures. Then, there's me. Joe Mitchum, professional antifisherman.

You've never heard of my particular <u>trade</u>? Well, first, a little about myself.

I was just like any other normal kid. I liked marbles, baseball, skipping school, and fishing. Especially fishing. I would spend long hours down at the Third Street bridge with my line in the water, baited with morsels no self-respecting bluegill could turn down. Except they did.

It never bothered me, because my friends always seemed to do lousy, too. It was strange, though. Almost invariably, they would have fish on their stringers when I arrived. Yet, I wouldn't see them catch anything. After a while, the boredom would get to me, and I'd leave to go play baseball or something. When I'd get a hundred yards or so down the road, I would start hearing whoops of delight as bobbers began vanishing beneath the waves. I'd shake my head and keep walking.

Eventually, I began suspecting that something strange was going on. For instance, there was the trip to Marineland. Now, my favorite TV show when I was a kid was Flipper, so naturally I wanted to see the dolphins. I was in my seat promptly for the 10:00 a.m. performance. The trainer came out and stood on the platform above the water and clicked his clicker two times. A grey shape lazily rolled to the top of the water, stuck its head out, and looked wearily upward at its master. The trainer gave some sort of hand signal. The dolphin sank out of sight. More clicking. No sign of the dolphin. The trainer, clearly agitated, reached in a bucket and grabbed a fish and held it over the water, all the time clicking furiously. At last, the dolphin leapt out of the water and grabbed out of the trainer's hand...the clicker! With a flick of its head, the noisemaker shot over the crowd into the parking lot. The trainer wept. The show was over.

I stepped out of the arena and walked about a hundred yards away. I turned around to see the dolphin furiously flipping, somersaulting, and diving before an amazed crowd and a still weeping trainer. Obviously, its appetite had returned.

At last I faced the truth. My appearance near underwater life caused instant loss of the desire to eat.

Well, as they say, if life hands you a lemon, make lemonade. Today, I am a very wealthy man, thanks to my dubious situation. You see, being an antifisherman happens to be a very marketable talent.

When game and fish authorities need to set limits on certain species, they call me. Fish and game employees walk up and down rivers distributing pieces of my old socks in locked pedestals every 100 yards along the shoreline. They are also sunk in sealed recoverable containers evenly distributed across the restricted waterways. My powers are so potent, in fact, that all that is needed is an article of clothing that I wore for a few seconds to provide a no-feeding zone for the fish. When authorities raise the fishing limits, they merely remove my clothing from the containers.

Now, my powers are not unlimited. There is a minimum size requirement of one square inch of clothing for the appetite removal to take effect. This means, however, that one pair of my jeans is adequate to protect the Snake River from Twin Falls to Glens Ferry. One oversized sweat shirt can cover the entire area of Lake Okeechobee.

Now, don't worry. Extensive studies have been performed showing that there is no ill effect upon the fishes from their fast. As a matter of fact, it seems to cleanse their systems, improve their karma, and lower stress, especially among the salmonids.

So, if you're fishing a good looking stretch of water but you aren't having any luck, look around for a locked container that says "Warning! Keep clear!" What you probably have is a piece of my underwear that was missed from the last time the trout spawned. Just move upstream a hundred yards, things should pick up.

Go on to the next page.

1. What did the fish do whenever the narrator was in the area?

   A. jump into his boat

   B. nibble on his friends' lines, but not on the narrator's

   C. refuse to eat at all

   D. die

2. How did the narrator use his "problem" to help the fish and game authorities?

   A. Since he never caught any fish, the authorities didn't have to worry about him going over his limit.

   B. He let them use his clothing to help protect species from over-fishing.

   C. The narrator visited areas where the fish supply was low, to prevent fisherman from catching any fish.

   D. He sold his story to the fish and game authorities so they could make an antifishing movie.

3. What is the meaning of the word <u>innate</u> as it is used in line 1?

   A. existing naturally, rather than acquired

   B. secret

   C. to stimulate to movement or action

   D. prisoner

4. If you want to find out if someone had understood what the story is mainly about, which of the following questions would be the best one to ask?

   A. Why couldn't the narrator catch any fish?

   B. How did the narrator turn his problem into a business which helps the fish population?

   C. Why was the narrator sad when the dolphin didn't perform?

   D. How large a piece of clothing is needed for the appetite removal to take effect on the fish?

5. If you went swimming in a shark-infested area, what would happen if you wore a piece of the narrator's clothing during your swim?

   A. The sharks would leave you alone.

   B. The sharks would eat you.

   C. You would drown.

   D. It would be easy to catch a shark.

6. What is the meaning of the word <u>trade</u> as it is used in line 5?

   A. the buying and selling of commodities

   B. customers

   C. a purchase or sale

   D. occupation, work, or line of business

Go on to the next page.

7. The story describes a series of events in the narrator's life. Select the answer that gives the events in the order in which they occurred in the narrator's life.

   A. He becomes an anti-fisherman. He discovers that his presence makes fish not hungry. He gives his clothing to the fish and game authorities. He becomes wealthy.

   B. He has trouble catching fish. The dolphins don't perform when he visits. His father takes him hunting. He helps the fish and game authorities.

   C. He has trouble catching fish. The dolphins don't perform when he visits. He helps the fish and game authorities. He becomes wealthy.

   D. He becomes wealthy. He donates his clothing to the fish and game authorities. The fish and game authorities discover his clothes cause fish to lose their appetite. The fish population is saved from over-fishing.

8. If you read a biography of Ron Enderland, the author of this story, which of the following statements is **NOT** likely to be included in the biography?

   A. Enderland grew up in the desert regions of the southwest United States.

   B. Enderland enjoys fishing, hiking, and working with animal conservation agencies.

   C. A bit of a practical joker, Enderland has a wonderful sense of humor.

   D. While growing up, Enderland enjoyed inventing a wide variety of gadgets.

Go on to the next page.

Pioneering Poet
by Karinne Heise

The Bars Fight
"August 'twas the twenty-fifth
Seventeen hundred forty-six
The Indians did in ambush lay
Some very valiant men to slay...."

Early in the morning, the Abenakis hid in a thicket, waiting for the settlers to return to their hay making in a field outside the village fort. Meanwhile, inside the fort, Lucy Terry, the woman who eventually composed "The Bars Fight," was most likely doing chores. Lucy was not, however, doing chores in her own house, for she was a black slave woman.

Lucy's poem records the events of the last Indian raid on the frontier town of Deerfield, Massachusetts. She notes everything from the decapitation of Simeon Amsden—
"Simeon Amsden they found dead/Not many rods off from his head—"
to the kidnapping of Samuel Allen—
"Young Samuel Allen, Oh! lack-a-day/Was taken and carried to Canada."

"The Bars Fight" does not only record history; it makes history. Lucy's poem is the first poem credited to an African-American. It is unknown whether Lucy actually wrote down "The Bars Fight," or whether she composed it in her head and recited it from memory. While she may have known how to read and write, no manuscript of the poem has ever been uncovered. Certainly, there were numerous obstacles preventing African-Americans from becoming writers in 1746. Although it was legal for black slaves in Massachusetts to read and write, people need more than just knowledge of their ABC's to become writers. They need time to practice writing. Few slaves had the leisure time to become masters of the craft of writing.

Literature comes in many forms— not all stories are written. Lucy was born in Africa, and lived in a storytelling culture. She would have inherited an oral literature from her African tribe. It would be fitting if the first African-American poem on record involved combining the African storytelling tradition with tales of events in America.

Although Lucy recorded history in her poem, there are few primary sources recording her life. When she obtained her freedom from her master, Ebenezer Wells, is unknown. The town books of Deerfield do note her baptism, first communion, marriage to Abijah Prince and the births of her six children: Caesar, Duroxa, Drusilla, Festus, Tatnai and Abijah. The

Franklin Herald of Greenfield, Massachusetts and The Vermont Gazette of Bennington, Vermont also published notices of her death: "At Sunderland, Vt., July 11th, Mrs. Lucy Prince, a woman of colour....97 years of age."

Lucy crafted stories, and many stories about Lucy have been crafted. Myths usually do hold some grains of truth. We know that Lucy and her husband, Abijah Prince, were among the pioneering homesteaders in two Vermont towns: Guilford and Sunderland. Another legend claims that Lucy, in a lawsuit against a Sunderland neighbor, argued her case before the United States Supreme Court and won. These legends, many unverified, add to the evidence of her remarkable nature.

Lucy's obituary not only gives notice of her death, but also hints at her storytelling skill, complimenting her "volubility" and "the fluency of her speech" as well as complimenting her for being a "remarkable woman...much respected among her acquaintance, who treated her with a degree of deference." Such praise in the local press for a black woman, at a time in America when few blacks were treated with any deference, shows just how extraordinary Lucy must have been.

Lucy, who lived on the edge of many frontiers, was every bit the pioneer as the "valiant men" she eulogizes in "The Bars Fight." The stories about Lucy are certainly as captivating as the stories told by Lucy. It is no tall tale to say that Lucy Terry Prince was a pioneering poet.

9. Which of the following sentences is **NOT** directly stated but is an inference you could make from the selection?

   A. Lucy Terry Prince was known for her "volubility" and her "fluency of speech."

   B. Lucy lived in Deerfield, Massachusetts, Guilford, Vermont and Sunderland, Vermont.

   C. Lucy may have represented herself in a legal case held before the United States Supreme Court.

   D. In the eighteenth century, it was unusual for an African-American woman to make her mark on history.

10. According to the reading selection, which of the following statements represents an opinion, rather than a fact?

   A. "The Bars Fight" records the events of the last Indian raid on the frontier town of Deerfield, Massachusetts.

   B. It would be fitting if the first African-American poem on record involved combining the African storytelling tradition with tales of events in America.

   C. Lucy's poem is the first poem credited to an African-American.

   D. There are few primary sources recording Lucy's life.

Go on to the next page.

11. What is the author's purpose for writing this selection?

    A. to tell about the history of Deerfield, Massachusetts

    B. to discuss American poetry

    C. to tell about one of the first African-American poets

    D. to present examples of battle poetry

12. Which of the following statements best describes the author's view as presented in the selection?

    A. You cannot make any character judgments about a person based on legends.

    B. Lucy Terry Prince overcame the prejudices of her time to make an impact on her community.

    C. Lucy Prince was a troublemaker.

    D. Lucy should have become a lawyer.

13. If the author of this passage were speaking to a group of first grade students about this topic, which of the following statements would most likely **NOT** be included in the talk?

    A. Lucy was every bit the pioneer as the "valiant men" she eulogizes in "The Bars Fight."

    B. Not all stories are written, many are shared through storytelling.

    C. Lucy's poem tells about the last Indian raid on the town of Deerfield, Massachusetts.

    D. Lucy was born in Africa, and lived in a storytelling culture.

14. Which of the following statements about Lucy has **NOT** been verified?

    A. Her master was Ebenezer Wells.

    B. She married Abijah Prince, and had six children.

    C. Lucy and Abijah were homesteaders in Guilford and Sunderland, Vermont.

    D. Lucy argued and won a case before the United States Supreme Court.

15. Which of the following statements is true?

    A. Lucy wrote "The Bars Fight," and submitted it for publication.

    B. In 1746 in Massachusetts, it was illegal for black slaves to learn to read and write.

    C. No manuscript of "The Bars Fight" has ever been found.

    D. "The Bars Fight" records the kidnapping of Simeon Amsden.

16. Lucy Terry Prince was an extraordinary African-American woman who lived in 18th century New England. Which of the following statements does **NOT** support this main idea?

    A. Lucy and Abijah Prince had six children.

    B. "The Bars Fight" is the first poem credited to an African-American.

    C. Lucy and Abijah were pioneering homesteaders in Vermont.

    D. Lucy's obituary hints at her storytelling skill, and calls her a "remarkable woman...much respected among her acquaintance, who treated her with a degree of deference."

Go on to the next page.

Questions 17 through 20 are NOT based on a reading selection.

17. Which statement below uses propaganda?

A. Beginning January 1, 1996, "baby boomers" began turning 50 at the rate of eight per minute.

B. Candidate Jones is out to rob you blind— save your tax dollars and vote for Smith.

C. The black widow spider is so named because the female eats her mate.

D. Automobile accidents are one of the leading causes of death among teenagers.

18. Emily is preparing a slide presentation about Japan for a group of travelers. She needs to:

✓ prepare a map, labeling the seven cities covered in her presentation
✓ find the latest exchange rate from U.S. dollars to Japanese yen
✓ write a brief history of the Japanese city of Kyoko
✓ locate a photo shop which can make copies of several slides

To find this information, which resources will Emily need to consult?

A. a dictionary, a telephone book, an encyclopedia, and a map

B. a table of contents, an encyclopedia, an atlas, and a newspaper

C. a train schedule, a newspaper, a dictionary, and a telephone book

D. an atlas, a newspaper, an encyclopedia, and a telephone book

1.	Register to win a trip to Paris!
2.	Name:
3.	Address:
4.	Preferred means of travel?
5.	Telephone:

19. What is the meaning of the words on line 4 of the registration form above?

A. How do you like to get from one place to another?

B. What areas of the world do you like to visit?

C. Do you have enough money to take a trip?

D. Do you usually pay by cash or credit card?

Go on to the next page.

20. To load software into your Macintosh computer: Insert the floppy disk into the floppy disk drive. Double-click on the "install" icon. Click the "OK" box. Once installation is complete, quit the installer program. Before using your new software, restart your computer.

Which answer shows some of the software installation steps in the proper order?

A. insert floppy disk, double-click install, quit the installer, restart computer

B. insert floppy disk, quit the installer, restart computer, click OK

C. click OK, double-click install, quit the installer, restart computer

D. restart computer, double-click install, click OK, quit installer

College Day Information:
Tuesday is College Visiting Day. Representatives from 30 colleges will be at school from 9:00 a.m. until 5:00 p.m. Please observe the following changes in school routine: students should arrive at school by 8:00 a.m.; please park cars in the lower lot, so that representatives may use the upper lot; registration for information sessions will take place in the gym, and should be completed by 8:30 a.m.; please spend any free time in the dining hall, or in the courtyard. Thank you for your cooperation. Enjoy your information gathering!

21. If you want to attend a college information session, you need to register by

A. 8:00 a.m.

B. 9:00 a.m.

C. 5:00 p.m.

D. 8:30 a.m.

22. If a student parks his car in the upper lot, which of the following statements will be true?

A. The student will not be able to participate in College Day.

B. He will find the gym door locked.

C. There will be less room for college representatives to park.

D. He will not be able to leave school until 5:00 p.m.

Go on to the next page.

Anno Matins
by Lawrence Schimel

Let the clarion snowbell <u>herald</u> spring.
The sun is drawn by its tinkling chimes
of pistil on petal. Snow melts on
the earth's warm tongue. The river licks
its parched lips. Silhouetted against the dawn,
a lone crocus stands like a town crier
announcing the time of year.

23. What is the meaning of the word <u>herald</u> as
    it is used in the first line?

    A. a messenger

    B. to announce or foretell

    C. an official in charge of genealogies

    D. an official who makes proclamations

24. Which of the following is the main idea of
    the poem?

    A. the beauty of rivers covered with snow
       and ice

    B. types of flowers for a garden

    C. the events which mark the arrival of
       spring

    D. the duties of a town crier

25. Which of the following sentences is
    NOT directly stated, but is an inference
    you could make from the selection?

    A. Crocuses announce spring.

    B. As the snow melts, the river rises.

    C. Snow melts on the warm earth.

    D. Flowers are the only signs of spring.

Go on to the next page.

Ahhh, the cool crisp air of
— the BMV office

We've moved. Period. No exclamation point. In fact, the Bureau of Motor Vehicles and their Licensed Agents are quickly destroying my enthusiasm for the entire state.

Now, we've seen BMV bureaucracy in action before– we used to live in Massachusetts, and we're still arguing with them over whether or not we actually moved from the state six years ago. I figured that no state could be as complicated as Massachusetts, and until now I've been right.

When we moved here, we picked up a brochure detailing how to transfer car titles, get tags, and get driver's licenses. It all looked pretty simple— deceptively so, as I was soon to discover.

Step One. "Let your fingers do the walking," as the old ad said. I called the License Agent in town and asked what I needed to do to get tags for our cars, since they both have my husband's name on the registration. I was told to get the pink power of attorney slip off the counter and have him sign it. Fine. Done.

Step Two. Wait in line for 45 minutes with two young children in tow. Wrong power of attorney form. I needed the white one, which must be witnessed by a notary public. Ahh.

Step Three. Drag husband and the two young children to the License Agent's on Saturday morning. This did not go over well. Wait, again, for 55 minutes. Pay lots of money to have titles transferred and to get 30 day tags. (I questioned why the amount we paid differed from the amount in the brochure. Apparently if we went downtown we would pay the quoted amount, but of course "You'd have to pay at least $5 for parking." I think I just did.) They will call us when the tags arrive.

Step Four. They don't call us (were you surprised?). The 30 day tags expire, and I call them. I told them I'd be right down to pick them up. "Oh, no. Your husband must be here since his name is on the title." (Didn't we already solve this problem?) So, it's either the *white* power of attorney form, or another Saturday morning at the BMV, checkbook in hand.

Now that we've licensed our cars, we need to license ourselves. I'm really not looking forward to this. Rumor has it that we go to one location, wait in line of course, and take our test. We then receive a slip of paper saying we passed (I'm assuming here). We must take this paper to *another* location, wait in yet another line, and have our photo taken. Oh, I forgot. We'll have to pay money, too. At both places.

The really bad part of all of this is that we are planning to buy a house next year. You'd think we'd be excited, but it's hard. Maybe we just won't tell the BMV.

Go on to the next page.

26. Which of the following statements best represents the author's attitude towards theBureau of Motor Vehicles?

    A. The BMV is well-organized and efficient.

    B. There is no reason to register cars with the BMV.

    C. The BMV waiting room is a boring place.

    D. The BMV complicates a simple process.

27. If the author wanted to summarize her BMV experience for the state governor, which of the following statements would be most appropriate?

    A. You should spend a day at the BMV—what a zoo!

    B. The process of transferring car titles from another state is far too complicated.

    C. The BMV is a waste of time; you should cut the department from the payrolls.

    D. I've never seen such an efficient operation as the BMV.

28. According to the selection, which of the following statements is **NOT** true?

    A. The author is looking forward to getting her driver's license.

    B. The white power of attorney slip was needed to transfer the car titles.

    C. The author's children and husband did not enjoy waiting at the License Agent's.

    D. The author was required to pay more for a title transfer than was stated in the BMV brochure.

29. In the third paragraph, what is the meaning of the word <u>deceptively</u>?

    A. misleadingly

    B. truthfully

    C. beautifully

    D. honestly

Go on to the next page.

Look Out, Alice Webster!
by David Howard

Laura came up with me through Pony and Mustang League. She played third base when I was shortstop on the Dodgers Pony Team. Every spring we couldn't wait for the season to start, and I guess we thought we'd play together forever. We followed the Giants in the Big Leagues and always planned to go to a game together. San Francisco is the closest city to us, 100 miles south. We live in Norwood, pop. 25,000, like the sign says.

Last year, Laura started wearing short skirts and tank tops and counting calories instead of RBI's. There was no way she wanted to go out for softball. Me either. I was going for boy's hardball or nothing.

Lots of times when the corridors at school empty out, I go to the area near Principal Wilson's office where all the photos of the teams are. It goes back to the 1950s. Some of these guys are grandpas already.

In all the pictures there's only one girl, a gangling black girl named Alice Webster. She was on the boy's hardball team way back in the eighties. A couple of girls have tried out since then and warmed the bench. Coach Benson admits that when he started out at Lincoln in 1975, he didn't think girls should or could play baseball. Then Alice Webster came along, and changed his mind forever. She batted .400 in her sophomore year and probably could be playing Triple A minor league ball today, if she wanted to. She still lives in Norwood and even came to the tenth-year reunion of her class in 1995.

Coach Benson now says, "Sure a girl can play for Lincoln. But she'd better be half as good as Alice Webster. And I ain't seen one of those yet."

30. If you wanted to discover if someone had understood what this story is mainly about, which of the following questions would be the best one to ask?

A. What was the narrator's and Laura's favorite sport while they were growing up?

B. Why wouldn't Coach Benson let girls play baseball?

C. Why is Alice Webster important to the narrator?

D. What year did Alice Webster graduate from high school?

31. If this story continued, which of the following is most likely to happen?

A. Alice Webster will sign on for Triple A minor league baseball.

B. Coach Benson will retire.

C. Laura and the narrator will try out for the softball team.

D. The narrator will be on the baseball team.

Go on to the next page.

32. Based on the reading passage, which statement would most likely be an entry in the narrator's journal?

   A. Coach Benson told me that I can't try out for baseball.

   B. I am frustrated that Laura has lost interest in softball, but I am determined to try out for the baseball team this year.

   C. I'm considering giving up sports so I have more time for my friends.

   D. I met Alice Webster, and she encouraged me to try out for baseball.

33. What made Coach Benson decide that maybe girls could play baseball?

   A. The male players had become grandfathers.

   B. Alice Webster graduated and played Triple A minor league baseball.

   C. Alice Webster batted .400 during her sophomore year.

   D. The softball coach retired, and the baseball team was forced to become coed.

34. In the fourth paragraph, what is the meaning of the word <u>gangling</u>?

   A. thin and tall

   B. a member of a gang

   C. beautiful

   D. shy

Go on to the next page.

Map of the Library

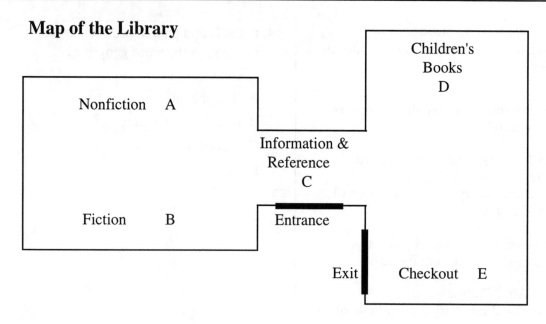

35. Conor wants to borrow the following books from the library:

   ✓ a biography of Frederick Douglass
   ✓ the picture book *Harold and the Purple Crayon*, for his sister
   ✓ the novel *Trinity*, by Leon Uris
   ✓ a biography of the artist Van Gogh
   ✓ a children's novel, *Trumpet of the Swans*, by E.B. White

   What route should Conor take through the library, so that he won't retrace his steps?

   A. D, A, B, A, then E
   B. C, B, A, C, D, then E
   C. C, D, then E
   D. B, A, D, then E

36. If Matthew wants to find the C volume of an encyclopedia, which area of the library should he visit?

   A. the children's area
   B. the reference area
   C. the nonfiction area
   D. the fiction area

Go on to the next page.

Travel Tips: Telephones in Japan

In Japan, pay telephones are different colors, depending on their function. The chart below shows the function of each color telephone.

	Blue	Green	Pink	Red	Yellow
domestic calls	✓	✓	✓	✓	✓
in-country long distance calls	✓	✓	✓	✓	✓
international calls		✓			
accept telephone cards		✓			
accept 100-yen and 10-yen coins		✓			✓
accept only 10-yen coins	✓		✓	✓	
offer travel information	✓	✓			✓

37. Which color telephone can be used for all of the listed functions?

    A. pink

    B. red

    C. green

    D. blue

38. What is the purpose of this chart?

    A. to explain the different functions of Japanese pay phones for travelers

    B. to convince Japan to make their pay phone system simpler

    C. to discourage travelers from using Japanese pay phones

    D. to entertain travelers

Go on to the next page.

Idyllic Idyllwild

As you wind your way up the mountain road, try not to look over the edge. Nothing separates the road from the precipitous cliffs. The views upwards, however, are magnificent— glimpses of the peaks of the San Jacinto Mountains. The cars struggle uphill: past 4,000 feet above sea level, then 5,000 feet. Finally, at a mile above sea level, you enter the town of Idyllwild, California.

Idyllwild rests in the middle of the San Jacinto National Forest, and has become a haven for those seeking to escape the summer heat of the California valleys. The village population doubles with the arrival of the summer visitors. The town is located thirty minutes from the nearest city (all downhill), so Idyllwild has developed a self-sufficient core of stores, along with many gift and specialty shops.

Leisure activities abound in this small town. The town is world famous among rock climbers for the rock face known as Tahquitz. Hiking and mountain biking trails are plentiful. Once you have exhausted yourselves outdoors, take a stroll through the quaint shops, or stop for a meal at one of the many restaurants.

Day trips from Idyllwild take full advantage of the scenic routes to and from town. Look for mountain goats among the rocks as you drive to Palm Desert. Visit The Living Desert, or tour the shops in nearby Palm Springs. If you want a truly different perspective of the San Jacinto Mountains, you can take a tramway ride from Palm Springs to a spot not far from Idyllwild. Be adventurous, and hike back to the village to complete your tour of the area.

Go on to the next page.

Refer to the passage on the previous page to answer the following questios.

39. Which of the statements below is not directly stated but is an inference you could make from the reading selection?

   A. You can ride a tram from Palm Springs up into the mountains.

   B. Rock climbers know Idyllwild for the rock face Tahquitz.

   C. The charm of Idyllwild is well worth the scary trip up the mountain.

   D. Idyllwild has many restaurants and quaint shops.

40. If a travel agent wanted to promote Idyllwild to tourists, which of the following facts is **NOT** likely to be mentioned?

   A. July temperatures are cooler in Idyllwild than in Los Angeles.

   B. When biking or hiking on mountain paths, use extreme caution if you see a mountain lion or bobcat.

   C. Most of the restaurants are open seven days a week.

   D. Idyllwild is home to several galleries featuring California artists and craftsmen.

41. Which statement best represents the main idea of this passage?

   A. Mountain roads are safe, but sometimes scary.

   B. Idyllwild is a good place to stay if you want to visit Palm Springs.

   C. Mountain towns are a great escape from the heat of summer.

   D. Idyllwild is a beautiful mountain town with a variety of recreation opportunities.

Go on to the next page.

THE NANNY CONNECTION: CANDIDATE APPLICATION

1. Name _____

2. Address _____

_____

3. Telephone _____

4. References_____

_____

_____

_____

5. Languages _____

6. Driving Record _____

7. Date Available _____

---

42. What information is asked for on line 5?

    A. the subjects you can tutor

    B. whether you speak English

    C. whether you swear in front of children

    D. the languages you speak

43. What is meant by "driving record" on line 6?

    A. How fast can you drive?

    B. Have you had any tickets or car accidents?

    C. Are you a professional race care driver?

    D. Do you listen to music when you drive?

44. What is meant by "Date Available" on line 7?

    A. When could you begin a new job?

    B. Do you date often?

    C. Would you like to go to a movie next week?

    D. Are you available for a driving test?

STOP.

Answer Key

Answer	Learning Outcome
1. C	1g
2. B	1c
3. A	1a
4. B	1j
5. A	1f
6. D	1b
7. C	1d
8. A	1i
9. D	2d
10. B	2e
11. C	2h
12. B	2j
13. A	2f and 2i
14. D	2a
15. C	2e
16. A	2g
17. B	3d
18. D	3b
19. A	3c
20. A	3a
21. D	2a
22. C	2c
23. B	1a
24. C	1e
25. B	1h
26. D	2j
27. B	2i
28. A	2a
29. A	1a
30. C	1j
31. D	1f
32. B	1i
33. C	1c
34. A	1a

Answer	Learning Outcome
35. D	3a
36. B	3b
37. C	2a
38. A	2h
39. C	2d
40. B	2f
41. D	2b
42. D	3c
43. B	3c
44. A	3c

Mathematics

Ninth Grade Proficiency Test: Mathematics

The Ohio Ninth Grade Proficiency Mathematics Test is designed to test your overall understanding of mathematics and its application to the real world. You will need to combine your knowledge, which is everything you have ever learned in and out of school, with test-taking skills and confidence to be successful on the proficiency test. This chapter will cover the content of the test by reviewing the material and by setting up simulated proficiency test questions with an analysis that will help you learn the powerful thinking skills in solving the problems, and ultimately in choosing the correct answer. The mathematics required is not difficult on the ninth grade proficiency test. But, the difficult part is knowing how to take everything you know, everything that you have learned, and know how to use it on the test. You will perform well on the test if you can come to realize that the test is an <u>opportunity</u> for you to *Show What You Know*!

About the Mathematics Test

The mathematics test will consist of 40 multiple-choice items. There will be at least one test item to assess each learning outcome. Test questions will be distributed, as follows.

Category	Learning Outcome	# of Items	% of Items
Arithmetic	1, 2, 3, 4, and 5	12	30%
Measurement	6, 7, and 8	10	25%
Geometry	9, 10, and 11	6	15%
Data Analysis	12, 13, and 14	6	15%
Algebra	15 and 16	6	15%

What You Need To Know About the Mathematics Test

- Each test item will have four answer choices, but only one answer will be correct. There will not be a penalty for choosing an incorrect answer.
- Answer choices such as "None correct," "All correct, " or combinations of responses will not be used.
- It is possible to solve each problem in no more than three steps.
- Students will do their figuring in the test booklet. Answers will be recorded on a separate answer sheet. Your test booklet will not be scored.
- The symbol "X" is used to signify multiplication, but not to indicate a variable. Other letters will be used to indicate variables.
- Students will not be permitted to use calculators, rulers, compasses, or any other such devices on this test.
- For application and problem solving questions, only simple calculations will be necessary.
- Students will have a maximum of two and one-half hours to finish the test. Most students will be able to complete the test in approximately one hour.
- Charts and other materials that could assist students with test items will be covered or removed from the classroom during the test.

Test-Taking Strategies For Mathematics

The way to succeed on the mathematics proficiency test is to use everything you know to answer the question. For example, if you do not remember a formula required to answer the question, then use everything you know to 1) eliminate answer choices that you know are incorrect, or 2) try using your common sense and solve the problem using good sound logic. The key is not to panic or give up. Keep trying or skip the question and go back to it later.

On the next page are a list of test-taking strategies that will help you PASS!

For the Mathematics test, following these strategies:

1. Read the question carefully. Ask yourself, "What is the "Real Question?" or "What is the question asking me to do?"
2. Circle or underline the important words in the question. These will help you see clearly what you are being asked to do to answer the question correctly.
3. Read all the answer choices. There are no trick questions on the proficiency test but there may be trick answers that have been chosen because they are popular wrong answers. (i.e. answers that you can get if you make a simple mathematical mistake)
4. Cross out any answers you know are wrong. Knowledge is not only knowing the correct answer but knowing the incorrect answers too.
5. If you don't know the answer to a question, and you can't eliminate any incorrect answer, make your *best* guess. There is **no** penalty for an incorrect guess. NEVER LEAVE AN ANSWER BLANK!

Other Tips To Remember:

- Use common sense. The correct answer sometimes just makes sense.
- Watch out for absolutes. Be careful of words like "never" or "always." It is rare that something is so absolute. This may be a clue for an incorrect answer.
- It is OK to write in your test booklet. Make notes, figure your problems, or draw diagrams to help you answer the question.
- Be careful when you transfer your answer to your answer sheet. Make sure that you have given an answer for each question. Fill in the bubble, completely shading it in. Do not erase the answer sheet. Check your answers before you transfer. The answer sheets are scanned electronically when scored, so be neat and accurate.

Field Test Results

While the number of students responding to each test item was limited, the results of the field test summarized here provide indications of student achievement on groups of test items. Students performance was highest on items measuring outcomes 1, 6, 12, and 15. The symbol "✔" will be used in this book to identify the highest performance outcomes. These are outcomes that students seem to grasp the concepts of more easily. Students performance was lowest on items measuring outcomes 2, 3, 5, 9, and 10. The symbol "✍" will be used in this book to identify the lowest performance outcomes. These outcomes are worth reviewing a little more. If you find these outcomes are your weak areas, spend extra time on them.

> **Key:**
> ✔ = Student performance was HIGH during field tests.
> ✍ = Student performance was LOW during field tests.

The Mathematics Learning Outcomes

Strand – Arithmetic

✔ **1. Compute with whole numbers, fractions, and decimals.**

Each test item will require you to add, subtract, multiply, or divide whole numbers, fractions, or decimals. The set of whole numbers contains zero (0) and positive numbers, such as 34, 675, and 2. Fractions on the proficiency test will have denominators of 25 or smaller, but they may be negative; such as –3/4. Decimals will have no more than three decimal places, or numbers through to the thousandths place.

A Review of Computations
For correct computations, be sure you know all the rules for adding, subtracting, multiplying, and dividing whole numbers, fractions, and decimals. Some of these are:

To add or subtract fractions, first find a common denominator. The answer will have that same denominator. Just add or subtract numerators. Change to lowest terms, if possible. If a numerator is too small for the subtraction, you can increase it by re-grouping the whole number. For example:

$7\frac{1}{6} - 2\frac{5}{6}$ can become, $6\frac{7}{6} - 2\frac{5}{6}$ which equals, $4\frac{2}{6}$ or $4\frac{1}{3}$.

Try this one! $2\frac{1}{8} - 1\frac{3}{4}$ WORK HERE

Did you use a
denominator of 8?

The answer is $\frac{3}{8}$.

To add or subtract decimals, arrange numbers vertically with decimal point under decimal point. Then add or subtract. The answer will have a decimal point directly under the other decimal points.

Try this one!   7.46 + .8 = ?   WORK HERE

Did you write
the .8 under .4?

The answer is 8.26

To multiply fractions, first re-write the example with each fraction in simplest form. Then multiply, left to right - numerator times numerator, denominator times denominator.

Try this one! $\frac{3}{6}$ x $\frac{3}{9}$ = ?   WORK HERE

Did you write the
problem as $\frac{1}{2}$ x $\frac{1}{3}$?

The answer is $\frac{1}{6}$.

To multiply decimals, it is not necessary to arrange numbers decimal point under decimal point. Just multiply! Then count the numerals to the right of each decimal point. Fix your answer with a decimal point, so that there are the same number of numerals to the right of the decimal point as there are altogether in the two original numbers.

Try this one!   .4 x .12 = ?   WORK HERE

4 x 12 = 48, so the digits in the product
are 4 and 8. Did you count three decimal
places? (One is the 4 and two are the 1 and
the 2.) You only had 48, so a zero is needed
for the third decimal place.

The answer is .048   How did you do?

To divide fractions, invert (turn upside down!) the second fraction. Then multiply.

Try this one! $\frac{5}{6}$ ÷ $\frac{1}{3}$ = ?   WORK HERE

Did you flip the second fraction and
change $\frac{1}{3}$ to $\frac{3}{1}$?

The answer is 2 $\frac{1}{2}$.

To divide decimals, move the decimal point in the divisor all the way to the right. (If it's already there - or a decimal point doesn't show - you can skip this step!) Then, under the division symbol, move the decimal point the same number of places to the right. Put a decimal point above that new point before you divide the numbers. Then divide.

Try this one!   6.18 ÷ .3 = ?   WORK HERE

Did you move the decimal points
one place each? Did you see the
need for a zero in the answer?

The answer is 20.6

Beware of ZERO in all multiplications and divisions! Zero is a tricky number.
Practice all kinds of computations that include zero.

Things to Remember
- Most computations will be described in story problems. It is very important that you read each problem carefully. Then re-read the problem. You may even need to read it several more times until you really understand both the situation and the question you are asked.
- It is often helpful to draw figures or pictures in order to be able to understand the meaning of a problem. Making a table is another helpful strategy.
- After you understand the problem, decide how best to solve it.
- Work the problem first. Then select your answer choice. Even if your answer is given as a choice, check to be sure the other answers cannot be correct.

Examples:

1. Mr. Prince is on a low-calorie diet. If his breakfast contained 200 calories; lunch, 600; dinner, 1300; how much above his 2,000 calories limit was he?

   A. 100
   B. 1900
   C. 2100
   D. 4100

Analysis:

On first reading, you may think that since there are four numbers involved, you should add the four numbers to identify the answer. (This is a common mistake made by persons who read a problem only once!) However, on second reading, you may realize that three of the numbers were related to his meals and the fourth number was a daily limit for his calories. So, then it becomes clear that by adding the number of calories he ate that day (200 + 600 +1300 = 2100), you could compare that total to his allowed limit (2000). This leads to the conclusion that he went over the limit by 100 calories. Now let's look at the answer choices. You already think he has gone over by 100 calories, so "A" is probably the correct answer. But it's safer also to check the others. "C" is the total number of calories he consumed. He was allowed 2000, so he didn't go over by 2100. Eliminate "C." "D" is the total, if you had added all numbers as you had thought about doing after only one reading; but it doesn't make sense to add daily calories to his limit of 2000! So, eliminate "D." "B" is too large. If he went over his limit by 1900, he would have eaten 3900 calories altogether. You know he ate only 2100; so eliminate "B." Now, you know for sure the correct answer is "A."

2. The human heart beats 360 times in 5 minutes. How many times will it beat in 11 minutes?

    A. 72

    B. 376

    C. 720

    D. 792

Analysis:

On first reading, you may think you should add the three numbers. But when you re-read and think about what is asked, you will know that before you can figure out how many times the heart will beat in 11 minutes, you must first know how many times it beats in 1 minute. Since the first sentence gives the information that the heart beats 360 times in 5 minutes, you could either divide 360 by 5 to determine that it beats 72 times in 1 minute or you could find 1/5 of 360 by multiplying 1/5 x 360. This multiplication, of course, leads to dividing 360 by 5, and also provides the answer of 72 beats per minute. Now, it is clear that 72 must be multiplied by 11 to obtain the answer to the problem's question (72 x 11 = 792). Now let's look at the answer choices. When you worked the problem, you got 792 for the answer; so it seems like "D" is correct. But it's safer to check the others. Answer choice "A" cannot be correct, because, if the heart beats 360 times in 5 minutes, it can't beat fewer than 360 times in 11 minutes. Answer choice "B" is not correct because, 376 is simply the sum of all the numbers. Answer choice "C" is incorrect because 720 is the number of beats in 10 minutes, not 11 minutes. Therefore, "D" is the correct answer.

3. Jill's mother purchased a 12-inch pizza for lunch. She ate 1/4 of the pizza. Jill ate 1/3 of the pizza and her brother ate the rest. What part of the pizza did Jill's brother eat?

   A. 2/7

   B. 5/7

   C. 7/12

   D. 5/12

Analysis:

If you draw the pizza and divide it into slices, it may help to visualize the situation. The question becomes: How many slices? If you cut it into four equal parts (fourths), the mother's part is obvious, but not Jill's.

If you cut it into three equal parts (thirds), Jill's part is obvious, but not her mother's.

So what size pieces should be cut? This is really what you determine when you decide on a common denominator of 12. If the pizza is cut into 12 pieces, Jill's mother will eat 3 pieces or 3/12 which equals 1/4, and Jill will eat 4 pieces or 4/12 which equals 1/3. That leaves 5 pieces for Jill's brother. Since each piece is 1/12, he eats 5/12 of the pizza. Drawing pictures is a very useful technique when solving fraction problems. The correct answer is "D."

✍ 2. Compare, order, and determine equivalence of fractions, decimals, percents, whole numbers, and integers.

Questions include the symbols <, =, > and involve comparisons using number line applications. You may encounter several types of number representations (e.g. fractions, decimals, and percents) in the same problem.

Things to Remember
- To compare or order numbers represented as decimals, be sure all decimal representations have the same number of decimal places. To accomplish this, you may have to fill some places with zeroes. If you do need to fill with zeroes, never put them in near the decimal point. Always put them to the far right!
- To compare or order numbers represented as fractions, either change all the fractions so they have a common denominator or change the fractions to decimals before comparing them.

More Things to Remember

- A fraction is really a division. (Did you know that?) The numerator is divided by the denominator. The result is the decimal form of the original fraction. (e.g. 5/8 means "5 divided by 8". When 5 is divided by 8, the quotient is .625; so 5/8 = .625).
- Percent is based on 100. In fact, "per cent" means "per 100". (e.g. 4% means 4 per hundred. So, 4% of 200 would be 2 sets of 4, or 8. 4% of 500 would be 5 sets of 4, or 20.)
- "All" of a number is 100% of the number. Half of a number is 50% of the number. One fourth of a number is 25% of the number. One tenth of a number is 10% of the number. Similarly, any fractional part of a number can be expressed as a percent of that number.
- Often, when it is necessary to compare or order numbers, it is helpful to arrange the numbers on a number line. That makes it easier to see which number is larger, because it will be farther to the right. The smaller numbers will be farther left on the number line.
- Negative numbers are all to the left of zero on the number line. Any negative number is smaller than any positive number. This is very helpful, especially if you are trying to order three or more numbers.

Examples:

1. Which of the following numbers is the smallest?

   A. .3
   B. .314
   C. .29
   D. .2

Analysis:
Fill the places with zeroes, to be sure all numbers represented in decimal form have the same number of decimal places. The numbers then look different, but they are equal to the original four numbers shown above. Here's how they look after you fill with zeroes.
 A. .300
 B. .314
 C. .290
 D. .200
They are read, "300 thousandths, 314 thousandths, 290 thousandths, 200 thousandths. The last number is the smallest, so answer choice "D," or .2 is the correct answer.

2. Which of the following numbers is the greatest?

    A. $\frac{3}{5}$

    B. $\frac{7}{10}$

    C. $\frac{3}{4}$

    D. $\frac{1}{2}$

Analysis:
Here are two ways to find the solution:

1) Identify a common denominator. Since 20 is a multiple of each denominator, 20 can be the common denominator. The "new look" for the four fractions becomes:

    A. $\frac{12}{20}$ B. $\frac{14}{20}$ C. $\frac{15}{20}$ D. $\frac{10}{20}$

Obviously, 15/20 is greater than any of the other three. Answer choice "C" is the correct answer because 3/4 is the greatest of the four numbers.

2) Divide to change the four fractions to decimal form. The answer choices now look like: A. 0.6   B. 0.7   C. 0.75   D. 0 .5   Because the third one has two decimal places, you must fill with zeroes in the others. Now compare .60, .70, .75, and .50 and you see that .75 is the greatest of the four numbers. The correct answer is "C" or 3/4, the same answer you identified when you used the common denominator method.

3. Which of the following is true?

    A. $1/2 < 1/8$

    B. $.85 > 85\%$

    C. $40\% = 2/5$

    D. $.8 < .789$

Analysis:
Check the meaning of each answer choice. Here is one way.
"A" 1/2 = 4/8 and 4/8 is not less than 1/8, so "A" is not true.
"B" .85 = 85%, so .85 is not greater than 85%. "B" is not true.
"C" 40% = .40 = 40/100 which, in simpler form, is 2/5. Therefore, "C" is true.
"D" When zeroes are filled in, .8 becomes .800 and .800 > .789 ; so "D" is false.

4. Order these numbers, from greatest to smallest:

$$\frac{4}{5}, \quad .62, \quad -8, \quad \frac{1}{3}, \quad \frac{-1}{2}$$

    A. –8, –1/2, 1/3, .62, 4/5

    B. 4/5, .62, 1/3, –8, –1/2

    C. 4/5, .62, 1/3, –1/2, –8

    D. .62, 4/5, 1/3, –1/2, –8

Analysis:

Look at the two negative numbers first. On a numberline, –8 is farther to the left from zero than –1/2; so –8 is smaller than –1/2 (or –1/2 is greater than –8). Since you are to arrange the numbers from greatest to smallest, -1/2 should be in the list before -8. In both "A" and "B", -8 is before -1/2; so "A" and "B" can be crosses out and eliminated. Now look at the three positive numbers. Change them to decimal form. 4/5 = .80 and 1/3 = .33333333... The third number (.62) is between .80 and .33, so .80 (4/5) is the greatest. Only "C" begins with 4/5, so check it to be sure. The two negative numbers are correctly ordered and the three other numbers in decimal form are correctly ordered from greatest to smallest, so "C" is the correct answer.

5. Each of four barbecue recipes requires vinegar. The amounts to be used in the recipes are: Recipe A – 1/4 cup, Recipe B – 1/2 cup, Recipe C – 1/8 cup, Recipe D – 3/4 cup. Which recipe requires the least vinegar?

    A. Recipe A

    B. Recipe B

    C. Recipe C

    D. Recipe D

Analysis:

Using a common denominator of "8", the fractions become: Recipe A – 2/8 cup, Recipe B – 4/8 cup, Recipe C – 1/8 cup, Recipe D – 6/8 cup. Since 1/8 is the smallest fraction, "C" is the correct answer. Recipe C uses the least vinegar.

✍ **3. Solve and use proportions.**

You must be able to set up a proportion and to find a missing number in a proportion.

Things to Remember
- A proportion is a true statement that two fractions are equal.

  For Example: $\frac{4}{5} = \frac{16}{20}$ IS a proportion, because the two fractions are equal.

  $\frac{2}{3} = \frac{5}{9}$ IS NOT a proportion, because the two fractions are not equal.

- Here's one way to figure out whether fractions are equal to each other.
  a) Multiply the numerator of the first fraction by the denominator of the second fraction.
  b) Then multiply the denominator of the first fraction by the numerator of the second fraction.
  c) If the two products are equal, then the two fractions are equal (also called equivalent).

  For Example: Are $\frac{2}{3}$ and $\frac{8}{12}$ equivalent fractions?

  Multiply 2 x 12 and 3 x 8. Both products are 24; so 2/3 and 8/12 ARE equivalent. This method is called cross-multiplying. It is very useful for solving proportions.

- If one of the four numbers in a proportion is unknown, you can identify the unknown number by cross-multiplying as described above (c).

  For Example: $\frac{n}{6} = \frac{1}{2}$

  For these two fractions to be equivalent, 2 x n must equal 6 x 1. It seems that the unknown number must be 3, because 2 x 3 = 6 x 1. Now put 3 into the original proportion and see if the statement is true: $\frac{3}{6} = \frac{1}{2}$. True! So, 3 is the missing number in the proportion.

- When setting up a proportion, it is very important to keep the same type of information as numerators of both fractions. Similarly, for denominators. For example: If a problem involves cost and number of bags, then the two numerators should both be cost or both be number of bags. Otherwise, your proportion will not make sense, because it will not show similar relationships in the fractions.

- After you identify a missing number in a proportion, always take time to put the number back into the original proportion. Then, cross-multiply. The products should be equal, if you have identified the correct number.

Examples:

1. A printing machine turns out 45 copies in 2 minutes. How long will it take to print 270 copies?

    A. 10 min.

    B. 12 min.

    C. 90 min.

    D. 135 min.

Analysis:
Express the information as two fractions,.

$$\frac{45}{2} \quad : \text{ number of copies / number of minutes}$$

and $\dfrac{270}{m}$ *: number of copies / number of minutes (as yet unknown)*

Now you can set up and solve a proportion:

$$\frac{45}{2} = \frac{270}{m}$$

$$45 \times m = 2 \times 270 \text{ (cross-multiplication)}$$

$$45m = 540$$

$$m = 12 \text{ (after division by 45)}$$

Since "m" represented the number of minutes to print 270 copies, the answer appears to be 12 minutes. Answers "C" and "D" are far too large to make any sense. "A" is 5 x 2 minutes, so you would be able to print 5 x 45 copies (which is not 270). So, the correct answer is "B." Now re-write the original proportion, putting 12 into the fraction instead of "m". Cross-multiply. The products are both equal to 540. Now you are absolutely sure that "B" is the answer.

2. A recipe for 6 servings calls for 1/2 (also written .5) teaspoon of cinnamon. If this recipe is used for 15 people, how much cinnamon should be used?

    A. .2 tsp.

    B. 1 tsp.

    C. 1 1/4 tsp

    D. 180 tsp.

Analysis:

Express the information as a proportion. Be sure to keep the same type of information as numerators and the other type of information as denominators. In this problem, the two types of information are: number of servings and amount of cinnamon. We choose to use the number of servings as numerators. The proportion can be written and solved as follows:

$$\frac{6}{.5} = \frac{15}{a} \text{ (numerators are number of servings)}$$
(denominators are amounts of cinnamon)

$$6 \text{ x } a = .5 \text{ x } 15 \text{ (cross-multiplication)}$$

$$6a = 7.5$$

$$a = 1.25 \text{ (after division by 6)}$$

It seems that 1.25 (1 1/4) teaspoons of cinnamon is needed for the recipe. When you put that number back into the original proportion and cross-multiply, both products are equal to 7.5. So, you know for sure that the answer is 1 1/4 ("C"). Let's look at the other answer choices! "A" (.2) is less than .5, so it isn't even enough for the original six servings. "B" (1) is twice the original amount of cinnamon, so it would be used for 2 x 6 (12) servings. "D" is far too much to make any sense at all. So, "C" is the correct answer.

4. Round numbers to the nearest thousand, hundred, ten, one, tenth, and hundredth.

The proficiency test may include applications of rounding in situations where fractional parts, regardless of size, must be rounded to the next higher whole number. Students will not be asked to make rounding decisions based on the number five (5) alone.

Things to Remember
* So that you will understand questions which involve rounding, you must know the names of each column in our numeration system. Questions on the proficiency test will include:

  (left of the decimal point) ones, tens, hundreds, thousands
  (right of the decimal point) tenths, hundredths, thousandths

  For example, consider the number: 6,273.158

  Left of the decimal point -
  a) 3 is in the ones place and means: 3 x 1, or 3 sets / one in each set.
  b) 7 is in the tens place and means: 7 x 10, or 7 sets / ten in each set.
  c) 2 is in the hundreds place and means: 2 x 100 or 2 sets / one hundred in each set.
  d) 6 is in the thousands place and means: 6 x 1000 or 6 sets / one thousand in each set.

Again, consider the number: 6,273.158

Right of the decimal point -
a) 1 is in the tenths place and means 1/10.
b) 5 is in the hundredths place and means 5/100.
c) 8 is in the thousandths place and means 8/1000.

- One way to think of "rounding" is to picture a number (say, 48) on a numberline. It is between 40 and 50, but closer to 50; so 48 rounds to 50.

- Another way to think of "rounding" is to picture your number (say, 4178) with some digits replaced by zero (0). If you are to round to thousands, all digits will be replaced by zero (0) except the front-end digit which is the thousands digit. That would be 4000. Your number, 4178, is between 4000 and the next higher thousand which is 5000. On a number line, or in your head, you can see that 4178 is closer to 4000; so 4178 rounds to 4000 (if you're rounding to thousands). If, instead, you were to round to hundreds, then you would keep the two front-end digits and replace the two others with zero (0). That would be 4100. 4178 is between 4100 and the next higher hundred which is 4200. You can probably see that 4178 is closer to 4200; so 4178 rounds to 4200 (if you're rounding to hundreds).

- Fractions can be rounded in one of two ways. Either change the fraction to its decimal form and proceed as described above, or consider the fraction on a numberline between 0 and 1. If it is closer to 0, the fraction rounds to 0. If it is closer to 1, the fraction rounds to 1.

Examples:

1. Round 6789 to the nearest ten.

   A. 6000
   B. 6780
   C. 6790
   D. 6700

Analysis:
The tens column is second from the right, so keep the first 3 digits and replace the 9 with a 0. Now you have 6780. The given number (6789) is between 6780 and the next higher multiple of ten, 6790. It is closer to 6790; so 6789 rounds to 6790 (because you are rounding to the nearest ten). Easy to pick <u>wrong</u> answer choices are; "A" because you used only front-end estimation; "D" because you rounded to hundreds instead of tens; and "B" because you chose the lower number instead of 6790.

2. Round $\frac{7}{8}$ to the nearest whole number.

    A. 0

    B. 1

    C. 7

    D. 8

Analysis:
On a numberline, 7/8 is between 0 and 1. It is closer to 1; so 7/8 rounds to 1. That means, 7/8 is almost 1. Draw a numberline, and you will see why "B" is the correct answer. "7" and "8" are far away from 7/8 on a numberline.

3. Tasha buys a CD for $4.59. The tax rate is 5 1/2% (.055). When the clerk multiplies $4.59 by .055 to compute the tax, the calculator display is .25245. For tax purposes, all states consider any part of a cent to be another cent. How much tax will Tasha owe?

    A. 26¢

    B. 24¢

    C. 27¢

    D. 25.2¢

Analysis:
Using the rules for rounding, the number .25245 would be rounded to .25 (25 cents). However, the remaining digits represent part of another cent; so the tax will be 26 cents. In this case, the rules of rounding are ignored.

5. Solve problems and make applications involving percentages.

Questions may require you to find what percent one number is of another; to find a given percent of a number; and to solve problems involving discounts, interest, and tip/gratuity. Problems may involve more than one step.

Things to Remember
- To find a certain percent of a number means to find a certain part of a number. You should first change the percent to a decimal or to a fraction. Then multiply the number by the percent which is now written in a new form (decimal or fraction).

For example: 13% of 68   becomes .13 x 68   or 8.84

                6% of 90   becomes .06 x 90   or 5.4

          120% of 86   becomes 1.20 x 86   or 103.2

Notice that, because the last percent is greater than 100%, the answer is greater than the number you multiplied (86).

More Things to Remember

- When asked to find what percent one number is of another number, use a proportion. Write the 2 numbers as one fraction and the percent as another fraction with denominator of 100. Set the two fractions equal to each other and solve for the unknown number.

    For example: 22 is what percent of 88?

    $$\frac{22}{88} = \frac{n}{100}$$

    You can cross-multiply, if you wish; or you can express 22/88 in simpler form as 1/4. Then 1/4 = n/100, and when you find the common denominator (100), you see that n = 25. Therefore, 22 is 25% of 88.

- To solve a discount problem, always think, "The amount of discount plus what I pay must equal the original price."

- To solve a tax problem, always think, "The amount of tax plus the cost of the item must be greater than the cost of the item."

- To figure a tip (gratuity), always think, " I must multiply the cost of the meal(s) by whatever percent I wish to tip the server."

- To determine interest, multiply the amount of money by the percent of interest (just like a tip/gratuity). When figuring interest, though, there is sometimes another step. If the interest rate is for 1 month or year and the question asks for 2 months or years, you must multiply by 2 to find the total interest. If the interest rate is given for 1 year and the question asks for 6 months, you must multiply by 1/2. In other words, unless the question asks for the interest in the same time period for which the rate is given, you will have to multiply the interest you compute by the number of months or years (or parts of months or years) to find the correct amount of interest. This is tricky; so be careful!

Examples:

1. A person's monthly housing cost should not be greater than 25% of the person's monthly income. According to this rule, if Mr. Ellis earns $24,000 per year, which of the following monthly rents can he afford?

    A. $500
    B. $600
    C. $2000
    D. $6000

Analysis:
Read carefully. Notice that the question is about <u>monthly</u> rent related to <u>monthly</u> income. However, the salary is given as "per year." Think, "How much does Mr. Ellis make <u>per month</u>?" Since there are 12 months in a year, divide $24,000 by 12 and you see that he makes $2000 per month. You might be tempted to stop here; but the question does not ask how much he makes per month. So, go on. The first sentence says that the rent should not be greater than 25% of monthly pay ($2000). 25% of $2000 or 1/4 of $2000 is $500. Now you can look at the answer choices. All except "A" are greater than 25% of $2000; so "A" is the correct answer.

2. Seven horses on a merry-go-round are cracked. If that is 20% of the horses, what is the total number of horses on the merry-go-round?

    A. 7
    B. 28
    C. 35
    D. 80

Analysis:
Always think first, to get a "feel" for the problem. 20% is less than 100%, so not all the horses are cracked. Not even half of the horses are cracked, because that would be 50% cracked. Because 20% of the horses are cracked and 20% = 1/5, 1/5 of the horses are cracked. That means 4/5 of them are not cracked; or four times as many horses are in good shape as are cracked. So, multiply 4 times the number of cracked horses to find the number of horses which are not cracked. (4 x 7 = 28; so 28 horses are not cracked.) Don't stop here! You didn't answer the question yet! (Answer "B" is there to trick you!) The question asks, "What is the total number of horses on the merry-go-round?". Add: 7 (cracked) + 28 (not cracked) = 35. There are 35 horses on the ride. Good job!

3. Beth estimates 15% of her dinner bill and leaves a tip of $2.00. How much was her dinner bill?

    A. $ .30
    B. $ 2.15
    C. $13.40
    D. $30.00

Analysis:
Answer choices "A" and "B" cannot be correct. If $2.00 is 15% of the meal's cost, the meal had to cost more than $.30 or $2.15. So, one way to decide upon the correct answer is to multiply "C" by 15% (.15 or 15/100) which provides $2.01 as a product. Then multiply "D" by 15%. That gives a product of $4.50 which is too large. "C" then is the meal cost which requires a $2.00 tip. Another way to think about this problem is to say to yourself, " 15% is $2; so I can add six 15%'s (six $2's) and still be under 100%, but close to it. Six $2's is $12.00 which is under, but close to, answer "C". The correct answer is "C."

4. 15% of a number is 2. Which of the following is closest to the number?

   A. .30

   B. 2.15

   C. 13.4

   D. 30

Analysis:
Mathematically, this is exactly the same as problem #3. Besides the methods used in #3, another way to calculate the missing number is to create a proportion. 15% = 15/100; so 15/100 = 2/some number. Let n stand for "some number". Then, you have 15/100 = 2/n and, by cross-multiplying, you get 15n = 200. Since 15 times some number = 200, you can divide 200 by 15 to identify the unknown number. Try this way to solve #3. You should get an answer close to $13.40. Answer choice "C" is correct.

5. A motorbike is on sale at 20% off. If the original price is $92.00, what is the total cost of the bike after a 5% sales tax is added?

   A. $ 4.60

   B. $ 18.40

   C. $ 73.60

   D. $ 77.28

Analysis:
Think through the problem first.
Step 1:   20% of $92 = $18.40   (Compute the amount of discount)
Step 2: $92.00 -18.40 = $73.60   (sale price)
Step 3:   5% of $73.60 = $ 3.68   (amount of tax)
Step 4: $73.60 + $3.68 = $77.28   (total amount you pay)

Problems will not require four steps to solve, because results of one of the four steps will already be given in the question statement. In this problem, the amount of discount could have been given or the amount of tax could have been given. But, the process is still the same - Steps 1, 2, 3, and 4. If one of the parts is already finished for you, just use the given information. Answer choices "D" is the correct answer. If you do not finish all the steps you may stop and pick the wrong answers "B" and "C." If you choose answer choice "A" you may have mistakenly multiplied the tax rate by original price instead of sale price.

6. When a credit card bill is not paid on time, there is a 1 1/2% monthly interest charged on the amount owed. Luann owes $60.00 and is totally unable to pay. How much interest will she be charged after the first month?

   A. $ .90
   B. $61.50
   C. $67.20
   D. $90.00

Analysis:
First check to determine if the periods of time for the interest rate and for the charge to be made are the same. In this problem, both charge and interest rate are based on one month. Therefore, you simply need to find 1 1/2% of $60.00 and you will know how much interest Luann will be charged.

Here are two ways to find your solution:
1. *1 1/2% is tricky to change to a decimal; but you know it is between 1% and 2%. 1% = .01 and 2% = .02; so 1 1/2% is half-way between .01 and .02 or 5 thousandths larger than .01. So, 1 1/2% = .015 and you can now multiply. $60.00 x .015 = $ .90, the interest Luann will be charged.*

2. *Another way to think about this problem is, as follows: 10% of $60.00 is $6.00, so 1% is 1/10 of $6.00 or $ .60. That means 2% (2 x 1%) would be $1.20 and 1 1/2 % (halfway between 1% and 2%) is .90. – Now look at the answer choices! Three of them are greater than the amount Luann owes. It would not make sense to say that the interest for one month would be more than the amount owed; so you could have known immediately that "A" was the correct answer. The other three are actually the result of not knowing what to do with 1 1/2%!*

Strand – Measurement

✔ **6. Select and compute with appropriate standard or metric units to measure length, area, volume, angles, weight, capacity, time, temperature, and money.**

You will need to know when a particular measurement unit is appropriate. You will also need to know approximate measurements of common items. Questions will focus on your ability to solve problems using standard or metric measurement units. Problems do not involve converting from one measurement system to another, but may require converting within a measurement system.

Things to Remember

- **To measure length**, the following units are commonly used.

Standard	Metric
inch (in)	millimeter (mm)
foot (ft)	centimeter (cm)
yard (yd)	meter (m)
mile (mi)	kilometer (km)

- **To measure weight,** the following units are commonly used.

Standard	Metric
ounce (oz)	milligram (mg)
pound (lb)	centigram (cg)
ton (t)	gram (g)
	kilogram (kg)

- **To measure time**, the following units are commonly used in both standard and metric measurement systems: second, minute, hour, day, week, month, year, decade, century.

- **Area** is measured in square units (length x width).

Standard	Metric
square inch (in^2)	square millimeter (mm^2)
square foot (ft^2)	square centimeter (cm^2)
square yard (yd^2)	square meter (m^2)
square mile (mi^2)	square kilometer (km^2)

- **Volume** is measured in cubic units (length x width x height).

Standard	Metric
cubic inch (in^3)	cubic millimeter (mm^3)
cubic foot (ft^3)	cubic centimeter (cm^3)
cubic yard (yd^3)	cubic meter (m^3)
cubic mile (mi^3)	cubic kilometer (km^3)

- **To measure capacity**, the following units are commonly used.

Standard	Metric
fluid ounce (fl oz)	millileter (ml)
cup (c)	centiliter (cl)
pint (pt)	liter (l)
quart (qt)	kiloliter (kl)
gallon (gal)	

- **Temperature** is measured in degrees. A degree is the unit of coolness or warmth. There is a Fahrenheit (standard) scale and a Celsius (metric) scale.

	Fahrenheit	Celsius
Freezing point	32°	0°
Boiling point	212°	100°

- **Angles** are also measured in degrees. In this case, a degree is a unit of rotation between the two rays of the angle. Imagine two rays, one on top of the other, attached at the end point of each (similar to the two hands of a clock at noon). As one ray moves away from the other - still attached - it sweeps through an area forming an angle between the two rays. The amount of rotation is the degree measure of that angle.

- It is helpful to have a mental picture of some examples of common units of measure. Here is a brief list of examples. Maybe you can think of others.

Unit	Example(s)
millimeter	approx. thickness of a dime ($.10)
centimeter	approx. width of the nail of one's little finger
inch	approx. width of a quarter ($.25) approx. width of a 9V battery
foot	approx. length of a man's shoe approx. length of a football
ounce	approx. weight of an envelope with letter
pound	approx. weight of a loaf of bread
square foot	approx. area of a floor tile
square yard	approx. area of a cardtable top

Examples:

1. What is the approximate height of a can of Pepsi?

    A. 11 mm

    B. 11 cm

    C. 11 m

    D. 11 km

Analysis:
Think about the size of each metric unit. A millimeter (mm) is about the thickness of a dime, so "A" approximates the thickness of 11 dimes stacked up. - certainly not the height of a can of Pepsi! "B" is about 11 small fingernails side by side. That seems like a reasonable height for the Pepsi can. Since a meter (m) is longer than a yardstick and a kilometer (km) is almost a mile, "C" and "D" are far too large to be the height of a Pepsi can. So, "B" is the correct answer.

2. Which of the following is likely to have a capacity of 2 liters?

    A. shampoo bottle

    B. milk carton

    C. cough syrup bottle

    D. juice can

Analysis:
To answer this, you must have some idea of the amount of liquid in 1 liter. You may think, "A liter is a little less than a quart, so 2 liters is about a half-gallon;" or you may think, "Soft drinks are sold in 2-liter bottles." Either way, when you look at the answer choices, you see that shampoo bottles, cough syrup bottles, and juice cans are not big enough to hold a half-gallon of liquid. Nor could you pour the contents of a 2-liter bottle into any of those three. Therefore, answer "B"– milk carton – makes the most sense. Milk is sold in half-gallon containers, and you could pour the contents of a 2-liter soft drink bottle into an empty milk carton. (Note: The type of thinking in this problem will be necessary, when you take the proficiency test.) The correct answer is "B."

7. Convert, compare, and compute with common units of measure within the same measurement system.

Questions will involve common units for measuring length, weight, capacity, time, and money. You may be asked to solve problems involving conversion of units within the same measurement system, either standard or metric. Each computation will be within one system or the other, but not both.

Things to Remember
- Common units of measure are listed under the previous outcome (6).
- When computing with units of measure, it will sometimes be necessary to change a larger unit, such as a yard, to a number of smaller units, such as feet; that is, instead of thinking about a "yard," it might be more useful to consider the yard as "3 feet." Similarly, you may want to express a set of smaller units, such as 60 seconds, as one larger unit of measure, such as 1 minute.
- Here are some equivalences you will need to know.

Length / Height
1 foot = 12 inches.
1 yard = 3 feet or 36 inches.
1 mile = 5280 feet.
1 centimeter = 10 millimeters.
1 meter = 100 centimeters or 1000 millimeters.
kilometer = 1000 meters.

Capacity
1 cup of liquid = 8 fluid ounces of liquid
1 pint of liquid = 2 cups of liquid or 16 fluid ounces of liquid
1 quart of liquid = 2 pints of liquid or 32 fluid ounces of liquid
1 gallon of liquid = 4 quarts of liquid or 128 fluid ounces of liquid
1 liter of liquid = 1000 milliliters of liquid or 100 centiliters of liquid

1 quart is also equal to 2 pints for dry measure (e.g. a quart of berries)

Time
60 seconds = 1 minute
60 minutes = 1 hour
24 hours = 1 day
7 days = 1 week
52 weeks = 1 year
10 years = 1 decade
100 years = 1 century

Examples:

1. A recipe for fruit punch requires 16 ounces of lemonade, 1 gallon of orange juice, and 1 quart of water. If the recipe is doubled, how much lemonade is required?

    A. 1 pint

    B. 3 pints

    C. 1 quart

    D. 1 gallon

Analysis:
First recall the relationship among ounces, quarts, and gallons (4 quarts = 1 gallon and 32 ounces = 1 quart). When the recipe is doubled, the amount of lemonade will be 16 ounces + 16 ounces, or 32 ounces. This is not an answer choice. However, 32 ounces = 1 quart and "1 quart" is an answer choice. So, "C" is the correct answer.

2. There are 4 lamps in a room. Their heights are: 30 inches, 1 yard, 2 feet, and 6 feet. If the lamps are arranged in order of height, from tallest to smallest, what is the correct order?

    A. 30 inches, 2 feet, 6 feet, 1 yard

    B. 6 feet, 1 yard, 30 inches, 2 feet

    C. 6 feet, 1 yard, 2 feet, 30 inches

    D. 1 yard, 6 feet, 2 feet, 30 inches

Analysis:
Think " 3 feet = 1 yard, so 6 feet = 2 yards." That means 6 feet > 1 yard, so 6 feet should appear before 1 yard in the list. Now you know answer "D" is not correct. Now think, "36 inches = 1 yard, so 30 inches < 1 yard and it should appear after 1 yard in the list." So, "A" is not correct. Only "B" and "C" are left as choices. They each begin with 6 feet followed by 1 yard. The only question is: Which is larger, 30 inches or 2 feet? Since 12 inches = 1 foot, 24 inches must equal 2 feet; so 30 inches is larger than 2 feet. "B" is the correct answer.

8. Read the scale on a measurement device to the nearest mark and make interpolations (estimates) where appropriate.

You will be asked to read pictures of measurement devices which are used to measure length, angles, weight, time, and temperature. You may also be asked to use such information to solve problems. Measuring devices will not always include a zero point.

Things to Remember

• These measurement devices are commonly used: ruler (metric and standard), protractor, balance scale, spring scale, digital timepiece, circular timepiece, Celsius thermometer, Fahrenheit thermometer.

• Carefully study the units and divisions on a pictured measurement device before trying to answer a question about it. You might ask yourself:

      a. Is this device metric or standard?
      b. What is the smallest unit shown on this device?
      c. How many of the smallest unit are in the next larger unit?
      d. What part of a unit is represented by each division on the device?
      e. Where is zero on this device? Is it shown?
      f. Are any negative numbers shown on the device?

• The protractor is probably the trickiest measurement device to use. Always "eyeball" the angle first to determine whether it is an acute angle (< 90°), a right angle (90°), or an obtuse angle (> 90°). Then decide whether to use the inner or outer numbers on the circular edge of the protractor. Be sure to keep in mind what kind of angle you are measuring (acute or obtuse), so you choose the correct number of degrees where the angle's ray crosses the protractor edge.

Examples:

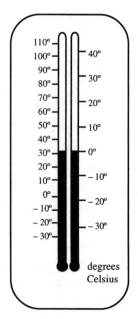

1. Consider the pictured thermometer. Which of the following statements seems to be true?

    A. The thermometer is not working correctly.

    B. The thermometer is working correctly.

    C. The thermometer is hanging inside a warm room.

    D. A heater may be near this thermometer.

Analysis:
This device is really like two thermometers. One measures according to the Celsius scale; the other, the Fahrenheit scale. The temperature shown is 0° (Celsius) and 32° (Fahrenheit). These are the freezing points on both scales. Therefore, only "B" could be correct. "C" and "D" imply warmth near the device, and "A" would mean that 0° (C) does not mean the same as 32° (F). So, "B" is the correct answer.

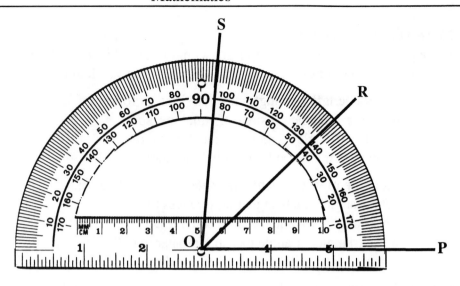

2. What is the measure of angle SOR?

   A. 30°

   B. 42°

   C. 85°

   D. 137°

Analysis:

Angle SOR appears to be an acute angle, so its measure is less than 90°. (Therefore, answer "D" is not correct.) Use the inner scale. Ray S crosses at 85° and Ray R crosses at 43°. If Ray R were not there, the measure of angle SOP would simply be 85° (answer "C"). But Ray R cuts off part of angle SOP; in fact, it cuts off 43°. So, angle SOR = 85° – 43° OR 42°. Now you can see that "B" is the correct answer.

Strand – Geometry

✍ 9. Recognize, classify, and use characteristics of lines and simple two-dimensional figures.

Students must be familiar with concepts such as perpendicular, parallel, vertical, and horizontal. They should be knowledgeable about triangles, quadrilaterals, pentagons, and circles.

Things to Remember

• A **line** stretches indefinitely in both directions. A **line segment** is part of a line which has 2 endpoints. A **ray** is also part of a line. A ray has only 1 endpoint.

• Two lines either intersect or they are **parallel**. If 2 lines intersect, they either form a right angle or they do not form a right angle. If the 2 lines do form a right angle, the lines are said to be **perpendicular**.

More Things to Remember

- If a picture of a line runs left to right with no slant, then it is a **horizontal** line. If a picture of a line runs up-down with no slant, it is a **vertical** line.

- Based on **side lengths**, triangles are classified as follows:
    equilateral triangle - 3 sides of equal measure
    isosceles triangle - 2 sides of equal measure
    scalene triangle - 0 sides of equal measure

- Based on **angle measurements**, triangles are classified as:
    acute triangle - each angle measure less than 90°
    right triangle- 1 angle measure equal to 90°
    obtuse triangle - 1 angle measure greater than 90°
    equiangular triangle - 3 angles of equal measure

- A **quadrilateral** is a 4-sided closed figure. Any quadrilateral can be divided into 2 triangles by connecting one pair of opposite corners (vertices).

- If a quadrilateral has 2 pairs of opposite sides parallel, it is called a **parallelogram**. **Squares** and **rectangles** are special parallelograms which have right angles besides 2 pairs of opposite parallel sides. (Actually, a square is a rectangle which happens to be equilateral; i.e. all 4 sides are of equal length.)

- A **pentagon** is a 5-sided closed figure. It may be equilateral; i.e. all 5 sides are of equal length. If it is equilateral, then its 5 angles also have equal measures. A pentagon can be divided into 3 triangles by connecting 1 vertex with the 2 vertices which do not neighbor it. (Try it!)

- The sum of measures of the three angles in any triangle is 180°. To determine the sum of angle measures in a quadrilateral (4 sides) or a pentagon (5 sides), divide the figure into triangles as described above. A quadrilateral divides into 2 triangles; a pentagon, 3 triangles. Since there are 180° in the measures of the angles of each triangle, the sum of measures of the angles of a quadrilateral will be 2 x 180° (360°) and the sum of measures of the angles of a pentagon will be 3 x 180° (540°).

- If you select 2 points on a circle and connect them, you will have drawn a **chord** of the circle. A chord which contains the center point of the circle is a **diameter**. A line segment having the center of the circle as one endpoint and a point on the circle as its other endpoint is called a radius of the circle.

Now try the examples on the next page.

Examples:

1. Choose an answer which correctly completes this sentence.

Two parallel lines _____?_____.

    A. could be perpendicular (form right angles).

    B. are at equal distance from each other wherever the distance is mea
       sured.

    C. could not be vertical lines.

    D. are sides of an obtuse triangle.

Analysis:
Draw a picture of 2 parallel lines. Can they intersect to form a right angle? No. So "A" is not correct. Can your lines be connected by one more line to form a triangle? No. So "D" is not correct. "C" means that parallel lines cannot be vertical lines; but you can prove that's wrong by holding 2 pencils side by side and vertical to a table. They will be parallel to each other. Therefore, "B" is the correct answer. If distance between the 2 lines was not the same measure everywhere, the lines would eventually meet and, therefore, would not be parallel.

2. What is the sum of the interior angles of a pentagon?

    A. 180°

    B. 270°

    C. 360°

    D. 540°

Analysis:
Draw a 5-sided figure (pentagon). Divide it into 3 triangles by connecting one vertex to the 2 vertices which are not neighbors to it. You will have 3 triangles.

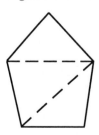

Since the sum of angle measures in each triangle is 180°, multiply 3 x 180°. The product is 540°, so the sum of the interior angles of a pentagon is 540°. The correct answer is "D."

✍ 10. Find the perimeters (circumference) and areas of polygons (circles).

You must know formulas for calculating the areas of triangles, rectangles, and circles. You should also have knowledge of formulas or strategies for finding the perimeter of a polygon and the circumference of a circle. You will need to know that the approximate value of π is between three and four.

Things to Remember
- ALWAYS draw a figure and label the parts of the figure before beginning to calculate an area or perimeter (circumference).
- The perimeter of a figure is the measure of the path around the figure. Remember - **2 P's!** **P**erimeter – **P**ath around! This will help you, so you don't confuse perimeter with area.
- If the figure is a circle, the perimeter is called by a special name - circumference. The circumference of a circle (distance around) is always about 3 times the diameter (distance across through the center). (e.g. If the diameter of a circle is 7, then the circumference of that circle is about 21.)
- The area of a figure is the count of the squares needed to cover the figure. This is true whether the figure is a polygon or a circle. The size of the squares usually depends on the units given for dimensions of the figure (e.g. If the dimensions are given in centimeters, then each "covering" square is a square centimeter. If the dimensions are given in feet, the "covering" squares are square feet.)
- An oddly-shaped figure can sometimes be divided into a set of smaller figures. Then, you can find the area of each small figure and add the areas together.
- π is a Greek letter used to represent a number between 3 and 4. π is approximately 3.14 or, as a fraction, π is approximately 22/7.
- The symbols " and ' are sometimes used instead of the word **inches** or **feet**. (e.g. 6' is read as six feet. 6" is read as six inches.)
- You should know definitions for the following terms: (Except for the last two, each is defined under **Things to Remember** in the section for Outcome 9.) radius, diameter, quadrilateral, parallelogram, rectangle, square, pentagon, hexagon (6-sided figure), octagon (8-sided figure)

- Here are some formulas you should know.

	Perimeter	Area
triangle	$P = a + b + c$ (a, b, and c are the 3 side lengths.)	$A = 1/2\ bh$ (b is the length of the base and h is the height of the triangle.)
rectangle	$P = 2l + 2w$ (l is a side length; w is the other side length.)	$A = lw$ (l is a side length; w is the other side length.)

More formulas you should know:

	Perimeter	Area
square	p = 4s	$A = s^2$ (s times s)
	(s is a side length.)	(s is a side length.)

	Circumference	Area
circle	C = πd or 2πr	$A = \pi r^2$ (π x r x r)
	(d is the measure of diameter;	(r is the measure
	r is the measure of radius.)	of radius.)

Examples:

1. The radius of a circle is 2.5 centimeters. Approximate the circumference of the circle.

   A. 3.14 cm

   B. 15.8 cm

   C. 75 cm

   D. 157 cm

Analysis:
Use the formula C = πd. Since π is a number close to 3 and d = 5 (because r = 2.5), choose the answer close to 3 x 5. That, of course, is "B." "A" is π; "C" and "D" are too large and are not near 3 times the diameter. So, eliminate "A", "C", and "D." The correct answer is "B."

2. If you look at an open TV tray from the side, you see a triangular shape made by the intersection of the two legs and the floor. If the perimeter of that triangle is 38 inches and the legs are 12 inches apart at the floor, how long is each leg from the point of intersection to the floor?

   A. 12"

   B. 13"

   C. 24"

   D. 36"

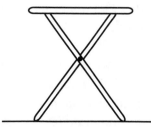

Analysis:
First draw the picture. You can see that the two legs must be equal length or the table would tip. The perimeter (38") of the triangle is the sum of the 3 sides. You know that the base side (on the floor) is 12". So, the problem becomes: 12" + length of leg + length of leg = 38" or 2 times the length of a leg must be equal to 26". Because the legs have equal measures, each one is 13" (answer "B") To check, try the other choices in the

3. A rectangular table measures 3' by 2.5'. Which of the following will cover the table?

    A. a 2' by 3.5' tablecloth

    B. a 3' by 2' party cloth

    C. a 4' by 2' newsprint page

    D. six 1' by 1.5' placemats

Analysis:

Drawing a picture of the tabletop will help you visually solve the problem. Label the tabletop's dimensions. Try to draw each answer choice, to see which one will cover the table. "A","B", and "C" are each long enough, but not wide enough. It is possible to draw the placemats in "D", so that the table is covered. Try it! It's like a puzzle! "D" is the correct answer.

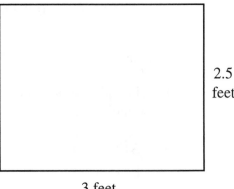

2.5 feet

3 feet

4. A mother spreads a 3' by 2.5' baby blanket on a rug which is 8' by 10'. How much of the rug shows around the baby blanket?

    A. 7.5 sq ft.

    B. 23.5 sq ft.

    C. 72.5 sq ft.

    D. 80 sq ft.

Analysis:

First draw a picture. You can find out how much of the rug is covered by finding the area of the blanket, and then subtracting that area from the area of the rug. Since both are rectangles, use A = lw twice. Blanket: A = 3' x 2.5' or 7.5 sq ft. Rug: A = 8' x 10' or 80 sq. ft. Subtract 7.5 from 80 and you see that 72.5 sq ft. of the rug shows around the baby blanket. Now check the answer choices. "A" is the area of the blanket, so it doesn't answer the question. Eliminate it. "D" is the area of the entire rug, which also doesn't answer the question. Eliminate it. "C" is the answer you computed, and "B" is not clearly evident what it represents; so the correct answer is "C."

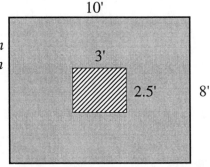

10'

3'

2.5'

8'

11. Find surface areas and volumes of rectangular solids.

Questions will require knowledge of formulas and strategies for finding the surface area and volume of a rectangular solid.

Things to Remember

- Another name for "rectangular solid" is "rectangular prism." Below are some pictures of rectangular solids (prisms). They look like boxes. Notice that all six sides are rectangles.

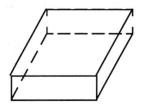 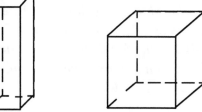

- The surface of the rectangular solid (prism) is like the 4 sides and the 2 ends of a box. Each of the 6 parts is a rectangle; so to find the surface area of the rectangular prism, you need to calculate the area of each of the 6 rectangles. Luckily, there are 2 of each size; so you need only to calculate 3 areas ($A = l \times w$, $A = l \times h$, and $A = w \times h$). You can then either double each one (because each has an identical side opposite it in the prism) and add the 3 doubled areas together; or you can add the 3 original areas together first and then double the sum to get the area of all 6 sides.

- A formula for surface area of a rectangular prism is:
  Surface area $= A_1 + A_2 + A_3 + A_4 + A_5 + A_6$
  (A_1 to A_6 are the areas of the 6 rectangles which form the prism.)

- The volume of a rectangular prism is like the space inside an empty box. You could also picture the volume as the space an end would move through, if you pushed it evenly and carefully through the box to the other end.

- A formula for volume of a rectangular prism is: $V = lwh$ or Volume equals length times width time heigth. (l,w, and h represent length, width, and height of the prism.)

Examples:

1. Mr. Keller wants to redecorate his office which has no windows and a single door. He will carpet the floor, but paint the ceiling and walls. His office is 8 feet high, and has a floor which measures 9 feet by 12 feet. What is the approximate area to be painted? (Assume his office is rectangular.)

   A. 29 sq ft

   B. 276 sq ft

   C. 444 sq ft

   D. 552 sq ft

Analysis:
First, sketch a picture. Number the walls: 1, 2, 3, and 4. Number the ceiling: 5. Use the formula A = lw to find the area of wall #1. The opposite wall in the room will have that same area. Enter that area on each of those 2 walls. Then use the same formula to find the area of another wall. Its opposite wall will have that same area, so label those 2 walls with the second area you computed. Now use the formula to figure out the area of the ceiling, and write it on your sketch. If you add the five areas, you will know the total area to be painted. There are 2 walls which measure 9' by 8'. Each of their areas is 9' x 8' or 72 sq ft. There are 2 walls which measure 12' by 8'. Each of their areas is 12' x 8' or 96 sq ft. The ceiling measures 9' by 12' (same as floor), so its area is 9' x 12' or 108 sq. ft. Now add, as follows: 72 + 72 + 96 + 96 + 108 = 444, so the area to be painted is 444 sq ft. You do not need to subtract out the area of the door since you are only looking for an approximate area and the measurement of the door was not given. The correct answer is "C."

2. A videotape in its cover measures 1" x 4" x 7.5". It is protected by an outer layer of plastic cellophane. Approximately how large is the piece of plastic cellophane?

    A. 12.5 sq in

    B. 30 sq in

    C. 41.5 sq in

    D. 83 sq in.

Analysis:
This problem is like #1 (above), except you need to figure the surface area of all 6 sides instead of skipping one as you skipped the floor in #1 (above). So, find the 3 areas by using the formula A = lw three times: A = 1" x 4" or 4 square inches, A = 1" x 7.5" or 7.5 square inches, and A = 4" x 7.5" or 30 square inches. Add the 3 areas and double the sum: 4 square inches + 7.5 square inches + 30 square inches = 41.5 square inches. When doubled, that becomes 83 square inches. So, the piece of plastic cellophane has an area of 83 square inches. Can you figure out why the other answer choices are used? (Hint! Look at the reasons why you eliminated answer choices for #1 above.)

3. To wash a rectangular sandwich box, it is filled with soapy water. The dimensions of the box are: height - 3 cm, width - 12 cm, length - 13 cm. How much water completely fills the box?

    A. 28 cm^3

    B. 56 cm^3

    C. 468 cm^3

    D. 936 cm^3

Analysis:

This is a volume problem, because you are considering the inside space of the box. The formula for volume of a rectangular prism is: V = lwh, where l is the length of the prism, w is the width of the prism, and h is the height of the prism. You know all of those dimensions; so replace the three variables with the given measurements. Then, multiply. In this problem, l x w x h becomes 13 cm x 12 cm x 3 cm, so the volume of the box is 468 cubic centimeters. Not let's check the answer choices! "A" is the sum of the dimensions; "B" is the double of "A" (in case you were in the habit of doubling from #1 and #2 above); "C" is the volume; "D" is the double of "C" or twice the volume. So, "C" is the correct answer.

Strand - Data Analysis

✔ **12. Read, interpret, and use tables, charts, maps, and graphs to identify patterns, note trends, and draw conclusions.**

Questions are designed to measure your ability to use coordinates (letter, number); to solve problems using information presented in tables, charts, or graphs; to use maps; and to interpret meanings, identify patterns or trends, and draw conclusions from tables, charts, and graphs.

Things to Remember

• Study the table, chart, or graph carefully, BEFORE you even read the question you are asked.

• The title of a graph tells you what kind of information is displayed. Side and bottom labels (if any!) indicate two types of data for which relationships are shown on the graph.

• To make good predictions from tables or graphs, always look for a pattern.

• If there is an unusual section on a graph - maybe a disruption to a pattern - ask yourself, "What does this really mean?"

• Circle graphs usually involve use of percent. (Be sure you know which fractions are equal to which percents!) All the percents pictured on the circle graph must add up to 100% (the entire circular region).

• Sometimes it is helpful to use a straight edge (such as a pencil, edge of a paper, etc.) when reading a graph or chart. Laying the straightedge along the line of the graph or chart makes it easier to keep your eye in the correct row or column of the display.

Try the examples on the next page.

Examples:

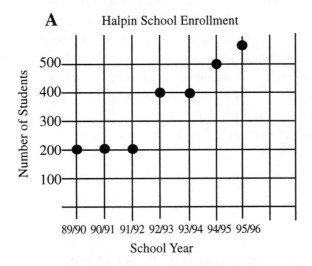

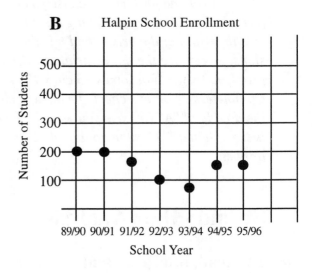

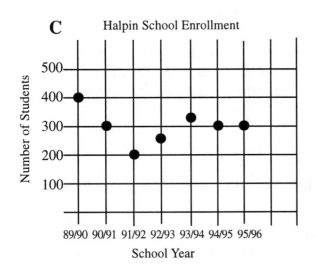

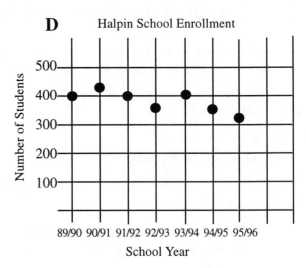

1. Which graph displays an increasing enrollment at Halpin School?

    A. Graph A

    B. Graph B

    C. Graph C

    D. Graph D

Analysis:

Study the four graphs. Each one is entitled " Halpin School Enrollment." Across the bottom are the years from 1989 to 1996, and the side are the number of students. "Increasing" means "getting larger." So, the graph which shows the number of students getting larger each year is the one you are asked to find. Graph A is the only one that show a steady increase. The correct answer is "A."

Use the graph below to answer questions 2, 3, and 4.

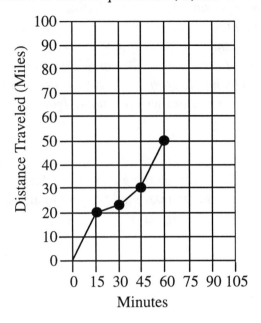

2. Josh left Columbus at 1:00 p.m. Approximately how far is he from his starting point an hour later?

   A. 30 mi

   B. 50 mi

   C. 60 mi

   D. 100 mi

Analysis:

Time is across the bottom of the graph, so look over to the 60 minute point (1 hr). Above that will be the distance traveled in one hour. The point above 60 minutes is across from 50 miles on the side where distance is indicated. So, in one hour, Josh will be 50 miles from where he started. In other words, at 2:00 p.m., Josh will be 50 miles from his starting point. Answer "B" is correct. The other choices do not correspond to points above 60 minutes.

3. Josh left Columbus at 1:00 p.m., but encountered a construction delay on the trip. According to the graph, at which time was he slowed by construction?

   A. 1:00 - 1:15

   B. 1:15 - 1:45

   C. 1:45 - 2:00

   D. 2:00 - 2:30

Analysis:

A delay means that time is passing, but not much distance is being covered. Look at the graph. In the first 15 minutes, 20 miles were traveled. In the next 15 minutes, about 2 miles were traveled. From then on, the distance was covered more quickly. So, the delay must have been between 1:15 and 1:45. The correct answer is "B." "A" represents his first 15 minutes, during which time Josh was traveling at regular speed. The "C" time interval shows 20 miles in 15 minutes which is not a delayed speed, and "D" shows times which are not even on the graph.

4. According to the information on the graph, and if Josh has no further delays, at what time could he reasonably expect to arrive in Cincinnati which is 100 miles from Columbus?

    A. 2:00

    B. 2:45

    C. 3:15

    D. 4:00

Analysis:

The answer to #1 indicates that, at 2:00, Josh will be only 50 miles from his starting point; so eliminate "A". After the delay (#3), Josh resumed speed and was traveling at the rate of 20 miles in 15 minutes. On the graph, imagine the line moving upward to the right until it reaches the point across from 100 miles (side markings). That will be between 90 minutes (1 1/2 hrs) and 105 minutes (1 hr 45 min). So, answer "B" is a good estimate of arrival time in Cincinnati. Answers "C" and "D" indicate times after a reasonable expected arrival time.

13. Use elementary notions of probability.

Questions will measure your knowledge of simple probability principles and your ability to apply such principles to solve problems involving randomly occurring events or equally likely outcomes.

Things to Remember

- A probability is a ratio (fraction). To identify the ratio (fraction), first determine the number of <u>all</u> possible outcomes in the given situation. That number is the denominator of the fraction. Then determine the number of possibilities for the desired outcome in which you are interested. That number is the numerator of the fraction. Thus, the probability of an event is:

        number of desired outcomes ÷ number of possible outcomes.

For Example: When flipping a coin, there are 2 <u>possible</u> outcomes altogether - heads or tails; so the denominator is 2. If you want heads, there is only one possibility on a single coin; so the numerator is 1. Therefore, the probability of heads, when flipping a single coin, is 1/2.

- A desired outcome is called an <u>event</u>. An abbreviation for probability of an outcome or probability of an <u>e</u>vent is P(E). In the above example, P(E) = 1/2.

- Any fraction can be written as a decimal or as a percent (%), so any probability can be written as a decimal or as a percent (%).

- If an event is certain to occur, the numerator is equal to the denominator so the probability of the event is 1 or P(E) = 1. No probability can be greater than 1, because an event cannot be more than certain to occur.

- If an event cannot possibly occur, the probability of the event is 0 or P(E) = 0. No probability can be less than zero.

- Any probability is between 0 and 1, or it is equal to 0 or 1. The closer the probability is to 0, the <u>less</u> likely an event is to happen. The closer the probability is to 1, the <u>more</u> likely an event is to happen.

Examples:

1. Sweatshirts come in Extra-large, Large, Medium, and Small. An equal number of sweatshirts were bagged individually but, by mistake, the labels were not attached. If you open one bag, what is the probability that the sweatshirt will be your size?

    A. 1/4

    B. 1/3

    C. 1

    D. 4/1

Analysis:
There are four equally likely possibilities for the size of each bagged sweatshirt; so the denominator of the fraction is 4. Only one of the 4 sizes is your size, so there is only one possible way to get your size. That means the numerator is 1. So, the probability of getting your size is 1/4. Now, let's check the answer choices! "A" - seems to be the correct answer, but check the others to be sure. Answer choice "B" has a denominator of 3 which means only 3 possible sizes. Eliminate "B." Answer choice "C" indicates that you are certain to get your size, and you aren't sure of that; so eliminate "C." Answer choice "D" has a probability of greater than 1, so "D" cannot be correct. "A" is the correct answer.

2. Josh drops some jelly beans - 3 red, 4 green, and 1 orange. His colorblind dog eats one of them. What is the probability that the dog ate a green jelly bean?

    A. 1/8

    B. 1/4

    C. 1/3

    D. 1/2

Analysis:

This one is tricky because a different number of each color was dropped. A person might think that the probability is 1/3 or one of three colors. But there isn't the same chance for the dog to eat each color, so you can't just consider color. 8 were dropped altogether, regardless of color, so there are 8 possible jelly beans for the dog to eat. Therefore, the denominator is 8, not 3. There are 4 green candies, which is the color we are now interested in. So, there are 4 possibilities for the dog to eat a green jelly bean. Therefore the numerator is 4. The probability of the dog eating a green jelly bean is 4/8 or 1/2. Now, let's look at the answer choices! Answer choice "A" indicates that only 1 of the 8 jelly beans is green. Not true! Eliminate "A." Answer choice "B" uses the number of greens as all possible jelly beans. But there are 8 possibilities. Eliminate "B." Answer choice "C" uses the number of colors, rather than the number of jelly beans. So, eliminate "C." The correct answer is "D.".

3. A picture of each U.S. president hangs in a museum. What is the probability that one of the pictures is a picture of a woman?

    A. -1

    B. 0

    C. 1/12

    D. 1

Analysis:

Since there have been no female presidents, there is no possibility that one of the pictured presidents is a woman. Therefore, you can be sure that the probability is zero (0). "B" is the correct answer!

4. A weather forecaster announces, "60% chance of rain tomorrow." What is the probability that it will not rain tomorrow?

A. 0

B. 2/5

C. 3/5

D. 1

Analysis:

A percent can be written as a fraction. In this case, 60% = 60/100 = 6/10 = 3/5. So, the probability of rain tomorrow is 3/5. With a 60% chance of rain, there is only a 40% chance of "no rain," (because rain % + no rain % must equal 100%.) But 40% = 40/100 = 4/10 = 2/5. So, the probability of "no rain" is 2/5. Now, what about the answer choices? Zero probability means "no chance that it will not rain. This is not true! Eliminate "A." Answer choice "C," 3/5 = 60 % which is the probability of rain instead of no rain. Eliminate "C." In answer choice "D," the probability of 1 means there certainly will be no rain. Not true! Eliminate "D." Therefore, "B" is the correct answer.

5. At a carnival, the probabilities of winning certain games are not equal. In which one of the following games are you most likely to win?

Game Title	Probability of Winning
SpinWheel	5/12
Catch-a-Star	1/2
Ring Toss	2/5
Dice Drop	1/6

A. SpinWheel

B. Catch-a-Star

C. Ring Toss

D. Dice Throw

Analysis:

Whichever game has the probability closest to 1 is the game with the best chance of winning. Catch-a-Star has a 1/2 probability which is exactly in the middle between 0 and 1. All of the other probabilities are closer to 0 than to 1; so Catch-a-Star is the game with the best chance of winning. If you aren't sure, draw a number line and place a point for each of the four fractions on the number line. You will see that 1/2 is closest to 1, making "B" the correct answer choice.

14. Compute averages.

You will be required to find averages of as many as five numbers using numerical information (data) presented in word problems, tables, charts, or graphs. You may also be asked to find a missing data element (e.g. a score or number), given the average and other data elements.

Things to Remember

- Another name for "an <u>average</u>" - as used in this proficiency outcome - is "a <u>mean</u>."

- An average (mean) is the number each data element would be, if all the data elements in a given set were equal. (e.g. The average score on a test is 80. This means that, if all the students' test scores were equal, each score would be 80.)

- An average is never larger than the largest data number. The average is never smaller than the smallest data number. (Always check this!)

- To compute an average, add the numbers which represent given data. Then divide the sum by how many data numbers you added. (Brief rule: Add, then divide.)

- If you know an average and are given all the data numbers but one, just work in reverse to find the unknown data number. The average (which you know) times the total number of data numbers - including the one you do not know - determines the sum of all the data numbers (known and unknown). After that, you can add the data numbers you know and subtract that total from the sum of <u>all</u> data numbers to identify the missing number. (Rule: Multiply the known average (a) times the total number of data numbers (d) or "a" times "d". Subtract the sum of the data numbers you know from the product just obtained.

- Be careful when you are asked to compute an average by using information from a table, chart, or graph. Use only data numbers related to the question you are asked. Ignore other data. It is probably not needed.

Examples:

1. Your scores on four exams are 70, 80, 90, and 96. What is your average exam score?

   A. 68
   B. 84
   C. 94
   D. 336

Analysis:

Add the four data numbers. The sum is 336. Divide that sum by 4 to determine the average which is 84. This means that, if you had had the same score on each exam, it would have been 84. Now, check the answer choices! "A" is smaller than any of the scores and "D" is larger than any of the scores. Forget "A" and "D"! "C" is too close to the top score. The average will not be that close to the top score, because the four numbers are spread far apart. So, "B" is the correct answer.

2. Your average test score is 84, but you only know your first three grades. They are 70, 80, and 90. What is your fourth grade?

    A. 80

    B. 81

    C. 84

    D. 96

Analysis:

You can see that this problem is #1 in reverse! So, work in reverse. Multiply 84 by the total number of test scores (4). The product is 336. The three scores which you know add up to 240. Subtract 240 from 336 and you have the fourth score which is 96. In # 1, you first added; then, you divided. In #2, you first multiplied; then, subtracted the sum of the known scores from 336. You just worked in reverse! No matter what the answer choices are, you now know that the fourth score must be 96. Another way to identify the correct answer is to compute the averages using each of the 4 answer choices as "fourth grade" with the 3 grades you already know. By this method, "A" creates an average of 80; "B," 80.25; "C," 81; "D," 84. So, "D" must be correct!

Strand - Algebra

✔ **15. Solve simple number sentences and use formulas.**

You will be asked to solve number sentences involving one variable with integer co-efficients. Questions will measure your ability to make simple substitutions in formulas or equations that are given. Some questions may require you to find a missing dimension by applying knowledge of simple formulas.

Things to Remember

- A variable is any letter which can be replaced by a number in a number sentence (equation). The challenge is to identify the correct number to put in place of the variable so that the given number sentence (equation) is true. (e.g. If n - 4 = 10, then n = 14.)

- When you think you know the correct number for a variable, put that number into the original number sentence to see if it "works." (e.g. In #1 above, we said n = 14. Put 14 into the original number sentence and you have 14 - 4 = 10. That's true, so n does equal 14.)

- The multiplication and division symbols are not used in equations. For multiplication, a number is written just before a variable. (e.g. 5t means 5 times t.) For division, the number and the variable are written as a fraction. (e.g. n/6 means "n" divided by 6.)

- A formula is a rule which "works" for all figures or situations of a similar type. (e.g. A = 1/2 bh is a formula which tells how to figure the area of a triangle. If you already know the area and one of the dimensions, you can also use the same formula to figure the base or height of the triangle.)

- Make a list of all the commonly used formulas. Be sure you understand <u>what</u> they mean, <u>how</u> to use them, and <u>when</u> to use each one. Include formulas for perimeter, circumference, area, volume, distance, and any others you think are important. Most textbooks have formulas listed; but write out your personal copy. By writing them, you'll probably understand them better! (Hint! Some formulas are listed under Outcomes 10 and 11.)

Examples:

1. Solve this equation: $15 - t = 6$

   A. $t = 6$
   B. $t = 9$
   C. $t = 12$
   D. $t = 15$

Analysis:
The "mystery number" is represented by "t." In your own words, this equation means "If I subtract a mystery number from 15, the remainder will be 6." So, you might think, "6 plus what number is 15?"   6 + 9 = 15, so 15 - 9 = 6. Therefore, t = 9. To check the answer choices, put each of them into the original equation.   "A" gives 15 - 6 = 6. Wrong! "B" gives 15 - 9 = 6. Right! "C" gives 15 -12 = 6. Wrong! "D" gives 15 - 15 = 6. Wrong! So, "B" is the correct answer. It's the only one which makes the equation true.

2. Solve this equation: $\dfrac{2s}{3} = 4$

   A. $s = 3$
   B. $s = 4$
   C. $s = 6$
   D. $s = 8$

Analysis:

2s means 2 times s. $\frac{2s}{3}$ *means 2 times s, then divided by 3. Now, the question becomes "What number divided by 3 is equal to 4? You probably know it is 12. That means 2 x "s" is 12, so s = 6. When you put 6 instead of "s" into the original equation, you get 2 times 6 which is then to be divided by 3. Since 2 x 6 = 12 and 12 / 3 does equal 4, it seems that 6 is the correct number for s. If answers "A," "B," or "D" are put in for "s", you do not get a true number sentence. (Try it!) So, "C" is the answer for this one.*

3. Mrs. Gwinter bought a number of $200.00 airline tickets and three travel books which sell for $20.00 each. If her bill was $860.00, how many airline tickets did she buy?

   A. 4

   B. 60

   C. 260

   D. 860

Analysis:

It is easy to see that $60.00 is the cost of the three books. The "mystery number" is the number of airline tickets, so use a variable to stand for that number. Let's use "t" (for tickets). " t" times $200.00 (or $200.00 times "t") will be the cost of all the airline tickets. So $200t + $60 = $860. Subtract the book cost of $60 from $860 total cost and you see that the ticket cost ($200t) is $800. Now it seems like t = 4, or Mrs. Gwinter bought 4 tickets. Let's see if that makes sense! 4 tickets at $200 per ticket is $800. 3 books at $20 per book is $60. That means her bill should be $860 which is the amount she was charged. What about the other answer choices? "B", "C", and "D" are all too large to be the number of airline tickets. "B" is the cost of the books. "C" is the amount you pay for one ticket and three books. "D" is her total bill, not the number of tickets purchased. So, "A" is the correct answer.

4. The following formula may be used to determine the total number of rides at an amusement park.

$$R = A + C + \frac{5C}{2}$$

   Where R = total number of rides, A = number of rides preferred by adults, and C = number of rides preferred by small children. If a park has 4 rides preferred by adults and 18 rides which small children like, how many rides does the park have altogether?

   A. 22

   B. 31

   C. 45

   D. 67

Analysis:

Replace the variables in the original formula with the numbers you know after reading the problem. This is what you will then have.

R = 4 + 18 + 5 x $\frac{18}{2}$ *which equals* 22 + $\frac{90}{2}$ *which equals* 22 + 45 *or* 67.

Because R = 67 and R = total number of rides, you now know that there are 67 rides at the amusement park. Before leaving this problem, put 67 into the original formula in place of "R" to make sure it works. Also check the other answer choices in this way. The correct answer choice is "D."

16. Evaluate algebraic expressions (simple substitutions).

You will be asked to evaluate algebraic expressions containing as many as three variables by using simple substitutions. When an expression includes two or more variables, values will be given for all but one.

Things to Remember
- To "evaluate" an algebraic expression, substitute known numbers for variables; then add, subtract, multiply, or divide as indicated. Sometimes the directions may say, "Find the value of" instead of the word "evaluate."
- To evaluate expressions, you must know correct order of operations. The first thing to do is determine the number in the parentheses (if there are any parentheses.) Then, move from left to right in the expression, doing any multiplication or division you find. Finally, move again from left to right, doing all additions and subtractions.
- Some additional rules for evaluating expressions are listed above, under Things to Remember for Outcome 15.

Examples:

1. If a = 4 and b = 2, evaluate 3a – 2 + ($\frac{a}{4}$ – 1) + 6b.

   A. 13
   B. 17
   C. 22
   D. 37

Analysis:

In parentheses, a/4 - 1 becomes 4/4 - 1 which is the same as 1-1 and that equals 0. From left to right, there are two multiplications: 3a and 6b. 3a is 3 x 4 which equals 12. 6b is 6 x 2 which also equals 12. So, in the original expression, put 12 for 3a and 12 for 6b. Remember, there is a 0 in the parentheses. Now, the expression looks like this: 12 - 2 + 0 + 12 which, when you add and subtract left to right, equals 22. This is answer choice "C." The three incorrect answer choices all result from not using correct order of operations.

Mathematics Practice Items

About The Practice Items: Mathematics

Now that you have a better understanding of the mathematics to be included in the Ohio Ninth Grade Proficiency Test, you can check your understanding by solving the following practice items which are very similar to problems you will find on the actual test. To make it easier for you to identify areas with which you might need help, the sample problems in this section are arranged by learning outcome. This will help you identify what learning outcomes you need to work on some more. You may want to ask your teacher, parent, or a friend to help you if you continue to have difficulty with the content of one or more learning outcome.

1. If round trip adult airfare to Salt Lake City is $600 and a child flies for 2/3 fare, what is the cost of tickets for one adult and one child?

   A. $ 400.00
   B. $ 666.00
   C. $ 800.00
   D. $1000.00

   $\frac{5}{8} + \frac{5}{8} \times \frac{5}{8} + \frac{5}{8} = \frac{20}{8} \quad 4\frac{2}{8}$

2. A contractor needs to carpet a floor which is 19 1/2 feet wide. If he uses four carpet panels which are each 4 5/8 feet wide, how wide should the final piece be?

   A. 1/2 foot
   B. 1 foot
   C. 4 5/8 feet
   D. 15 1/8 feet

3. On June 23, 1996, a U.S. Olympian broke the record in the men's 200 meter dash. Michael Johnson's time of 19.66 seconds bettered the old mark by .06 second. What was the old record?

   A. 19.06 sec
   B. 19.60 sec
   C. 19.72 sec
   D. 20.20 sec

4. Each issue of Funnybone Magazine contains at least 80 jokes. What is the minimum number of jokes contained in 12 issues of the magazine?

   A. 68
   B. 92
   C. 960
   D. 1280

5. How much change from a $20.00 bill should you receive, if you bought a sweatshirt for $11.99 and a belt for $4.39? (Tax is included in the prices.)

   A. $ 3.61
   B. $ 3.62
   C. $ 4.62
   D. $ 8.01

6. A printer who has 2 1/2 rolls of paper agrees to three jobs. One job requires 1/4 roll, another requires 1 1/2 rolls, and the third requires 1/2 roll. Which of the following statements is true?

   A. The printer has exactly enough paper for the three jobs.

   B. The printer does not have enough paper for the three jobs.

   C. The printer has more paper than he needs for the three jobs.

   D. The printer needs another 1/2 roll of paper for the three jobs.

7. On a customary numberline, which statement is true?

   A. Points which lie to the right of "2" represent numbers smaller than "2."

   B. Points which lie to the left of "7" represent numbers smaller than "7."

   C. A point representing "3.5" lies right of a point representing "3.6."

   D. A point representing 4/5 lies right of a point representing 9/10.

8. Which numbers are equivalent?

3.4, 6/8, .75, 6.8%, 7.5, 3/4, 7/5, .68, 34%

   A. 6/8, .68, 7/5

   B. 34%, 3/4, 3.4

   C. 7.5, .75, 7/5

   D. 3/4, 6/8, .75

9. Arrange these numbers from smallest to greatest: -2/3, 2/3, -4, .04

   A. -2/3, -4, .04, 2/3

   B. -4, -2/3, .04, 2/3

   C. .04, 2/3, -2/3, -4

   D. -2/3, -4, 2/3, .04

10. Which symbol ($<$, $=$, $>$, $\geq$) makes the statement true?   -7/8 ? 1/7

   A. $<$

   B. $=$

   C. $>$

   D. $\geq$

11. The numeral .08 means:

   A. 8 thousandths

   B. 8 hundredths

   C. 8 tenths

   D. 8

Use the following information to answer questions 12 - 14.

During a science experiment, each student poured 10 ounces of water into a separate jar. Jars varied in size and shape. Daily, the students measured the remaining water to determine from which jar evaporation was occurring most quickly. On the third day, measurements were as follows: Marcus - 8.103 oz; Terri - 7.8 oz; Pat - 8.09 oz; Jo - 8.7 oz.

12. Which student's jar contained the greatest amount of water after the third day's reading?

   A. Marcus

   B. Terri

   C. Pat

   D. Jo

13. If the jars are to be lined up according to the amount of water in each jar, what is the order of the jars from least to greatest?

   A. Marcus, Terri, Pat, Jo

   B. Terri, Pat, Jo, Marcus

   C. Terri, Pat, Marcus, Jo

   D. Pat, Marcus, Terri, Jo

14. If these measurements were graphed on a numberline, which student's measurement would lie to the right of Marcus' measurement?

   A. Terri

   B. Pat

   C. Jo

   D. Terri and Pat

15. Five cans of catfood cost $1.30. What is the cost of seven cans of catfood? Which proportion could be used to solve this problem?

A. 5/7 = c/$1.30
B. 5/$1.30 = 7/c
C. c/5 = $1.30/7
D. $1.30/c = 7/5

16. Aaron can deliver 100 weekly newspapers in an hour. If he increases the number of subscribers and has to deliver 130 newspapers, how long will it take?

A. 46 min.
B. 60 min.
C. 78 min.
D. 130 min.

17. A band charges $500 for a 4-hour performance. At this rate, how much would they charge for 2 1/2 hours of music?

A. $ 50.00
B. $250.00
C. $312.50
D. $750.00

18. A cleaning crew can thoroughly clean three rooms in four hours. At this rate, which of the following is the most reasonable estimate of how long it will take to clean eight rooms?

A. 1.5 hrs.
B. 6 hrs.
C. 8 hrs.
D. 11 hrs.

19. Solve for t: t/3 = 7/10

A. t = 2.1
B. t = 4 2/7
C. t = 21
D. t = 63

20. A drive-thru manager paid $6.00 for 48 packs of paper cups. At the same rate, how many packs of cups can he buy for $20.00?

A. 2.5 packs
B. 120 packs
C. 144 packs
D. 160 packs

21. Round 1369 to the nearest ten.

A. 1000
B. 1369.0
C. 1370
D. 1400

22. Round 647.83 to the nearest tenth.

A. 600
B. 647.8
C. 650
D. 650.83

23. (1 lb. = 16 oz.) A bag of chips weighs 18 ounces. To the nearest pound, how heavy is it?

   A. .5 lb.
   B. 1 lb.
   C. 1.8 lb.
   D. 2 lb.

24. Cedar Point is an amusement park in northwestern Ohio. On a July day, park managers estimated about 14,000 paid admissions at the park. Assuming that the managers used customary rules for rounding, which of the following could be the exact number of people who paid to enter the park?

   A. 13099
   B. 13444
   C. 14444
   D. 14544

25. By phone, a used car salesman is describing a car which has a sticker price of $659.00. To attract the customer to his car lot, he tells her that the car costs about $500.00. To the nearest hundred, what price should he have told the customer?

   A. $600.00
   B. $660.00
   C. $700.00
   D. $750.00

26. There are 51.7 million young people in the schools of the United States. If approximately 30% of these students are in the nation's high schools about how many students are in the high schools?

   A. 15.5 million
   B. 21.7 million
   C. 25.9 million
   D. 1551 million

27. At a shopping mall, 75% of the stores sell clothing or shoes. There are 48 stores altogether. How many sell clothing or shoes?

   A. 12
   B. 27
   C. 36
   D. 42

28. During a tornado, 68 of a motel's windows were broken. If there were 100 windows altogether, what percent of the windows were not broken?

   A. 25%
   B. 32%
   C. 67%
   D. 68%

29. At a discount store, there are 12 cashiers. When you arrive, 9 of the lanes are occupied by customers. What percent of the lanes are open for you?

    A. 3%

    B. 9%

    C. 25%

    D. 75%

30. A recent TV survey identified 60% of commercials as boring to viewers. If 15 commercials were used for the survey, how many did viewers find interesting?

    A. 3

    B. 6

    C. 9

    D. 12

31. There are 20 steps leading to Saundra's apartment. 10% of them are squeaky. How many steps squeak?

    A. 2

    B. 10

    C. 15

    D. 18

32. 80% of the area of one newspaper page displayed advertising. How much of the page was left for other material?

    A. 8%

    B. 20%

    C. 40%

    D. 60%

33. At a 25% discount, what is the sale price of an $8.00 belt?

    A. $ 2.00

    B. $ 4.00

    C. $ 6.00

    D. $ 7.75

34. Jack bought a $1000 motorcycle at a 20% discount. Jill bought a $1000 stereo unit at a 25% discount. Which statement is true?

    A. Jack's purchase cost more than Jill's purchase.

    B. Jill's purchase cost more than Jack's purchase.

    C. Jack and Jill spent the same amount of money.

    D. Jack received a better discount than Jill received.

35. The sales tax rate in Redberg is 5 1/2%. How much tax must be paid on a $ 6.00 purchase in Redberg?

    A. $ .33

    B. $ 3.30

    C. $ 5.45

    D. $33.00

36. If a hall is reserved at least 3 months in advance, there is a 10% discount on the rental rate. Under that arrangement, how much is the rent on a $350.00 hall which is reserved 4 months in advance?

    A. $ 35.00
    B. $210.00
    C. $315.00
    D. $350.00

37. The area of Ohio is recorded in an encyclopedia. Which unit is most likely used?

    A. sq in
    B. sq ft
    C. sq yd
    D. sq mi

38. Which unit is most appropriate for representing the weight of ten bananas?

    A. milligram
    B. centigram
    C. gram
    D. kilogram

39. A truck is filled with mulch which is to be sold by volume. If someone purchases the entire truckful, the cost will most likely be related to which unit of measure?

    A. square feet
    B. square yards
    C. cubic yards
    D. cubic inches

40. About how much does a family-size box of breakfast cereal weigh?

    A. 4 oz.
    B. 1 lb.
    C. 2 1/2 lbs.
    D. 10 oz.

41. Which of the following is the most likely weight of a large box of laundry detergent?

    A. 2.9 kg
    B. 2.9 mg
    C. 2.9 cg
    D. 2.9 g

42. About how long is a toothbrush?

    A. 12 mm
    B. 12 cm
    C. 12 in
    D. 12 ft

43. Terri walks to school. Which measurement is most reasonable for the distance from Terri's home to school?

    A. $\frac{3}{4}$ mm
    B. $\frac{3}{4}$ mi
    C. $\frac{3}{4}$ yd
    D. $\frac{3}{4}$ cm

44. Which of the following objects might have an area of 1.5 square centimeters?

   A. postage stamp
   B. TV screen
   C. kitchen door
   D. vitamin pill

45. Which is the correct order, showing units of time from smallest to largest?

   A. century, decade, year, week
   B. day, week, century, decade
   C. day, week, decade, century
   D. hour, decade, day, century

46. Which is the correct order, showing units of length from largest to smallest?

   A. km, m, cm, mm
   B. m, cm, km, mm
   C. mm, km, cm, m
   D. km, mm, m, cm

47. Two carpenters measure the same board, one measuring in feet and the other in inches. One of the two measurements is "3 feet." What is the other measurement?

   A. 12 in
   B. 24 in
   C. 36 in
   D. 48 in

48. Allen's 10 sheets of cookies are ready to bake. If each one must be in the oven for 12 minutes and the oven is too small to bake two at a time, about how long will it take to bake all 10 sheets of cookies?

   A. 1 hr 12 min
   B. 1 hr 30 min
   C. 2 hrs 10 min
   D. 10 hrs 12 min

49. How many decades are in a century?

   A. 2
   B. 10
   C. 60
   D. 100

50. A roll of dimes is worth $5.00. A dime is about 1 millimeter thick. About how long is a roll of dimes?

   A. 5 mm
   B. 5 cm
   C. 10 cm
   D. 1 m

51. When the captain on an airline flight announces, "Our altitude is now 23,000 feet," about how many miles above the earth's surface is the plane?

   A. 1 mile
   B. 3 miles
   C. 4 miles
   D. 10 miles

Use the drawing pictured below to answer questions 52 - 54 .

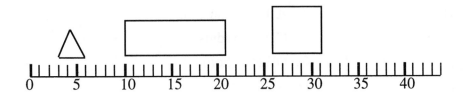

52. What is the length of the rectangle?

   A. 10 units
   B. 11 units
   C. 12 units
   D. 21 units

53. About how long is the base of the triangle?

   A. 3 units
   B. 4 units
   C. 5 units
   D. 9 units

54. Compute perimeter of the square. (Perimeter means "distance around".)

   A. 5 units
   B. 6 units
   C. 10 units
   D. 20 units

55. When John left school, his watch showed it to be 4:10. He arrived home 27 minutes later. Which timepiece shows the time when John arrived home?

A.

B.

C.

D.

56. An average January temperature is shown on the Fahrenheit thermometer pictured below. What is the average January temperature?

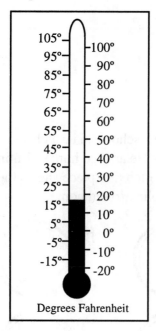

Degrees Fahrenheit

A. -20°

B. 13°

C. 15°

D. 17°

Use the figure below to answer questions 57– 59.

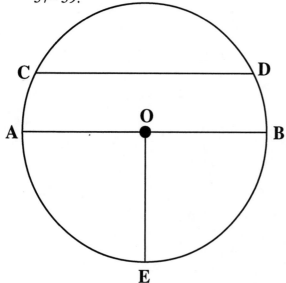

57. Which statement is true?

A. AB is a diameter.

B. CD is a radius.

C. OE is a chord.

D. AO is a chord.

58. Which statement is true?

A. The measure of OB is equal to the measure of OE.

B. The measure of AO is equal to half the measure of CD.

C. Each of the 4 segments (CD, OA, OB, OE) is a chord.

D. CD is perpendicular to AB.

59. OE is perpendicular to AB. The measure of angle BOE is 90°. Which statement is true?

A. OB is perpendicular to OA.

B. The measure of ∠AOE is less than 90°.

C. OE is perpendicular to AB.

D. The measure of ∠AOB is 0°.

60. How is any rectangle like any parallelogram?

A. Both figures have 4 right angles.

B. Each figure has an interior obtuse angle.

C. Both figures have 4 sides of equal measure.

D. Both figures have 2 pairs of parallel sides.

61. Two lines are perpendicular. If one of the lines is horizontal, what is true of the other line?

   A. It is also horizontal.
   B. It is parallel to the first line.
   C. It is vertical.
   D. It is shorter than the first line.

62. How many interior angles are inside a quadrilateral?

   A. 3
   B. 4
   C. 5
   D. 6

63. The radius of a circle is 3.5 centimeters. What is the length of the diameter?

   A. 1.75 cm
   B. 3.5 cm
   C. 7 cm
   D. 14 cm

64. When a ladder is placed on the ground and leaned against a building, a triangle is formed. The side of the building, the ground, and the ladder are the three sides. Which type of triangle is it most likely to be?

   A. right
   B. equilateral
   C. obtuse
   D. equiangular

65. A parallelogram is a special kind of:

   A. quadrilateral
   B. square
   C. rectangle
   D. triangle

66. The pages of most textbooks are the same general shape. Which geometric figure is the best representation of a page from a textbook?

   A. trapezoid
   B. rhombus
   C. pentagon
   D. rectangle

67. How long is a fence around an 8-foot square flower garden?

   A. 4'
   B. 16'
   C. 32'
   D. 64'

68. A step ladder has rectangular rungs which measure 3" by 18". What is the perimeter of each rung?

   A. 21"
   B. 36"
   C. 42"
   D. 54"

69. The area of a circle is approximately 28 cm^2. Which of the following is the best approximation for the radius of the circle?

   A. 3 cm
   B. 4 cm
   C. 7 cm
   D. 14 cm

70. What is the area of a triangle which is 8 meters high and has a base of 7 meters?

   A. 15 m^2
   B. 22 m^2
   C. 23 m^2
   D. 28 m^2

71. What is the area of this polygon?

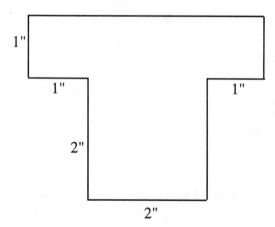

   A. 6 sq in
   B. 8 sq in
   C. 14 sq in
   D. 16 sq in

72. Certain medicines are sealed with a heavy plastic strip around the top of the bottle. If the diameter of the bottle cap is 4 centimeters, approximately how long is the plastic sealing strip?

   A. 3.2 cm
   B. 6.3 cm
   C. 12.2 cm
   D. 48.0 cm

73. The dimensions of a rectangular trash container are: width of .5 meter; length of .5 meter; and height of 1 meter. How much trash will the container hold?

   A. .25 m^3
   B. .5 m^3
   C. 1 m^3
   D. 2 m^3

74. A rectangular box is completely filled with papers for recycling. If the box measures 10" by 18" by 20", what is the volume of paper in the box?

   A. 48 in^3
   B. 360 in^3
   C. 3600 in^3
   D. 4800 in^3

75. A band member wants to paint the storage box for his keyboard. The dimensions of the box are: width of 4.5", length of 18", and height of 28". After the four largest sides are painted, what is the area of the remaining unpainted parts of the box?

    A. 50.5 sq in

    B. 162 sq in

    C. 252 sq in

    D. 1422 sq in

76. When computing surface area of a rectangular solid, the area of how many flat surfaces must be determined?

    A. 1

    B. 2

    C. 4

    D. 6

77. A toy box is shaped like a cube. One side is a 2 ft. by 2 ft. square. What is the surface area of the toy box?

    A. 4 sq ft

    B. 8 sq ft

    C. 16 sq ft

    D. 24 sq ft

Study this graph carefully. Use it to answer questions 78 – 80.

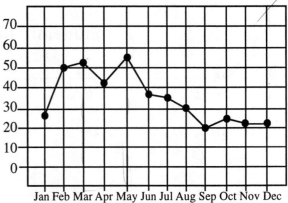

78. Flood stage for the Ohio River at Cincinnati is 52 feet. According to the graph, how many times did the river reach flood stage during 1996?

    A. never

    B. twice

    C. three times

    D. four times

79. During which two months was the river level continuously falling?

    A. Jan - Feb

    B. Mar - Apr

    C. July - Aug

    D. Oct - Nov

80. Based on this graph and thinking ahead to 1997, during which season does it seem most likely that the Ohio River will flood?

    A. winter

    B. spring

    C. summer

    D. fall

Study this graph carefully. Use it to answer questions 81 and 82.

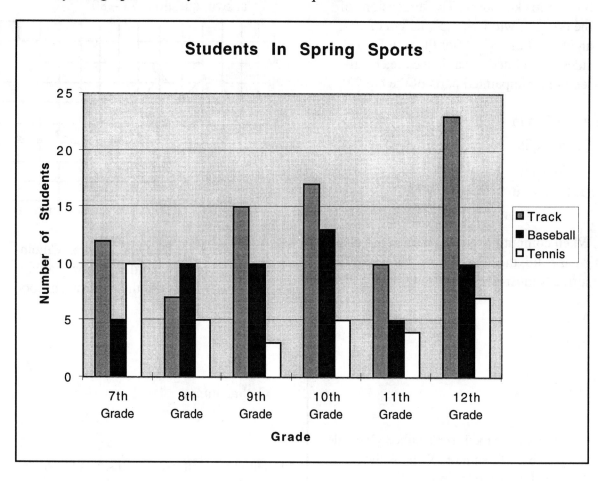

81. Which of the following statements is true?

A. There are more students in track than in any other sport.

B. Tennis has more participants than baseball.

C. Baseball is the least popular participatory sport.

D. Tennis is the most popular participatory sport.

82. Which statement is not true?

A. Tennis attracts fewer students than baseball.

B. There are more twelfth-graders than 10th-graders in sports.

C. Baseball is more popular than tennis.

D. When the seniors graduate, almost half of the track team will graduate.

83. An AM-FM radio is turned on. What is the probability that it is on the AM setting?

   A. 0

   B. $\frac{1}{2}$

   C. 1

   D. $\frac{2}{1}$

84. Some plastic chips are in a bag. All are the same size. 3 chips are brown, 2 chips are blue, and the other chip is white. If the bag is dropped and one chip falls out, what is the probability that it will be the white chip?

   A. $\frac{1}{6}$

   B. $\frac{1}{3}$

   C. $\frac{1}{2}$

   D. 1

85. Doug has ten coins in his pocket, but there are no pennies or nickels. If he reaches into his pocket and removes a coin, what is the probability that the coin he removes is worth more than five cents?

   A. $\frac{1}{10}$

   B. $\frac{1}{5}$

   C. $\frac{1}{2}$

   D. 1

86. Some cereal boxes contain prizes. On each box is printed, "20% chance of winning a valuable prize! 1% chance of winning the top award!" If you buy a box of cereal, which of the following is most likely?

   A. You will win a prize.

   B. You will win the top award.

   C. You will not win a valuable prize or the top award.

   D. You will win both a valuable prize and the top award.

87. A book has sixty-five pages. Three pages are torn, seven pages are spotted with ink, and a child's scribble marks are on four pages. When you open the book, what is the probability that at least one of the damaged pages will be showing?

   A. $\frac{3}{65}$

   B. $\frac{4}{65}$

   C. $\frac{7}{65}$

   D. $\frac{14}{65}$

88. Identify the average (mean) of the five listed numbers: 10, 11, 19, 20, 30

   A. 5

   B. 18

   C. 19

   D. 90

89. Jon's new employer will pay him the average hourly wage of the other three employees, if Jon can correctly compute that average. The others are paid hourly wages of $4.80, $5.00, and $5.11. What is their average pay per hour?

   A. $4.97
   B. $5.00
   C. $5.20
   D. $14.91

90. A trash collector complained that the 5 businesses on a certain street put out an average of 12 trash cans per day. Two of the businesses admitted to always putting out 15 cans; two others, 10. How many trash cans does the fifth business put out?

   A. 10
   B. 12
   C. 15
   D. 16

91. The average of a set of four numbers is 8. Three of the numbers are 2, 4, and 6. What is the fourth number?

   A. 8
   B. 12
   C. 20
   D. 32

92. On a weekly chart, a lunchroom manager keeps data about items sold in the lunch-room. Here is a copy of one part of last week's chart.

	Mon	Tues	Wed	Thurs	Fri
hot dog	60	50	71	80	55
pizza	74	70	70	68	59
hamburger	65	60	54	71	75

What was the average number of hamburgers sold last week?

   A. 43
   B. 65
   C. 68
   D. 73

93. Solve this equation: $8w + 1 = 33$

   A. $w = 4$
   B. $w = 4\ 1/2$
   C. $w = 32$
   D. $w = 34$

94. A soup can (with circular end) is 6 inches high. The diameter of the can is 4 inches. Use the formula $V = \pi r^2 h$ to determine the approximate amount of soup in the can.

   A. 12 cu. in.
   B. 24 cu. in.
   C. 72 cu. in.
   D. 96 cu. in.

95. A homeowner plans to cover a rectangular garden with topsoil. What is the total area to be covered, if the garden is 6 feet by 9 feet?

A. 15 sq. ft.

B. 30 sq. ft.

C. 54 sq. ft.

D. 81 sq. ft.

96. The amount of U.S. postage for first-class mail is computed by using this formula: p = .32 + .23n, (n>1) where "p" represents amount of postage and "n" represents the number of ounces more than the first ounce. How much postage must be used for a letter which weighs 3 ounces?

A. $ .78

B. $ .96

C. $ 1.01

D. $ 1.10

97. Find the value of 3d – e if d = 3 and e = 4.

A. –12

B. 4

C. 5

D. 12

98. Evaluate: z – 6y + 4 + 2z
(Note: y = 2, z = 8)

A. 10

B. 16

C. 18

D. 24

99. If a = 2, b = 3, and c= 4, what number is represented by ab + c?

A. 6

B. 9

C. 10

D. 24

100. If r = 3, s = 6, t = 8, which of the following represents the largest number?

A. r + s + t

B. rs – t

C. rs + t

D. r + st

101. If 3q – 1 = 20, what is the value of 2q – 5?

A. 7

B. 9

C. 21

D. 37

Answer Key

Learning Outcome #1
1. D
2. B
3. C
4. C
5. B
6. C

Learning Outcome #2
7. B
8. D
9. B
10. A
11. B
12. D
13. C
14. C

Learning Outcome #3
15. B
16. C
17. C
18. D
19. A
20. D

Learning Outcome #4
21. C
22. B
23. B
24. C
25. C

Learning Outcome #5
26. A
27. C
28. B
29. C
30. B
31. A
32. B
33. C
34. A
35. A
36. C

Learning Outcome #6
37. D
38. D
39. C
40. B
41. A
42. B
43. B
44. A

Learning Outcome #7
45. C
46. A
47. C
48. C
49. B
50. B
51. C

Learning Outcome #8
52. B
53. A
54. D
55. A
56. D

Learning Outcome #9
57. A
58. A
59. C
60. D
61. C
62. B
63. C
64. A
65. A
66. D

Learning Outcome #10
67. C
68. C
69. A
70. D
71. B
72. C

Learning Outcome #11
73. A
74. C
75. B
76. D
77. D

Learning Outcome #12
78. B
79. C
80. B
81. A
82. D

Learning Outcome #13
83. B
84. A
85. D
86. C
87. D

Learning Outcome #14
88. B
89. A
90. A
91. C
92. B

Learning Outcome #15
93. A
94. C
95. C
96. A

Learning Outcome #16
97. C
98. B
99. C
100. D
101. B

Citizenship

Ninth Grade Proficiency Test: Citizenship

Introduction: Strands and Learning Outcomes

The Citizenship Section of the Ninth Grade Ohio Proficiency Test is designed to test your *overall understanding* of the components, history, and functioning of the United States Federal and State governments. The test is based on a series of learning outcomes which define skills you will need for the ninth grade citizenship test. This introduction will discuss the test itself. The next section explains each learning outcome and gives you a chance to practice using your skills. Finally, the last section of this chapter contains 100 sample multiple-choice questions that simulate the questions on the actual test.

Show What You Know on the Citizenship Test

As you take the ninth-grade citizenship test, you will demonstrate your abilities by:

- demonstrating an understanding of the **history** of the development of the United States Government
- understanding the **geography** of the United States, and its impact on the government and its citizenry
- understanding the role and impact of **economics** in government
- demonstrating recall in the **components of government** and understanding the **functioning** of these components
- understanding the purpose and functioning of **law** as it pertains to the citizens of the United States
- showing a competency in knowledge necessary to be an **informed citizen**

About the Citizenship Test

The test covers the categories listed in the chart below. The learning outcomes that come from these categories are also listed in the chart with the number of test items that will come from the six categories. The test is comprised of 50 questions which will cover the six categories listed below. The number of questions representing each category is listed as well:

Category	Learning Outcome	Number of Test Items
History	1,2, and 3	7
Geography	4 and 5	6
Economics	6 and 8	5
Government	7, 9, 10, 13, and 14	14
Law	11 and 12	8
Citizen Knowledge	15, 16, and 17	10

All the learning outcomes will be reviewed in this chapter with example simulated proficiency test questions that will take you through an analysis of how the correct answer is found through test-taking and problem-solving skills combined with what you already know. You will increase your test performance in Citizenship by simply working through this chapter. But first there are some important test-taking tips, strategies, and skills that will give you the power to succeed in Citizenship!

Field Test Results

During field testing of the Citizenship test, the Ohio Dept. of Eduction identified the following: 1) Student performance was highest on items measuring outcomes 3, 4, 5, 12, 15, 16, and 17. 2) Student performance was lowest on items measuring outcomes 1, 7, 8, and 11. We have identified these results as shown in the key below.

> **Key:** ✓ = Students performance was HIGH during field testing.
>
> ✍ = Students performance was LOW during field testing.

Test-Taking Tips For Citizenship

- In preparing for the test be sure to study proportionally, based on the number of test items in each category. Primary focus should be on Government and Citizen knowledge.
- Each test item or question will have four answer choices, but only one answer will be correct. So, there is NO penalty for an incorrect answer. If you are not sure of an answer, it won't hurt your score if you guess. Answer every question on the test.
- Don't spend too much time on any one question; you are evaluated based upon the number of correct answers. Use your time wisely, so that you can answer ALL of the questions. If you get stumped, circle the question and come back to it later!
- You are not permitted to use references or tools other than writing instruments on this test. So, USE YOUR PENCIL! You are allowed to write in your test booklet, so scratch out incorrect answers and circle important information in test questions.
- You will have a maximum of two and one-half hours to finish the test. You will probably be able to finish in an hour. You are entitled to more time if you need it.

Test-Taking Strategies For Citizenship

The key to success on the proficiency test is to use what you know, whether you gained your knowledge in school, at home, or in the test question and its presentation. If you meet a question you can't answer, or simply don't understand, don't panic! Use what you know to attack the question in a logical manner. Use your knowledge to eliminate answers you know are wrong.

For the citizenship test, use the following steps:

1. Read the question carefully. If there is a map or chart examine it closely. Read and understand the key or legend.
2. Underline the key word(s) in the question. What is it asking you to do? Often the beginnings of a question's answer are found in the question itself.
3. Read the question for both content and context. Be sure to try to determine the perspective of the question. In the case of a primary source it is as important to know who spoke the words as it is to know the meaning of what is said.
4. Answer the questions:
   - Read the question.
   - Read *all* of the answers.
   - Cross out any answers you know are wrong. (There will be at least one, if not two answers, that will be easy to eliminate.)
   - If more than one answer remains:
      — be sure you know the meaning of the question.
      — quickly review all of the material contained in the question. Can you find the correct answer?
   - If you can't answer a question, make your *best* guess. There is **no** penalty for an incorrect guess.

- Use common sense. The correct answer will make sense. Don't over-analyze a question, just answer it.
- Watch the language. Be careful of words like "never" or "always." It is rare that life is absolute, so it will be rare for an absolute answer to be correct.
- Don't fall for "trick" answers. An answer might state a fact from the question or the question material, but it may not answer the question. These answers can "look right" because they use facts and language from the text. Make sure your answer *is* right — it must answer the question asked.
- It is OK to write on your test. If it helps you, make notes next to charts, maps, or graphs. This may help you in determining the correct answer.
- If you are not able to eliminate any answers in a question, take a guess. Circle the question in your test booklet and move on. If you have time at the end of the test, return to this question and try it again. If you do not have time, your guess will be your answer — if it's right, great; if not, you will not be penalized.
- Go over your answer sheet after you have finished to double-check that you have given an answer for each question asked.

The Citizenship Learning Outcomes

Strand: History

1. Identify the major significance of the following historic documents: Northwest Ordinance, Declaration of Independence, Constitution, Bill of Rights.

The preceding four documents were the basis for the establishment of the new government of the United States. The Declaration of Independence, written in 1776, gave a detailed reasoning as to why the thirteen colonies should be separated from England. The Northwest Ordinance described the establishment and governance of the new territories given to the United States by England after the Revolutionary War. The Constitution contained the basic structure and the processes of governance of the new country, the United States, and the Bill of Rights contained the first ten amendments (changes) to the Constitution. The Bill also defined some of the basic freedoms that citizens of the United States enjoy.

You will be asked to recall the specific documents, to recall and understand the content of the documents, and to determine the importance and significance of the documents to the new government of the United States. These four documents are the only historical documents which will be tested on the proficiency test.

Examples:

1. The first ten amendments to the Constitution can be found in:

    A. Bill of Rights

    B. Constitution

    C. Declaration of Independence

    D. Northwest Ordinance

Analysis:

The correct answer is "A," Bill of Rights. The content of the Bill of Rights is the first ten amendments to the Constitution. TIP: Be careful not to choose answer "B," Constitution. Although amendments are changes to the Constitution, they are not the Constitution itself.

2. In the Constitution it states that the making of laws is the responsibility of which branch of government?

    A. Executive

    B. Judicial

    C. Citizens

    D. Legislative

Analysis:

This question asks you to understand a process of governance described by the Constitution. Since the law-making is the sole responsibility of the Legislative Branch (The House of Representatives and the Senate), the correct answer is "D."

2. Know that many different peoples with diverse backgrounds (cultural, racial, ethnic, linguistic) make up our nation today.

The United States is comprised of peoples from around the world. Native Americans were on the North American continent when peoples from Europe came to colonize the East Coast of North America. In the following centuries, peoples from Africa, Asia, South America, Oceania, and Europe have come to the "New World." Each of these peoples and their beliefs are essential to the fabric of American society and government, despite the fact that at various points in our history certain ethnic groups were denied the rights of citizens (specifically Native, African, Hispanic, and Asian Americans).

Example:

1. The only ethnic group that did not immigrate to the United States was:

   A. Asian Americans

   B. African Americans

   C. Native Americans

   D. Hispanic Americans

Analysis:
With the exception of Native Americans, all other peoples of the United States have immigrated to this country in the last 500 years. Therefore the correct answer is "C," Native Americans.

✓ **3. Identify various symbols of the United States: flag, national anthem, Pledge of Allegiance, Independence Day.**

These four symbols are basic representations of the United States. The United States flag is distinct. The fifty stars represent the states which make up the union of the United States. The national anthem, written by Francis Scott Key during the War of 1812, is a song that displays pride in our country and our flag. The Pledge of Allegiance, written in the late 1800's, speaks to each citizen's loyalty to the United States. Independence Day, which is on the 4th of July, commemorates the signing of the Declaration of Independence, a document which pronounced the United States as a new and distinct nation.

Examples:

1. The following quotation is from which symbol of the United States?

   "and to the republic for which it stands,
   one nation, under God, indivisible,
   with liberty and justice for all."

   A. national anthem

   B. Pledge of Allegiance

   C. Gettysburg Address

   D. Constitution

Analysis:
The correct answer is "B," because the quotation is directly from the Pledge of Allegiance.

2. Which of the following flags is the flag of the United States?

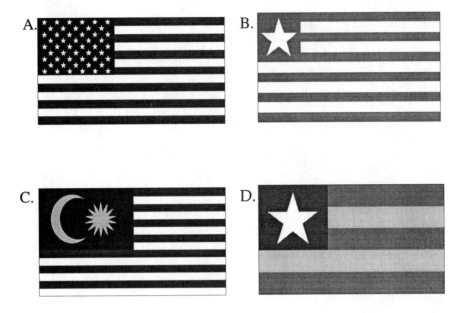

A.

B.

C.

D.

Analysis:
The correct answer is "A," because this shows the United States flag. TIP: Be sure to look closely at each flag, because there are several flags of countries and states that are similar to the flag of the United States.

Strand: Geography

✓ **4. Locate the United States, the nation's capital, the state of Ohio, and Ohio's capital on appropriate maps of the nation, hemisphere, or world.**

Geographical knowledge of these four locations is essential for success in this area of the test. You must be able to locate Ohio's Capital (Columbus), the Nation's Capital (Washington D.C.), and the United States on appropriate maps.

When locating countries and states, it often helps to know what borders the state or country you are trying to locate. For example, Ohio is bordered on the east by Pennsylvania, the southeast by West Virginia, the south by Kentucky, the west by Indiana, and the north by Michigan and Lake Erie. This knowledge will help you to locate Ohio.

Example:

1. The capital of Ohio, Columbus, is located in which location on this map of Ohio?

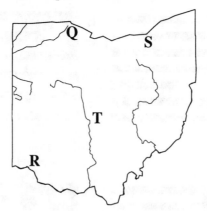

A. Q

B. R

C. S

D. T

Analysis:

The correct answer is "D," because the correct geographical location of the capital of Columbus, Ohio is at the position marked D. If you couldn't remember where Columbus was you could try eliminating the locations you know are NOT Columbus and narrow down your answer choices and take your best guess.

✓ **5. Demonstrate map reading skills, including finding directions, judging distances, and reading the legend.**

To master these skills it is necessary to have an understanding of the four main geographic directions; north, south, east, and west. It is important to first read the legend or key to a map in order to completely understand the map presentation. Most maps have a scale. The scale will enable map readers to determine the distances between points.

Be sure to read the legend completely before interpreting the map. It will give you the best chance to read the map correctly. Notice whether you are looking at miles, yards, feet, inches or looking at millions, thousands, hundreds. Take your time and do not answer the question without checking your answer.

Examples:

Answer the following two questions using this map:

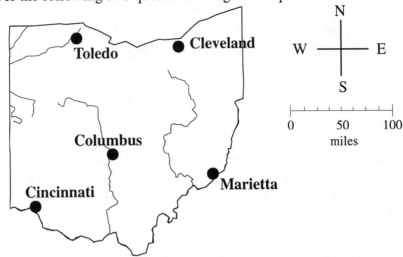

1. To fly from Cincinnati to Cleveland, one would need to travel in which direction?

    A. south

    B. west

    C. northeast

    D. southeast

Analysis:
The correct answer is "C," because in order to travel from Cincinnati to Cleveland you would need to go in a northern and also an eastern direction to get there. You can eliminate south beause Cincinnati is the most southern Ohio city listed.

2. Approximately, how many miles is Columbus from Marietta?

    A. 50 miles

    B. 100 miles

    C. 200 miles

    D. 500 miles

Analysis:
The correct answer is "B." By using the scale on the legend, you can determine the distance between the two cities is about 100 miles.

 Be sure to read the distance **measure** carefully. Not all scales are in miles, some are in kilometers, meters, yards or feet!

Strand: Economics

6. Know the following economic concepts:
   a. All levels of U.S. government assess taxes in order to provide services.
   b. Individuals and societies make choices to satisfy wants with limited resources.
   c. Nations become interdependent through trade.

Taxation is the means by which the United States government functions. Students must master the concept that taxes are a necessary part of a democratic system. Citizens are taxed by different government organizations: federal, state, and local. Taxes are imposed at different government levels because the taxes fund government services and needs at the different levels of American society.

As a product of an open democratic society, both the government and the private sector (citizens) have the opportunity to conduct their business affairs by using resources and making decisions as they see fit. The only exceptions are when restrictions and regulations are placed on the economy and businesses by laws at the federal, state, and local levels.

The United States economy functions in the United States, and it is an important part of the world economy. The United States becomes closely linked with other countries through international trade. Other countries depend on the United States, and the United States depends on them for all economies to thrive. This is known as **interdependence**. A major reason for trade is the natural imbalance of world resources.

Example:

1. A large proportion of Federal Taxes goes towards

   A. Town Parks

   B. Funding State Government

   C. Elementary Schools

   D. National Defense

Analysis:
The correct answer is "D." Town Parks, State Government, and Schools are primarily funded from taxes at the state and local levels. The National Defense (military) defends the entire country, therefore it is funded by federal taxes.

✍ **8. Identify major economic systems: capitalism, socialism, communism**

Capitalism, as a system, was first popularly identified by Adam Smith in the late 1700's. It is a system based on the belief of ownership by the individual. In the capitalistic system, capital (money) is invested in the system in order to bring about production, pay salaries or utilize resources. As a result of this investment, individuals will get increased amounts of money back (profit).

Socialism is a system in which economic production is controlled or owned by a government or other organization. In a socialist system, companies are owned and run by the government, not by individuals or groups of individuals.

Communism is a system that was popularized by Karl Marx in the late 1800's. He believed economic systems would historically evolve. The first step would be capitalism, the second socialism, and the third communism. Communism was a system in which everything would be shared communally. No one would own private property (capital), but all resources would be controlled and shared by society. There have been several countries (the former Soviet Union and China for example) that have tried to institute communist systems in their countries.

Example:

1. Communism is an economic system based on:

   A. private property

   B. shared property and wealth

   C. competition

   D. international trade

Analysis:
Answers "A," "C," and "D" all describe qualities of a capitalistic economic system. Answer "B" is correct, because shared property and wealth is a fundamental belief of the Communist economic system. Communism and Socialism are often mistakenly described as political systems. They are economic philosophies of certain governments, but they are not political systems in and of themselves.

Strand: Government

✍ **7. Identify the main functions of each branch of government (executive, legislative, judicial) at the national, state, and local levels.**

The executive, legislative, and judicial branches each have distinct purposes in the functioning of government in the United States. The executive branch sees that the government and the laws of the land function well. The head of this branch in the federal government is the President. The President is the equivalent of the CEO (Chief Executive Officer) of the government. The legislative branch makes the laws. Legislators are elected by the people to create laws that reflect the "will of the people." In this way, the laws of the land are made by the citizens of the United States. The judicial branch interprets the laws. People in this branch of government determine what the laws mean to the citizens of the United States. These three branches of government exist in all levels of government: federal, state, and local.

Examples:

1. Which branch of government has the power to change the law regarding speed limits on highways?

    A. Legislative

    B. Supreme Court

    C. President

    D. Executive

Analysis:
All laws are made by the legislative branch of government. The same is true for the changing of a law. Therefore the correct answer is "A," Legislative. It is often thought, incorrectly, that the President of the United States can create laws. This is not true. The President, like all other citizens, follows and honors the laws created by the legislatures. An important function of the President is to make sure that the laws are enforced.

2. Whose jobs are part of the executive branch?

    A. Supreme Court Justice and Judge

    B. President, Mayor, and Governor

    C. Senator and Representative

    D. Business Leaders

Analysis:
The correct answer is "B." The President is the head of the executive branch of the United States government, the governor is the head of state governments, mayors are often the heads of city and town (local) governments.

9. Demonstrate an understanding of the concept of federalism by identifying the level of government (local, state, national) responsible for addressing the concerns of citizens.

Federalism is the system of democratic government in which the national (federal) government controls some aspects of government, and state and local governments control other aspects and concerns of citizens.

For example, the federal government is exclusively responsible for the printing and regulating of money. Another area which the national government controls is the declaration of war, and the conduct of war when the United States is in conflict with another country.

State governments control whether or not someone is eligible to vote, determine marriage, divorce, and other domestic laws, and set the standards and development of education and school policy.

Local governments in Ohio are able to control zoning (where and what type of buildings can be built) and standards of size and safety regarding both new and old buildings.

Some parts of government are controlled by both State and National government. An example of this is environmental standards and regulations, and environmental safety laws.

Citizens' needs are many, and they are helped and controlled by all levels of government. In many cases several levels of government respond at the same time to citizens' needs.

Example:

    1. Laws regarding environmental water safety are controlled by:

       A. National Government

       B. State Government

       C. National and State Government

       D. Local Government

Analysis:
Issues concerning the environment are controlled at both State and Federal government levels. Environmental water safety pertains to the environment. Therefore the correct answer is "C," State and National government. Be sure to read all the answer choices before you select an answer. In this question both "A" and "B" are correct answers. However, "C" is the best and correct answer because it answers all aspects of the question.

10. Distinguish the characteristics, both positive and negative, of various types of government: representative democracy, monarchy, dictatorship.

Representative democracy is a democracy in which the power of the citizens is given to individuals elected to specific jobs and posts in government. This system enables all citizens to have a voice through their elected officials. At times, representative democracy is time-consuming because so many people are involved in the process.

Absolute monarchy is a system in which a single individual (a king or queen) has the total power of government. At the death of a king or queen, the new monarch will be a son or daughter of the former king or queen. In this system, decisions can be made quickly because only one person is involved. The citizens are dependent upon the good will and wisdom of the monarch.

In a dictatorship, power is controlled by one person. In many cases, these individuals have come to power by force. The rule of the government is based upon the whims of the dictator and the advisors. As with a monarchy, decisions can be made quickly. In the case of a dictatorship, the best interests of the dictator are considered, rather than the best interests of the people.

Example:

1. The voice of the citizens is represented most clearly in which form of government?

    A. representative democracy

    B. anarchy

    C. monarchy

    D. dictatorship

Analysis:
The correct answer is "A," representative democracy, because the people have the right to elect officials to represent their ideas and beliefs.

13. Understand that the major role of political parties in a democracy is to provide a choice in governmental leadership (i.e., candidates and platforms).

Political parties have always played an important role in the democratic process of the United States. They serve two very important functions in the political process at the national level.

1. They provide leadership in the form of candidates. Candidates who run for office are often recruited or encouraged to run by one of the two major political parties (Democrat and Republican). Once they become candidates they are given support by the party.

2. They provide leadership in the form of a political platform. The platform is a group of ideas and beliefs that the party supports. These ideas are then presented to the citizens through the candidates who are running for office.

Example:

1. The set of ideas and beliefs that the political party and candidates of the party support are called the:

   A. Constitution
   B. Bill of Rights
   C. Platform
   D. States' Rights

Analysis:
Although virtually all candidates would support the Constitution and the Bill of Rights, the correct answer would be "C," platform, because the platform is a collection of a party's ideas and beliefs.

14. Understand the role of public officials in government.
a. Distinguish between elected and appointed officials.
b. Describe the ways officials can be elected or appointed.
c. Evaluate the actions of public officials on the basis of a given set of criteria.

There are two forms of public servants in the United States: those who are elected by the citizens and those who are appointed to office.

Those who are elected at the national level are as follows:

> **President** (voters elect electors to the Electoral College; the Electoral
>   College elects the President)
> **Vice President** (same election process as President)
> **Senators and Congressional Representatives** (elected by voters)

Those who are elected by voters at the state level:

> **Governor**
> **Attorney General**
> **Secretary of State**
> **Legislators and State Judges**

Those who are elected by voters at the local level:

> **Mayors** (although some are appointed by city councils or commissions)
> **Council Members**
> **County Commissioners**

Those who are appointed at the national level are as follows:

> **Cabinet Members** (appointed by the President, confirmed by the Senate)
> **Federal Judges** (appointed by the President, confirmed by the Senate)

Appointments at local level:

> **Mayors** (who have been appointed by commissions or city councils)

All of the elected officials are evaluated by the citizens of the United States based upon various criteria which can include: performance, party platform, and public opinion.

Example:

> 1. Which of the following positions is elected?
>
>   A. United States Attorney General
>   B. United States Secretary of State
>   C. The Attorney General for the State of Ohio
>   D. Federal Judge

Analysis:
WATCH OUT! This is a tricky question. The correct answer is "C," Ohio Attorney General. Don't be fooled by the answer: U.S. Attorney General. The President's cabinet members are appointed and Federal Judges are appointed, too. Ohio's leading cabinet members are elected. When answer choices all look like very good answers, the answers may be designed to distract you into choosing a popular incorrect answer. Read each answer choice slowly and think carefully, trying to eliminate any answer choices that you can. Guess intelligently from what is left.

Strand: Law

✍ **11. Describe the process for making, amending, or removing laws.**

The making of laws is the responsibility of the legislative branches of the federal and state governments. For example, a bill is introduced to the House of Representatives of the United States. The bill is then sent to a committee to be studied and debated. After the committee has approved their version of the bill, they send it to the entire House of Representatives. The entire House debates the bill, and votes on it. If the bill is approved, it is sent to the Senate, where it follows the same process: debated by committee; approval by committee; debate and vote by Senate.

Many times, the version of the bill passed by the House is different from the version passed by the Senate. If this is the case, it is sent to a conference committee whose members are from the House and the Senate. This committee blends the differences of the two bill versions into a single bill. This revised bill is then sent to the House and Senate for final approval. The bill is then sent to the President (or in the case of the state government, it goes to the governor).

The President signs the bill into law or vetoes (rejects) the bill. Congress can override a veto by a two-thirds majority vote in both the House and Senate. In Ohio, the Ohio General Assembly can override a veto by a three-fifths majority vote.

Important things to note:
• Only a legislator — a member of the House or Senate — can introduce a bill.
• Lobbyists and special interest groups often draft bills to submit to their legislators.
• The executive branch, under the President, prepares many bills and has them introduced.
• In Ohio's state government, voters can propose laws by petitioning qualified voters and collecting enough signatures to have a law placed on the ballot. They can also petition to have an existing law passed by the legislature placed on the ballot for approval or rejection. Laws can be amended (changed) or removed most easily by the passing of a new or different law which will replace an existing law. Congress and the legislature can also abolish or remove an existing law through the same process as the making of a law.

An amendment to the Constitution can occur if the following happens:

1. Congress passes an amendment to the Constitution.

> The Constitutional Amendment is then taken to the State legislatures where they vote to approve or disapprove the amendment. The amendment needs to be approved (ratified) by 3/4 of the states before the Constitutional Amendment goes into effect.

2. A National Convention is called by Congress and the constitutional change is approved by that convention.

> This method for the amendment of the Constitution is rarely utilized

3. The third way in which a law is amended or removed is through the process of **judicial review**. The judicial branch of the federal government (specifically the Supreme Court) has the right to look over laws and determine if the laws are **constitutional**. If the Supreme Court determines that they are not, the laws can either be revised or removed.

Example:

    1. A Bill becomes a Law when:

        A. it passes both houses of Congress

        B. when it is signed by the President

        C. when it is vetoed

        D. when it gets out of Conference Committee

Analysis*:*
CAREFUL!! The correct answer is "B," because the President can sign a bill only AFTER it has passed both houses of Congress!

✓ **12. Know how the law protects individuals in the United States.**

a. Give examples of rights and freedoms guaranteed in the Bill of Rights.

Individuals in the United States are protected by laws that are based upon and are in agreement with the Constitution of the United States. The basic rights which all citizens in the United States enjoy are described in **The Bill of Rights** which were the first ten amendments to the Constitution. They are also known as **civil liberties**. The first ten amendments are:

1. The freedoms of speech, religion, and the press. It allows the freedom to assemble (meet in groups).
2. This declares the need for a state militia to protect the country and as a result, everyone should be given the right to "bear arms" (carry a gun). The United States at the time (1790), could not afford a full-time professional army.
3. Prohibits having soldiers housed in homes during peacetime. (It was common practice in the 1700's to "take over" a home at the end of a day's march.)

4. Prohibits unreasonable search and seizure of private possessions.
5. States that an individual cannot be tried twice for the same crime. This is known as **double jeopardy**. It also states that you cannot be forced to be a witness against yourself (give self-incriminating evidence).
6. The right to have a speedy trial, professional defense counsel (a lawyer), and to call witnesses in your own defense.
7. Gives one the right to have a trial by jury. (This jury is made up of randomly selected citizens who have registered to vote).
8. Prohibits excessive bail (a fee paid to get one out of jail before trial) and fines, as well as "cruel and unusual punishment."
9. The ninth amendment states that people's rights are not limited to the first eight amendments.
10. The tenth amendment states that all rights not specifically spoken to in the Constitution and its amendments can be defined and further refined by individual states and individuals.

b. Apply the concept of justice, including due process and equity before the law.

The concepts of justice, due process, and equity before the law were most recently defined by the 14th, 15th, 19th, and 26th Amendments. These are all further refinements of the original Bill of Rights.

- **The Fourteenth Amendment** states that all people born or naturalized in the United States are citizens. This amendment gave people the right of citizenship regardless of race or religion. (Prior to this amendment Native Americans and slaves were not allowed to be citizens.)
- **The Fifteenth Amendment** stated that all citizens (male) had the right to vote regardless of race, being a former slave, or color of skin.
- The passing of the **Nineteenth Amendment** in 1920 gave women the right to vote at last.
- **The 26th Amendment** defined the voting age as 18 or older. (Prior to this time it was 21 and older. This had been defined in the Constitution.)

c. Know the importance of a learning or work environment free of discrimination against individual differences.

There is always the potential that a work or learning environment is discriminating against individuals. It is important to know that the previous rights described apply in these situations and in all situations in the United States. (Much of the positive changes brought about in the 1950's and 1960's regarding civil rights were based upon these Constitutional protections.)

d. Identify legal means of dissent and protest against violation of rights.

There are several ways to express your dissent (disagreement) and protest against violations of rights. They include:

Petitions - a document describing dissent with signatures of citizens. This is then passed on to elected officials to influence them to make changes.

Lawsuits - When someone feels that their rights have been violated, they can sue the person, group, or organization that they think is responsible. The suit would go to trial, and the judicial system would determine justice.

Peaceful public protest - People assemble to speak out against the injustice.

Voting - People have great influence through voting: they help determine who represents them and how they vote on particular issues.

Oral and written communication to media and public officials - By using all forms of communication, the injustice and one's perspective on it can be spread widely amongst the people.

Examples:

1. The freedoms of speech, press, religion, and assembly are protected by:

    A. the first amendment
    B. the Declaration of Independence
    C. the Articles of Confederation
    D. the Gettysburg Address

Analysis:
The correct answer is "A." Those freedoms were specifically protected by the first amendment to the constitution.

2. Which came first: the right for eighteen-year-olds to vote, or the right for women to vote?

    A. women

    B. both groups received the right at the same time

    C. neither group has the right to vote

    D. eighteen year-olds

Analysis:
The correct answer is "A," women. Women received the right to vote by the 19th Amendment. Eighteen-year-olds received the right to vote by the 26th Amendment. The amendments are numbered in chronological order, therefore women's voting rights (19th Amendment) preceded eighteen-year-olds' voting rights (26th Amendment).

Strand: Citizen Knowledge

✓ **15. Know that voting is both a privilege and a responsibility of U.S. citizenship.**
    a. Recognize that property ownership, race, gender, literacy, and certain tax payments no longer affect eligibility to vote.
    b. Identify the qualifications for voting.

Voting in the United States is a privilege given to the citizens by the Constitution. At various points in United States history, people were restricted from voting based upon not owning land, being a slave, the color of their skin, or being a woman. These restrictions no longer apply. The voting opportunity is available to all citizens of the United States.

To qualify for voting in the State of Ohio one needs to:
- Be a citizen of the United States
- Be at least eighteen years of age at the November election
- Be a resident of the State of Ohio
- Be registered with the Board of Elections

Example:

1. Which of the following is NOT a qualification to vote in Ohio?

    A. be a citizen of the United States

    B. own land in the State of Ohio

    C. be a resident of the State of Ohio

    D. be eighteen years of age at the time of the election

Analysis:
The key word in this question is NOT. This word gives you the answer. The correct answer is "B," because you DO NOT have to own land in order to vote in Ohio. All of the other answers were qualifications for voting.

 There is often a key word in a question. Identify and underline it when you read the question the first time, then refer back to it when you go over the answers.

✓ **16. Demonstrate the ability to use information that enables citizens to make informed choices.**
   a. Use more than one source to obtain information.
   b. Identify points of agreement and disagreement among sources.
   c. Evaluate the reliability of available information.
   d. Draw conclusions by reading and interpreting data presented in charts and graphs.
   e. Identify and weigh alternative viewpoints.

The five skills mentioned above are all critical elements in helping a citizen make an informed choice regarding their government.

To illustrate this let's go through a hypothetical case found on the next page:

Hypothetical Situation:

You are a citizen of the United States and your town is putting forth a proposal to have recycling be mandatory (required) in the town. You, as an informed citizen, will use the five skills to make a decision as to how you will vote.

1. You will find out as much as you can regarding the issue of recycling. This information can be found in libraries, newspapers and magazines, radio and television, and from discussions that you could have with other citizens. All of this information gathering would be done in order to help you make a decision.
2. After obtaining this information, determine where the sources agree and disagree. This will be the area in which you can evaluate the differences of opinion regarding the issue of mandatory recycling.
3. Review the sources of information that you have obtained. Try to determine whether or not they are reliable. Many people or organizations have a bias or perspective. It is helpful in evaluating their opinion to determine what their perspective is.
4. A lot of data is presented in the form of graphs and charts. It is important that you become literate in reading this information in order to be able to evaluate it correctly.
5. Now you have obtained all information, identified the differences of opinion, and obtained, if possible, alternative viewpoints. It is now essential to weigh those differences and make a decision on the recycling issue based upon your informed, critically formed beliefs.

This process is helpful in making informed decisions at all levels of citizenship.

Example:

1. An informed citizen votes for a candidate based upon:

    A. who their neighbor is voting for
    B. the age of the candidate
    C. the platform of the party which the candidate is representing
    D. whether or not the candidate is a woman

Analysis:
The correct answer is "C," the party platform. If a candidate is running for a particular party, the candidate will believe in the party platform. This can be a basis for a decision, but an informed voter would look at other information as well. The other answers are not sound reasons for voting for a candidate.

✓ 17. Identify opportunities for involvement in civic activities.

Citizenship is a voluntary and active process and activity (meaning you do it of your free will) . One cannot sit back, do nothing, and be a "good citizen." There are a number of ways in which a person can become involved. They include: volunteering for a candidate's political campaign; volunteering to help with local, state, and national elections as a polling site volunteer; and generally keeping yourself informed about the issues, and engaging in discussions with others concerning the issues of the time.

Example:

1. Which of the following is NOT a constructive form of civic involvement?

    A. volunteering at a polling site

    B. watching the evening news

    C. refusing to vote

    D. running for political office

Analysis:
Volunteering , staying informed, and being a candidate are all positive ways in which a citizen can become involved. By not voting, a citizen's voice (through their vote) is not being heard. Therefore, the correct answer is "C," because refusing to vote would be a non-constructive form of civic involvement.

Now that you have reviewed all the learning outcomes and have tried a few sample test questions, try the next section of one hundred simulated proficiency test questions. As you identify the learning outcomes that cause you trouble, go back and review the material in this chapter. You may want to try *Pass In A Flash*, Ninth Grade Citizenship flash cards for more practice and review. (See order form at the end of this book.)

Citizenship Practice Items

What You Need to Know
Before You Begin Citizenship Practice Items!

There are 100 simulated proficiency test questions which represent the same number of two full proficiency tests in this practice item section of your book. (There are only 50 questions on the proficiency test.) You should be able to complete all the practice items in approximately two and one-half hours. Try to complete the practice items in one or two sittings. The answers to the questions are provided at the end of the items. The questions and answers identify the learning outcome that the questions comes from. If you missed questions from a learning outcome go back and review the learning outcome again or ask your teacher or tutor for some help in that area.

Remember these Test-Taking Tips!

1. Read the question carefully. If there is a map or chart examine it closely. Read and understand the key or legend.
2. Underline the key word(s) in the question. What is it asking you to do? Often the beginnings of a question's answer are found in the question itself.
3. Read the question for both content and context. Be sure to try to determine the perspective of the question. In the case of a primary source, it is as important to know who spoke the words as it is to know the meaning of what is said.
4. Answer the questions:
   - Read the question.
   - Read *all* of the answers.
   - Cross out any answers you know are wrong. (There will be at least one, if not two answers, that will be easy to eliminate.)
   - If more than one answer remains:
     — be sure you know the meaning of the question.
     — quickly review all of the material contained in the question. Can you find the correct answer?
   - If you can't answer a question, make your best guess. There is **no** penalty for an incorrect guess.

1. The governance for the new territories west of Pennsylvania, following the Revolutionary War, was set down in what document?

    A. the Declaration of Independence

    B. the Gettysburg Address

    C. the Northwest Ordinance

    D. the Constitution

2. The Declaration of Independence was signed in which year?

    A. 1783

    B. 1776

    C. 1789

    D. 1790

3. The document which most completely describes the governance of the United States is:

    A. the Bill of Rights

    B. the 26th Amendment

    C. the Declaration of Independence

    D. the Constitution

4. The first ten amendments to the Constitution comprise the:

    A. the Bill of Rights

    B. the Northwest Ordinance

    C. the Articles of Confederation

    D. the Shay's Rebellion

5. Which of the following was NOT a document written in the founding days of the United States?

    A. the Declaration of Independence

    B. the Bill of Rights

    C. the War Powers Act

    D. the Northwest Ordinance

6. The guarantee of a speedy trial is assured in which document?

    A. the Northwest Ordinance

    B. the 19th Amendment

    C. the Bill of Rights

    D. the Declaration of Independence

7. The United States is comprised of people from:

    A. Europe only

    B. Europe and Asia only

    C. Africa, Europe, and Asia only

    D. Peoples from diverse backgrounds

8. Which groups have NOT contributed to American society?

    A. Native Americans

    B. Hispanic Americans

    C. European Americans

    D. Indo-Europeans

Go on to the next page.

9. Which of the following groups of people did not immigrate to the United States?

A. African people

B. Native Americans

C. Asian people

D. Hispanic people

10. Independence Day is celebrated on:

A. July 4

B. the last Thursday of November

C. the first Monday of September

D. December 25

11. "O say can you see," is a line from which American symbol?

A. "America the Beautiful"

B. Pledge of Allegiance

C. National Anthem

D. "God Save the Queen"

12. Which of the following is NOT found on the American flag?

A. red, white and blue

B. thirteen stripes

C. 50 stars

D. the American eagle

13. Which of the following is a symbol of the United States?

A.

B.

C.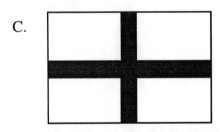

D.

14. "To the Republic for which it stands," is a quotation from which symbol of the United States?

A. the Constitution

B. Pledge of Allegiance

C. National Anthem

D. the Independence Day Address

Go on to the next page.

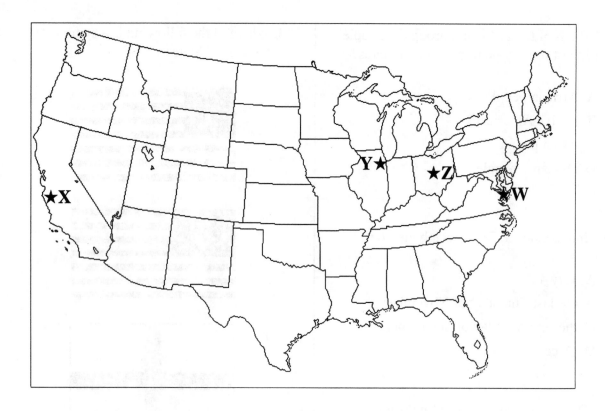

15. Which letter marks the location of the nation's capital?

    A. W

    B. X

    C. Y

    D. Z

16. Which letter correctly marks the location of Ohio's state capital?

    A. W

    B. X

    C. Y

    D. Z

Go on to the next page.

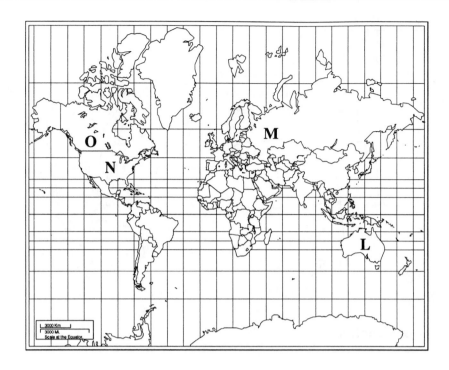

17. On the map of the world above, which letter marks the location of the United States?

    A. L

    B. M

    C. N

    D. O

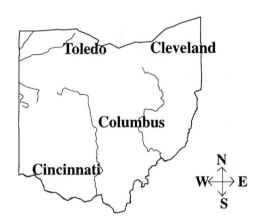

18. Refer to the map of Ohio above. Columbus, the capital of Ohio, is located southwest of which city?

    A. Columbus

    B. Toledo

    C. Cleveland

    D. Cincinnati

Go on to the next page.

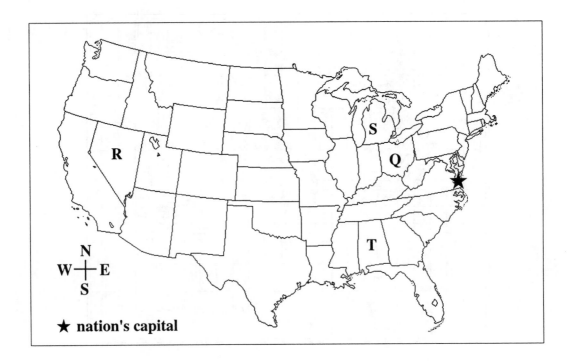

★ nation's capital

19. Refer to the map of the United States above. Which letter marks the location of Ohio on the map?

A. Q
B. R
C. S
D. T

20. Refer to the map of the United States above. To get to Ohio from the nation's capital, you would travel in which direction?

A. north
B. south
C. east
D. west

Go on to the next page.

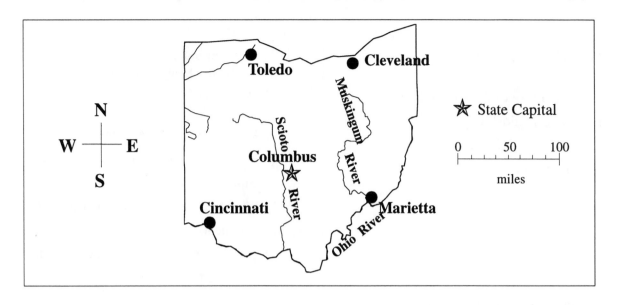

Refer to the map of Ohio for questions 21-26.

21. Where is Ohio's state capital in relation to Cleveland?

 A. 140 miles southwest of Cleveland

 B. 140 miles northeast of Cleveland

 C. 90 miles south of Cleveland

 D. 110 miles southeast of Cleveland

22. Which is the southernmost city labeled on the map?

 A. Cleveland

 B. Marietta

 C. Cincinnati

 D. Columbus

23. Which of these cities on the map is the closest to the state capital?

 A. Toledo

 B. Cleveland

 C. Marietta

 D. Ashtabula

24. According to the map, what city is the state capital of Ohio?

 A. Toledo

 B. Columbus

 C. Marietta

 D. Cleveland

25. Which is the longest river labeled on this map?

 A. Mississippi

 B. Scioto

 C. Ohio

 D. Miami

26. In which direction does the Scioto River flow?

 A. north to south

 B. south to north

 C. east to west

 D. west to east

Go on to the next page.

27. Federal taxes pay for:

A. the defense of the United States

B. city councilor's expenses

C. the Governor's salary

D. state parks

28. International trade helps to:

A. cause wars

B. reduce contact between countries

C. raise trade tariffs

D. have nations become more interdependent

29. If a nation does not have certain natural resources, how can the nation obtain them?

A. attack another nation

B. do without them

C. trade with other nations that have the resource

D. become isolationist

30. Which service is NOT paid for by taxes?

A. farm subsidies

B. Army supplies

C. local newspapers

D. preschool for disadvantaged children

31. The United States produces great amounts of wheat. How can this best be used for trade?

A. keep other countries hungry

B. trade wheat for resources the United States doesn't have

C. trade to another country that has lots of wheat

D. plow the wheat under if too much is produced

32. The main function of the executive branch of government is to:

A. make laws

B. interpret laws

C. carry out laws

D. control all the power

33. The main function of Congress is to:

A. make laws

B. impeach presidents and judges

C. find citizens guilty or innocent

D. interpret the law

34. The name of the institution which makes laws in the State of Ohio is:

A. Congress

B. Supreme Court

C. Appellate Court

D. The General Assembly

Go on to the next page.

35. The Chief Justice of the Supreme Court is a member of which branch of government?

    A. Executive
    B. Judicial
    C. Congress
    D. Legislative

36. The head of the executive branch of government in the State of Ohio is called:

    A. Senator
    B. President
    C. Mayor
    D. Governor

37. Which individual interprets the laws of the United States?

    A. the President
    B. a Judge
    C. a Senator
    D. the Secretary of State

38. This economic system is based upon private ownership of property.

    A. Communism
    B. Socialism
    C. Totalitarianism
    D. Capitalism

39. Socialism believes that:

    A. everyone should own private property
    B. production should be controlled or owned by the government
    C. good businessmen pay their employees poorly
    D. there should be a large gap between the wealthy and poor

40. A society in which all wealth is shared and there are no social classes is called:

    A. capitalism
    B. communism
    C. dictatorship
    D. anarchy

41. Making a profit is a major goal of which economic system?

    A. Capitalism
    B. Scientific Socialism
    C. Darwinism
    D. Communism

42. Capitalism is based on all of the following, EXCEPT:

    A. making a profit
    B. private ownership of property
    C. investment of money
    D. government owning and controlling the means of production

Go on to the next page.

43. Which of the following is NOT a responsibility of the federal government?

   A. declaring war

   B. negotiating treaties with foreign countries

   C. regulating commerce between states

   D. determining school district boundaries

44. Which is an action that state and national government are denied?

   A. declare war

   B. levy taxes on exports

   C. determine educational proficiency requirements

   D. govern marriage laws

45. Which level of government is able to establish zoning regulations?

   A. federal

   B. national

   C. local government of Ohio

   D. state

46. Which level of government is able to determine the qualifications of resident voters?

   A. federal

   B. local

   C. Interstate Committees

   D. state

47. Which of the following is not a responsibility of either the state or local government?

   A. building codes

   B. marriage laws

   C. the printing of money

   D. zoning regulations

48. A political system where power is exercised by elected officials is a:

   A. Representative Democracy

   B. Monarchy

   C. Absolute Monarchy

   D. Dictatorship

49. Which of the following is NOT a characteristic of a dictatorship?

   A. power in the hands of an individual

   B. force is often used to maintain power

   C. free and open elections are held

   D. rights are not guaranteed

50. When an absolute monarch dies, who succeeds them?

   A. an elected official

   B. a family member, usually a son or daughter

   C. a political coup always occurs

   D. whoever the nobility appoints

Go on to the next page.

51. Which of the following is a title given to an absolute monarch?

   A. President
   B. Commissar
   C. Chief Justice
   D. Queen

52. Which is a characteristic of Representative Democracy?

   A. rights are not guaranteed
   B. monarch has absolute power
   C. elections do not offer a choice
   D. the government and people follow the laws of the country

53. An absolute monarch:

   A. has limited power
   B. has total power
   C. is a figurehead
   D. has no power

54. How can the Constitution be changed?

   A. by Presidential decree
   B. through an Act of Congress
   C. through local elections
   D. with a Constitutional Amendment

55. For a bill to be approved, it has to:

   A. be passed by the Senate only
   B. be passed by both the House of Representatives and the Senate
   C. be passed by the House of Representatives only
   D. be introduced to Congress

56. Congress can override a Presidential veto by:

   A. a two-thirds majority vote in each house
   B. a three-fifths majority vote in each house
   C. a three-fourths majority vote in each house
   D. a one-half majority vote in the Senate

57. The Ohio General Assembly can override a veto by the Governor by:

   A. a two-thirds majority vote in each house
   B. a three-fifths majority vote in each house
   C. a three-fourths majority vote in each house
   D. a one-half majority vote in each house and approval of the State Attorney General

Go on to the next page.

58. Which of the following is NOT a step in making a law?

    A. a bill is introduced to the House of Representatives
    B. the bill is studied by a House committee
    C. the Vice-President provisionally signs the bill
    D. the bill is sent to Conference Committee

59. Judicial Review describes the process of:

    A. Congress reviewing laws
    B. the President vetoing laws
    C. the Supreme Court determines if a law is unconstitutional
    D. citizens voting down a law

60. A law can be abolished by all of the following methods, EXCEPT:

    A. Judicial Review
    B. Congress abolishes a law
    C. the General Assembly abolishes a law
    D. Presidential Decree

61. A national convention called by Congress could be to

    A. impeach the President
    B. propose a Constitutional Amendment
    C. draft new laws
    D. approve treaties

62. This amendment guaranteed the rights of 18-year-olds to vote.

    A. The Bill of Rights (Amendments 1-10)
    B. the 14th and 15th Amendments
    C. the 19th Amendment
    D. the 26th Amendment

63. This amendment guaranteed the right of trial by a jury of your peers.

    A. The Bill of Rights (Amendments 1-10)
    B. the 14th and 15th Amendments
    C. the 19th Amendment
    D. the 26th Amendment

64. These amendments guaranteed voting rights for recently freed slaves.

    A. The Bill of Rights (Amendments 1-10)
    B. the 14th and 15th Amendments
    C. the 19th Amendment
    D. the 26th Amendment

65. This amendment is know as the "women's suffrage" amendment.

    A. The Bill of Rights (Amendments 1-10)
    B. the 14th and 15th Amendments
    C. the 19th Amendment
    D. the 26th Amendment

Go on to the next page.

66. Discrimination in schools is:

A. unconstitutional
B. a law
C. guaranteed under the Constitution
D. not ever an issue

67. Which of the following is not a legal means of dissent?

A. lawsuits
B. petitions
C. terrorist acts
D. peaceful public protests

68. The 19th Amendment guarantees the right of:

A. people to vote regardless of race
B. 18 year-olds to vote
C. women to vote
D. land owners to vote

69. The Bill of Rights includes all of the following, EXCEPT:

A. freedom of religion
B. speedy trial
C. allows cruel and unusual punishment
D. freedom of assembly

70. The First Amendment guarantees:

A. voting rights for 18-year-olds
B. states have rights not implicitly described in the Constitution
C. freedom of speech, press, assembly, and religion
D. the right to "bear arms"

71. A speedy trial, a jury of one's peers, and no self-incrimination, are all examples of:

A. laws enacted by Congress
B. Due Process
C. Amendments 18 and 21
D. Executive Branch power

72. Political parties play what role in governmental leadership?

A. minor
B. none at all
C. no longer exist
D. major

73. What is a function of political parties?

A. provide leadership through developing political platforms
B. to get around laws
C. illegal means to raise money
D. enact laws of Congress

Go on to the next page.

74. Candidates almost always:

    A. run independently
    B. raise all their money themselves
    C. belong to a political party
    D. are over 50 years of age

75. Which of the following officials is NOT elected?

    A. State Attorney General
    B. United States Attorney General
    C. President
    D. Senator

76. Which of the following is a state elected official?

    A. President
    B. Mayor
    C. County Commissioner
    D. Legislator

77. Who appoints cabinet members?

    A. Supreme Court
    B. the Senate
    C. the House of Representatives
    D. the President

78. Who confirms federal judge appointments?

    A. the President
    B the Supreme Court
    C. the Senate
    D. the House of Representatives

79. Ohio state judges are:

    A. appointed by the Governor
    B. elected
    C. appointed by the State Attorney General
    D. appointed by the United States Attorney General

80. Who elects the President and Vice-President of the United States?

    A. voters
    B. Congress
    C. Electoral College
    D. citizens

81. Mayors, City Councilors, and County Commissioners are elected at which government level?

    A. local
    B. state
    C. inter-state
    D. national

Go on to the next page.

82. Attorney Generals, judges, and legislators are elected at which government level?

    A. local
    B. state
    C. national
    D. federal

83. To qualify to vote, one no longer needs to be:

    A. 18 years of age
    B. a citizen
    C. a land owner
    D. registered with the board of elections

84. The denial of voting based on gender was eliminated by:

    A. Congressional law
    B. Constitutional Amendment
    C. Presidential decree
    D. petition

85. Which of the following is not a requirement of voting in the state of Ohio?

    A. literacy
    B. age
    C. citizenship
    D. residency

86. To vote in Ohio, one needs to:

    A. petition the General Assembly
    B. show up at the polls
    C. write a letter to the Governor
    D. register with the Board of Elections

87. Voting is a privilege of citizens; this privilege is guaranteed by:

    A. Presidential decree
    B. Congressional law
    C. Supreme Court decision
    D. the Constitution

88. Which of the following is still a requirement for voting in the United States?

    A. literacy
    B. tax payment
    C. age
    D. race

89. Which piece of information is most reliable?

    A. one overheard in the check-out line at the supermarket
    B. one read in the opinion page of the newspaper
    C. one read in a magazine, and also in the news section of the newspaper
    D. one told to you by a political campaigner

Go on to the next page.

Candidate Smith	Candidate Zhou
believes in recycling	thinks recycling is unnecessary
supports President Espinosa	supports President Espinosa
wants to reduce taxes	thinks taxes should be raised to cover budget deficit
is against term limits	is in favor of term limits
believes in strong regula- tion of the environment	believes in some regulation of the environment
education should be federally controlled	education should be controlled by the state

Refer to the chart above for questions 90 – 94.

90. Which issues do Candidate Smith and Candidate Zhou agree upon?

    A. recycling

    B. education

    C. supports the President

    D. term-limits

91. Which issues do Candidate Smith and Zhou disagree upon?

    A. recycling and support of the President

    B. term limits and education

    C. strong military

    D. support of the President

92. Which of the following statements is true?

    A. Candidate Smith would like to run for many terms of office

    B. Candidate Smith believes taxes should be raise to cover the deficit

    C. Candidate Zhou would support all strong regulation of the environment

    D. Candidate Zhou would vote against a law requiring recycling

93. What is an issue that candidates Smith and Zhou have similar, but not quite the same, view upon?

    A. recycling

    B. taxes

    C. environment

    D. term limits

94. How would the candidates vote on a law passed by Congress establishing national high school graduation requirements?

    A. both candidates would support the law

    B. both candidates would not support the law

    C. Candidate Smith would support the law

    D. Candidate Zhou would support the law.

Go on to the next page.

Tracking Poll for Gubernatorial Candidates Wilson and Alvarez
(percentage of voters supporting the candidates)

	June 15	July 15	Aug 15	Sept 15	Oct 15	Nov 1
Wilson	15	30	45	50	50	50
Alvarez	10	20	30	40	45	50
Undecided	75	50	25	10	5	0

For questions 95 - 97, refer to the chart above.

95. What can one conclude about the June 15th poll?

   A. Most voters don't know enough about the candidates
   B. Wilson will win the election
   C. Alvarez will win the election
   D. The voter turn-out in November will below

96. If the election were held on August 15, who would likely win the election?

   A. Wilson
   B. Alvarez
   C. a write-in candidate
   D. it would be a tie

97. If the poll trends were to continue, which candidate would win the election on November 5?

   A. Wilson
   B. Alvarez
   C. neither, it would be a tie
   D. a write-in candidate

Go on to the next page.

98. Which of the following is the most active form of citizenship?

    A. volunteer to work on a candidate's campaign
    B. not voting
    C. watching the news
    D. reading the newspaper

99. Which of the following is not a positive form of citizenship?

    A. volunteering to work on a candidate's campaign
    B. watching the local news
    C. not voting
    D. discussing political issues with friends

100. If one wants to get involved in the civic life of the community, one could:

    A. be a volunteer at the polls
    B. refuse to vote
    C. leave the country
    D. encourage others not to vote

STOP.

Answer Key

Learning Outcome 1
1. C
2. B
3. D
4. A
5. C
6. C

Learning Outcome 2:
7. D
8. D
9. B

Learning Outcome 3:
10. A
11. C
12. D
13. B
14. B

Learning Outcome 4:
15. A
16. D
17. C
18. C
19. A
20. D

Learning Outcome 5:
21. A
22. C
23. C
24. B
25. C
26. A

Learning Outcome 6:
27. A
28. D
29. C
30. C
31. B

Learning Outcome 7:
32. C
33. A
34. D
35. B
36. D
37. B

Learning Outcome 8:
38. D
39. B
40. B
41. A
42. D

Learning Outcome 9:
43. D
44. B
45. C
46. D
47. C

Learning Outcome 10:
48. A
49. C
50. B
51. D
52. D
53. B

Learning Outcome 11:
54. D
55. B
56. A
57. B
58. C
59. C
60. D
61. B

Answer Key

Learning Outcome 12:
62. D
63. A
64. B
65. C
66. A
67. C
68. C
69. C
70. C
71. B

Learning Outcome 13:
72. D
73. A
74. C

Learning Outcome 14:
75. B
76. D
77. D
78. C
79. B
80. C
81. A
82. B

Learning Outcome 15:
83. C
84. B
85. A
86. D
87. D
88. C

Learning Outcome 16:
89. C
90. C
91. B
92. D
93. C
94. C
95. A
96. A
97. B

Learning Outcome 17:
98. A
99. C
100. A

Science

Ninth Grade Proficiency Test: Science

Introduction: Strands and Learning Outcomes

The Science Section of the Ohio Ninth Grade Proficiency Test is designed to test your overall understanding of scientific content and process. The questions on the test are developed from the learning outcomes and are based on the Ohio Model Competency-Based Science program and other related documents. The test will emphasize basic facts, an understanding of concepts, and the ability to analyze and apply information in a given situation.

About the Science Test
The science test will contain 45 multiple-choice items. It is designed to find out how well you can think about science; not how much science you know. The test covers basic science in four categories. Each area of science has 5 to 7 concepts that can be tested. Questions on science concepts can be at one of three different levels of thinking. Confusing? The following table can help you:

Category	Acquiring	Processing	Extending	Total
Life Science	3-5	3-5	1-3	9-11
Physical Science	3-5	3-5	1-3	9-11
Earth/Space Science	3-5	3-5	1-3	9-11
Nature of Science	3-5	3-5	1-3	9-11

About the Categories: Strands
On the proficiency test, there are four areas of science similar to courses you may have taken in school. These are the four strands or categories that the learning outcomes come from. You will review the four strands and all learning outcomes in this order.

Strand I – Nature of Science - Built into this science test is an assessment of your ability and thinking habits in investigating science ideas. Six outcomes (1, 2, 3, 4, 17, and 19) in this strand are taught in context-at every grade level, in every course and in nearly every unit.

Strand II – Earth and Space Science - Many of the phenomena of earth science are either too slow or too large to witness directly in action. These outcomes (5, 6, 7, and 18) generally involve events that you can witness, either directly or indirectly through television or film. Using someone else's observations and inferences made based on evidence collected is also useful.

Strand III – Physical Science - Commonly thought of as physics and chemistry, physical science includes the physical principles that can be observed and explored and the inferences that can be made based on concrete experiences in the classroom or witnessed by other means without complicated instrumentation or theories. Five outcomes (8, 9, 10, 1 1, and 12) are focused on this strand.

Strand IV – Life Science - Though life sciences (biology, environmental science) are the most familiar to us, these outcomes strike a balance between the life science concepts that are extremely complicated and full of terms with those that can be directly observed and explored. In these outcomes (13, 14, 15, 16 and 20), your ability to explain your choices and decisions are more important than your knowledge of terms.

About the Levels of Thinking
There are three levels of thinking that are tested on the proficiency test. All of the questions on the test were written at a particular level of thinking.

Acquiring Scientific Knowledge (about 40% of the questions on the test)
Questions of this type test your ability to make observations and collect and organize data. This may include the ability to make measurements; read graphs, charts, and tables; and classify objects on the basis of their characteristics. Basically, questions of this type test your ability to read and report data.

Processing Scientific Knowledge (about 40% of the questions on the test)
Questions of this type test your ability to interpret and analyze information. This may include the ability to make an inference from given information; recognize patterns and trends in data; and manipulate variables.

Extending Scientific Knowledge (about 20% of the questions on the test)
Questions of this type test your ability to apply knowledge and concepts to new situations. This may include your ability to develop models; draw conclusions; ask and evaluate questions; and make predictions.

What You Need To Know About the Science Test
The science test is set up so that you will be given some basic information to read or to observe, like a chart or a graph. Then, several questions are asked about this information. Generally, the first question is an acquiring type question, then a processing, and then, possibly an extending type question. In any case - **Read Carefully!**

- The questions will be grouped into two types: 1) a reading selection (passage) that may contain tables, charts, or figures followed by a series of related questions. This type of question will comprise 80% of the test questions. 2) questions that can be answered without referring to a reading selection. The stand-alone questions will comprise 20% of the test questions.
- Each test question will have four answer choices, but only one answer will be correct. There will not be a penalty for choosing an incorrect answer.
- While most questions will require students to interpret/analyze and apply information given to them, some questions may require students to recall specific information.
- Students will not be permitted to use references or tools other that pencils on this test.
- Students will have a maximum of two and one-half hours to finish the test. Most students will be able to complete the test within an hour.

Test-Taking Strategies For Science
- When you read multiple choice answer choices, read the up from the bottom! It will be much easier to spot the correct answer the first time.
- Read the entire question to find out what the "REAL" question is. What are you being asked to do or to give as an answer?
- Read all the answer choices and eliminate answer choices that you KNOW are incorrect by crossing them out.
- There is no penalty for guessing. On this test, it is to your benefit to guess if you HAVE to because you have a chance of getting the question correct. NEVER LEAVE AN ANSWER BLANK!
- If you do not know the answer, circle the question and come back to it. You will want to go back and check your answers when you are finished anyway.
- Be careful to fill in your bubble answer sheet neatly with a #2 pencil. Your test will be graded by an electronic scanner and erasing or using a mechanical pencil may affect your grade.
- You may write in your test booklet and it will not be graded. Use the margins of your test booklet to figure. Only your answer "bubble" sheet will be graded.

Field Test Results
Test questions based on the science learning outcomes were field tested in the fall of 1994. While the number of students responding to each test item was limited, some general observations regarding student achievement can be made.
- Student performance was highest on questions measuring outcomes 3, 4, and 7. We have used the symbol "✓" to identify these outcomes.
- Student perfomance was lowest on questions measuring outcomes 2, 10, and 20. We have used the symbol "✐" to identify these outcomes.

> **Key:**
> ✓ = Outcomes where student performance was HIGH during field tests.
> ✐ = Outcomes where student performance was LOW during field tests.

The Science Learning Outcomes

In this section, we will go concept by concept and give you an example of each type of question and how it might look on the test. Sometimes a question can be so obvious that not much information is needed. The outcomes may seem a little out of order; we are using the same number for the outcomes as the State uses. It will be easier to look at these by category.

The material for the ninth-grade test was drawnfrom science material from grades six through eight. In general, this proficiency test is designed to assess long-term memory of concepts, problem solving and thinking skills, and there is not much memorized fact.

Strand I – The Nature of Science

The Learning Outcomes in this strand are 1, 2, 3, 4, 17, and 19. These learning outcomes are covered together below using simulated proficiency test questions followed by an analysis that helps you find the correct answer. This process of review in the material will help prepare you to PASS the actual science proficiency test.

1. Devise a classification system for a set of objects or a group of organisms.

Use common characteristics to group items.

You should be familiar with methods of categorizing groups of objects and organisms based on their characteristics, such as simple keys and the periodic table. You should be able to tell if classification schemes work and identify the bases on which such schemes are developed. You should practice following written directions, reading keys, and making simple keys in groups. You should be able to improve and extend classification schemes that are used in a task. The construction of simple keys and charts and your use of keys in field guides and data in reference materials should be practiced as you explore the natural world.

Examples:

1. One day you are walking on the shore of a nearby lake and you find a shell. Follow this basic key to tell which shell is found above.

```
1. Shell is one piece ........................................................... Snail
   Shell is in two pieces ......................................................Go to 2

2. Shell is striped....................................................Zebra Mussel
   Shell is a solid color .....................................................Go to 3

3. Shell is dark.................................................Freshwater Mussel
   Shell is light...................................................Freshwater Clam
```

What shell did you find?

A. Snail
B. Zebra Mussel
C. Freshwater Mussel
D. Freshwater Clam

Analysis:
*You must start with number 1 and follow directions. The shell is in two pieces - go to 2; the shell is striped, it's a Zebra Mussel. STOP! You've got it! This is an example of a question that tests your ability of **Acquiring Scientific Knowledge**. The correct answer is "B."*

2. If you had a dark purple, solid colored, two-piece shell it might be a:

   A. Snail
   B. Zebra Mussel
   C. Freshwater Mussel
   D. Freshwater Clam

Analysis:
*This is an example of a question that tests your ability of **Processing Scientific Knowledge**. You have been asked to change your identification based on new information. This time, the correct answer is "C."*

3. Suppose the shell you found was gray (neither dark or light). How would you change the key to make it more useful?

   A. Start at the beginning with another characteristic
   B. Nothing, keys can't be wrong
   C. Guess if it is light gray or dark gray
   D. Find another key with more characteristics

Analysis:
*This is an example of a question that tests your ability of **Extending Scientific Knowledge**. It is asking you to take this situation further. It may seem that all of these are reasonable. However, because you know that there are many keys for things based on physical characteristics, you know that choice "D" is the most reasonable.*

✍ 2. Distinguish between observation and inference given a representation of a scientific situation.

Tell the difference between facts and assumptions

You should understand the difference between something that is directly observable using your own senses and something that may be inferred based on observed or given information. You should also be able to look at other people's statements and decide whether or not they are inference or observations. For example, you should be able to distinguish between an observation (e.g. rocks sink in water) and an inference (e.g. rocks are more dense than water). This outcome does not lend itself to very complicated questions. These are almost always at the acquiring level.

Examples:

1. You and your lab partner have been working outdoors and you find a small creature in the grass. Your task is to record your observations. Which is an observation and not an inference?

   A. It is a Snail.
   B. It has a curly shell.
   C. It is an animal.
   D. It came from the water.

Analysis:
Only "B" could be directly observed using your senses – in this case sight. The others are inferred from what you know or observed.

2. You are using a roller skate to investigate motion in your class. Which statement is an inference that you might make from your observations?

   A. The skate rolled 3 meters.
   B. The skate took 3 seconds to travel the course.
   C. The skate stopped on its own.
   D. Friction stopped the roller skate.

Analysis:
"A", "B", and "C" came from using your senses to state a fact from direct observations. "D" is an inference based on those observations. The correct answer is "D."

✓ 3. Identify and apply science safety procedures.

Identify the safety precautions needed when doing an experiment

You should be able to anticipate the need for and be familiar with the use of common laboratory safety equipment, such as safety goggles, and safety procedures as they relate to personal and group safety. You should be able to identify, and if necessary practice, the safety precautions needed in given classroom situations and school field studies. There are many safety guides and resources to help you think through these issues. In general, common sense should be followed and, always remember that your teacher should always be notified in case of an accident! These questions are usually not given as reading information. Often, because they are not too complex, they stand alone on the test.

Examples:

1. The student shown above is not ready to safely do a science activity that involves chemicals. What's missing?

   A. lab notebook
   B. safety goggles
   C. science textbook
   D. pan of water

Analysis:
Safety questions are generally pretty obvious. In this case, as with all lab exercises, safety goggles, "B" are very important. The other things are nice but not necessary for safety reasons. "D" might be needed for some activities, though not always.

2. While working in the lab on an activity, your lab partner gets something in her eye by wiping it with her hand. You are unsure what might be in her eyes. The first thing to do is to:

    A. Clean up the lab station

    B. Have your partner wash her hands

    C. Call the teacher for help

    D. Spray her face with water.

Analysis:

Always get help first! Since you do not know what is in her eyes, spraying water in her eyes, "D" could be harmful. The other two can wait until later.

✓ **4. Demonstrate an understanding of the use of measuring devices and report data in appropriate units.**

Choose an instrument to make a certain measurement

You should be familiar with using common laboratory equipment in and out of the classroom, such as scales, thermometers, balances, graduated cylinders, and rulers. Experience using the metric system of measurement is important. You will not be asked to convert units from English to metric. Your ability to use units of measure depends on the ability to think in those units, not in the ability to convert them.

Examples:

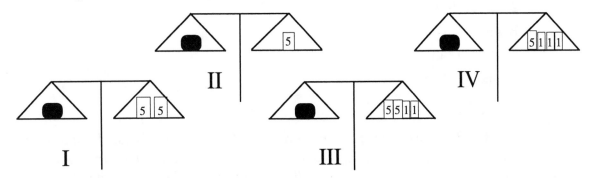

1. What is the mass of the object on balance II?

 A. 5 grams

    B. 5 liters

    C. 5 pounds

    D. 10 grams

Analysis:
This is an acquiring type question that asks you to simply know what a reasonable unit is for mass using a classroom balance. A balance measures in the metric system. Choice "C" is incorrect. A tricky answer like this shows how carefully you must consider each answer so that you get all the points you deserve. Liters is not a unit of mass so "B" is out. Reading the scale leaves you with choice "A."

2. Look at the illustrations of the balances in the previous question. Which choice shows the order of the masses on the balances from lightest to heaviest?

A. I, II, III, IV
B. IV, III, II, I
C. I, III, IV, II
D. II, IV, I, III

Analysis:
This may look like a trick, but it's not. It's simply a matter of adding up the standard masses to get the proper amounts. I is 10g; II is 5g; III is 12g; and IV is 8g. "D" is the correct order – lightest to heaviest. *READ CAREFULLY!*

3. What is the length of a new pencil?

A. about .18 m
B. about 1.8 m
C. about 18 m
D. about 1.8 cm

Analysis:
You need to know only what units are in the reasonable range and choose the appropriate one. Try it! The decimals might trip you up. "B" and "C" are much too large. A meter is longer than your arm. "D" is way too small. A centimeter is about the width of a thumbnail. This leaves "A."

17. Describe the ways scientific ideas have changed using historical contexts.

Describe how explanations of eclipses have changed over time

You should have an understanding of how and why scientific theories and methods have changed over time. For example, these may include, but are not limited to, models of the solar system, germ theory, models of the atom, heat, elements, and genetics. The study of the history of science helps you to connect significant examples of how the weight of accumulated evidence, technology, and creative thinking have overcome some of the constraints that have affected scientific thinking throughout the years. The focus of this outcome is on the dynamic nature of the scientific endeavor to constantly refine and extend scientific knowledge, not on historical facts such as names and dates. This outcome usually asks you to read a brief story or a couple of statements and compare them. It is important that you read these very carefully.

Examples:

The three questions which follow refer to this short paragraph:

> In the 1700's, Carol Linnaeus developed a simple logical system of classification to name and describe the relationships between animals and plants. He used measurements, shapes and similarities to give them their Latin names. In the 1990's we have many ways to describe animals and plants including electron microscopic techniques, genetics, and computers. This has called much of the Linnaean classification into question and has disagreed with many of the early Linnaeus ideas.

1. Which technology developed in the 1990's has extended our abilities to observe things?

    A. the telephone
    B. the microscope
    C. the electron microscope
    D. the metric rulers

Analysis:
A simple question if you read carefully. Read the choices up from the bottom. Metric rulers, microscopes, and the telephone were all developed long before the 1990's. The correct answer choice found in the reading is "C."

2. In Linnaeus' day, the only Kingdoms were animals and plants. Since that time, the Protist and Moneran Kingdoms have been added. Why might this be?

    A. scientists thought Linnaeus wrong.

    B. scientists used new tools to identify them.

    C. Protists and Monerans developed since Linnaeus' time.

    D. computers found these new life forms.

Analysis:
Using simple reasoning, and by reading the passage, "B" is the most reasonable answer. Right and wrong is not a scientific choice; Protists and Monerans (as well as Fungi) have been found in fossils; and these life forms were found before computers. This is a processing question.

3. Often new tools and technologies result in refinements of scientific ideas. Which is NOT an example of this?

    A. Submarines find organisms on the sea floor.

    B. The Hubble Telescope finds a new star.

    C. A cyclotron provides evidence of a new atomic particle.

    D. A scientists finds an exception to a mathematical theory.

Analysis:
Three of these have new tools – "A," "B," and "C." The correct answer is "D" because no tool is noted.

19. Describe the relationship between technology and science.

How do science and inventions affect each other?

You should understand the interactions between science and technology in society. You should be able to recognize advantages, disadvantages, and limitations of human actions intended to research, reshape, and control nature and the environment. For example, you should understand how electrical devices and energy sources may affect human health.

Try the examples on the next page.

Examples:

Use the following the passage to answer questions 1 – 3.

> Many new technologies and materials make people's lives easier. Plastics are an example of this. Plastics are made from oil and do not easily decompose. Many people say that plastics are a big environmental problem based on their view of the benefits and risks.

1. According to the passage, people may think plastics are a problem because:

   A. they are made from gas
   B. they do not easily decompose
   C. they are not useful
   D. they are too expensive

Analysis:
From the reading, only "B" is reasonable. You must be careful not to interject your own opinion into the situation.

2. A person will make choices about materials based on the risks and benefits of its use. Which of the following could be a risk of using plastic for shopping bags?

   A. low cost
   B. it's light
   C. it is strong even when thin
   D. it is dangerous to children

Analysis:
Thinking through the question, all except "D" are benefits. "D" is a risk for a person who has small children.

3. Recycling plastic could result in the need for:

   A. more oil
   B. new technologies
   C. larger landfills
   D. higher levels of pollution control

Analysis:
This is a basic concept. Technologies often result in the need for new technologies.
Answer choice "A,""C," and "D" are not reasonable choices. The correct answer is "B."

Strand II – Earth and Space Sciences

The Learning Outcomes in this strand are 5, 6, 7, and 18. These learning outcomes will be reviewed using simulated proficiency test questions.

5. Describe the results of earth-changing processes.

Describe changes taking place in the Earth's surface

You should be familiar with the theory and processes of weathering, erosion, glaciation, rock formation, and plate tectonics (volcanism, earthquakes, rifting, mountain building, etc.). You should understand how earth-changing processes are reflected in the land forms of the Earth's surface as presented in common situations, or on maps and diagrams.

Examples:

A large rock has been observed over a period of years. The following data has been collected.

Date	Mass	Surface	Height	other observations
1970	30.2Kg	smooth	1.20m	none
1975	29.9Kg	smooth	1.19m	none
1980	26.3Kg	sandy	.88m	moss covered
1985	26.0Kg	sandy	.88m	none
1990	25.7Kg	pebbly	.86m	seedlings growing
1995	25.4Kg	pebbly	.86m	none

1. The mass of the rock in 1985 was:

A. 29.9Kg
B. 26.3Kg
C. 0.3Kg
D. 26.0Kg

Analysis:
This question is as simple as it looks – according to the chart, the rock's mass in 1985 was 26.0Kg. The other choices are for other years or, in the case of "C," a difference is used as a choice. Read carefully. The correct answer is "D."

2. What may have caused the large loss in mass between 1975 and 1980?

   A. wind damage
   B. plants used the rock for food
   C. erosion by water
   D. ice damage in the winter

Analysis:
Only "D" could result in a large piece being broken off. This is probably what happened to make such a large loss of mass. The other answer choices could only result in slight losses over a short period of years.

3. If this pattern were to continue, how long might it be until the remaining rock had a mass of only 20Kg?

   A. 5 years
   B. 18 years
   C. 23 years
   D. can't predict from this information.

Analysis:
A simple pattern can be found in this data. Except for the large loss of mass in 1975–1980, the mass has been lost at a rate of about .3Kg every 5 years. At this rate, the rock would need around 18 years to lose the remaining 5.4Kg. This is an extension question. It calls for you to be able to look for the pattern in the data and to make a reasonable approximation from the data. The correct answer is "B."

6. Apply concepts of the Earth's rotation, tilt and revolution to an understanding of time and season.

Explain how seasons change

You should be familiar with the concepts of the tilt of Earth's axis, time of rotation and revolution, and orbital shape. Students should be able to relate these concepts to an understanding of seasons and how these factors influence our definition of time. This is basic, though difficult conceptually. In general, the spin of the Earth makes days and nights. The orbit around the sun combined with the tilt of the Earth make the seasons. We are actually closest to the sun in the winter, we are just tilted away from it. The phases of the moon are caused by its orbit around the Earth, not the Earth's shadow.

Examples:

1. The Earth's rotation determines the length of the day. How many times does the Earth rotate in one day?

   A. two times per day
   B. once per day
   C. once per two days
   D. can't predict from this information.

Analysis:
Since the information given states a direct relationship between days and rotations, it is reasonable that the Earth rotates once per day. The correct answer is "B."

2. The slant of the sun's rays and how direct the sunlight is determines the seasons on Earth. In which season would the Earth be tilted most toward the sun?

   A. Spring
   B. Summer
   C. Fall
   D. Winter

Analysis:
The more direct the sun, the warmer the season. Therefore, this answer is "B," Summer.

7. Describe interactions of matter and energy throughout the lithosphere, hydrosphere, and atmosphere.

Explain materials cycles (water, carbon, nitrogen), currents, and weather on the land, in the water, and in the air

You should be familiar with the concepts of weather and climate; the water, carbon, nitrogen and rock cycles; currents, including ocean currents and convection currents; and tides in relevant contexts from written passages, diagrams, pictures, charts, maps, graphs, and tables. Cycling of resources is best thought of as accounting for matter as it changes form and character.

Examples:

> Carbon is a vital part of life on Earth since it is in many of the vital chemical reactions necessary for life. There is only so much carbon. It is constantly recycled.

1. Which of the following is NOT a source of carbon?

   A. air
   B. distilled water
   C. plants
   D. animals

Analysis:
This is a recall question about the carbon cycle. Since air has carbon dioxide, and animal and plant tissues are made of carbon-based molecules, only choice "B" is reasonable and is the correct answer.

2. When sugars are broken down, carbon dioxide and water are released. Which is the most common source of these sugars ?

   A. air
   B. water
   C. plants
   D. animals

Analysis:
The question refers to something, like an animal, breaking down sugar. It is logical that this situation may be plants ("C") being broken down. "A" and "B" are out since they are listed in the question as products of the break down of sugar.

3. Water is also cycled in the atmosphere. Much of the water on Earth is trapped and temporarily out of the cycle. Which could trap water the longest?

    A. body fluid
    B. pond water
    C. ground water
    D. polar ice

Analysis:
"B" and "C" are flowing parts of the water cycle. "A" could be kept for a lifetime of an animal. "D" could trap water for centuries. Polar ice is the most logical choice. The correct answer is "D."

18. Compare renewable and nonrenewable resources and strategies for managing them

Compare oil and sunlight as sources of energy

You should be familiar with and be able to identify renewable and nonrenewable resources (includes energy sources). You should be able to relate resource use to existing supplies and be able to apply appropriate management strategies, such as conservation and recycling. You should be able to recognize and discuss the tradeoffs (including risks and benefits) represented as humans act to consume and/or conserve natural resources, while comparing this analysis from how social pressure and advertising may impact actions. The conservation or accounting of energy in a system is the focus of this outcome.

Try the examples on the next page.

Try the examples on the next page.
Examples:

1. Which of the following is a nonrenewable resource?

    A. oil

   B. water

   C. paper

   D. sugar

Analysis:
Oil is made over millions of years. Water is constantly recycled. Paper and sugar are plant products and quickly replaced. The correct answer is "A."

2. Deciding about which resource to use often depends on where you live. If you lived in a desert like in oil rich states like California or Texas where water is scarce would you choose a paper, styrofoam, or glass cup?

   A. paper because it can be shipped and recycled

   B. styrofoam because it is made from local oil resources

   C. glass because it can be cleaned with water

   D. glass because it can be crushed and recycled.

Analysis:
Based on the explanations given, the most reasonable seems to be "B." In the desert, water is scarce and oil may not be. "B" is the correct answer.

Strand III – Physical Sciences

The Learning Outcomes in this strand are 8, 9, 10, 11, and 12. These are the learning outcomes you will review next.

8. Apply the use of simple machines to practical situations.

Describe how a lever or pulley can make a task easier

You should have a basic understanding of how simple machines, such as levers, pulley systems, and inclined planes, change the effort and distance through which work is done. The simple principle that "You don't get something for nothing" is important here. You should be able to apply the use of these machines to simple, practical situations as shown in pictures, diagrams, and charts. You should be able to discuss the advantages and disadvantages of many simple technological devices as you explore the functions of those devices in relevant contexts.

Examples:

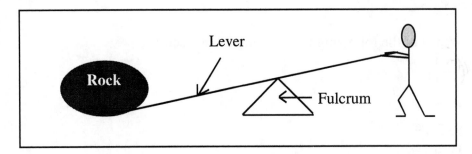

1. In the drawing above, the person is trying to move the large rock. How could the job be made easier?

    A. use a shorter lever

    B. move the fulcrum toward the rock

    C. move the fulcrum away from the rock

    D. push on the lever close to the rock

Analysis:
The best way to increase lever force is to move the fulcrum closer to the rock. The other choices make it harder to move the rock. The correct answer is "B."

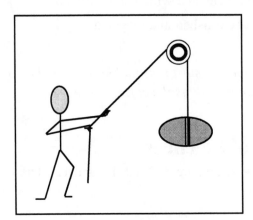

2. In the drawing above, which of the following would make the job easiest?

    A. get a longer rope

    B. use a larger pulley

    C. add another pulley

    D. get a shorter rope

Analysis:
In pulley systems, the additional wheels in the machine gives you greater advantage. Adding another pulley will make the job easier. The correct answer is "C."

3. If you choose a bottle opener to open a soft drink, which opener would make it the easiest?

    A. the one with the longest handle
    B. the one with the shortest handle
    C. the one with the widest blade
    D. the one with the least friction

Analysis:
In a lever with a fixed fulcrum (like a bottle opener), the best way to increase your mechanical advantage is to increase the length of the lever. You should choose the one with the longest handle. The correct answer is "A."

9. Apply the concept of force and mass to predict the motion of objects.

Describe the motion of a thrown ball

You should be familiar with the relationship between the change in motion of an object, the force applied to the object, and the mass of the object. This includes how Newton's three laws of motion relate to the motion of familiar objects. Law #1 – Nothing moves unless something moves it; nothing stops unless something stops it. Law #2 – The harder you push it, the faster it goes; the more mass it has, the harder it is to push. Law # 3 – for every push there is an equal push back.

Examples:

1. Which ball would move faster?

    A. a massive ball hit with a massive bat
    B. a massive ball hit with a light bat
    C. a light ball hit with a light bat
    D. a light ball hit with a massive bat

Analysis:
The larger the force, the faster the resulting movement. Answer choice "D," a light ball hit with a massive bat would move the fastest.

2. When a ball is thrown up into the air, several forces act on the ball. Which forces work to slow the ball?

          I. gravity
          II. momentum
          III. friction with the air

   A. I only

   B. II only

   C. III only

   D. I and III only

Analysis:
In the case of a thrown ball, the air and gravity work to slow the ball. Momentum works to keep the ball going. The answer in this case is "D."

3. When a rocket is launched, the momentum of the smoke, ash, and energy go in one direction and the momentum of the rocket goes in the other. How are these related?

   A. the smoke and ash have more momentum

   B. the rocket has more momentum

   C. the momentum in each direction is the same

   D. they are not related

Analysis:
In any system involving motion, momentum is the same in each direction. It balances out! Answer "C" is correct.

✍ 10. Apply the concepts of energy transformations in electrical and mechanical systems.

Describe how the energy in a flashlight battery is transformed into heat and light

You should be familiar with the concept of energy transformation. You should be able to distinguish between different forms of energy, such as chemical, electrical, and heat; potential and kinetic. You will be familiar with the conservation of energy, the major sources of energy, and the major losses of energy from different systems.

Examples:

1. What kind of energy is the source of light in a flashlight?

   A. motion

   B. chemical

   C. heat

   D. electrical

Analysis:
Since a flashlight is powered by a battery, the source is a form of chemical energy. The chemical energy is converted to electrical which is converted to light and heat. No energy is lost. It is all converted. The correct answer is "B."

2. If all energy on Earth is conserved, and more is coming in all of the time from the sun, why doesn't the Earth overheat?

   A. Heat is absorbed by rocks

   B. Plants lock in the energy

   C. Sea water holds the energy

   D. Heat is radiated into space

Analysis:
If energy is stored, it still adds to the total energy of the system. Much heat is radiated to space every day. Answer "D" is the most reasonable.

3. Which is an example of kinetic energy being converted to electricity?

   A. A water powered generator

   B. A nuclear power plant

   C. A coal-burning power plant

   D. A flashlight

Analysis:
Kinetic energy is energy of motion. The only case using motion to make electricity is a water powered generator. Answer choice "A" is correct.

11. Apply concepts of sound and light waves to everyday situations.

Describe how light and sound travel through different materials

You should be familiar with models of sound and light waves. This includes an experientially-rounded understanding of the concepts of frequency, wavelength, speed, energy, refraction, and reflection. You should be able to compare and contrast how different forms of wave energy are produced, transferred, and detected. For example, explorations of light and sound contribute to explanations of why we are able to see and hear. Contrasted with how other living things see and hear can be an engaging way in which to explore this concept.

Examples:

> Sound travels through a substance as a wave. The
> more dense the substance, the faster the sound waves travel.

1. Through which substance will sound travel the fastest?

   A. water

   B. steel

   C. air

   D. syrup

Analysis:
The densest substance in this question is steel so the sound will travel the fastest through the steel. Choice "B" is the best choice.

2. Both light and sound waves can bounce off of a barrier. This is called reflection. If a wave was reflected off of a barrier, how much energy is destroyed because of the change in direction?

   A. most of the energy

   B. about a tenth

   C. about half

   D. none of the energy

Analysis:
Since energy cannot be created or destroyed under any circumstances, the only reasonable answer is "D."

3. Energy is converted to other types in order for us to be able to perceive it in our brain. Which gives the types of energy transformations in the ear?

    A. light to mechanical to sound

    B. sound to mechanical to electrical

    C. sound to electrical

    D. mechanical to light to electrical

Analysis:
Sound energy enters the outer ear and is converted to mechanical energy in the ear bones. This mechanical energy is converted to electrical energy by the inner ear and transmitted to the brain. The correct answer is "B." You do need to know about the overall structure of the eyes and ears for this outcome.

12. Describe chemical and/or physical interactions of matter.

Describe how a cube of sugar dissolves in water, how metals rust, and how things burn

You should be familiar with the concept of matter. You should understand basic physical and chemical properties of matter, including phases, and be able to distinguish between a physical change and a chemical change. You should be familiar with models of atomic and molecular structure, and understand how these models can be used to explain the structure and interactions of matter. Simple physical changes, in general, do not result in irreversible changes in the properties of matter. Simple chemical changes are very difficult to reverse, and usually result in a change in the properties of the material. Often, chemical changes give off or absorb heat on their own. Common devices such as chemical cold or heat packs are examples of chemical changes.

Examples:

1. Which of the following is an example of a chemical change?

    A. lighting a match

    B. melting an ice cube

    C. freezing milk

    D. vaporizing water with a laser

Analysis:
"B," "C," and "D" are simple changes in phase and are therefore physical changes.
"A'" is a chemical change. The main hint here is that energy is released and the physical characteristics of the match are changed by the burning. "A" is the correct answer.

When cooking on a gas stove, black soot (carbon) can become deposited on iron cooking pans. There are both physical and chemical changes involved in this situation. Think of this situation to answer the next two questions.

2. Where did the soot (carbon) likely come from?

    A. the bottom of the pan becoming oxidized

    B. the carbon dioxide in the air surrounding the pan

    C. not properly cleaning the pan

    D. carbon is released when the gas is burned

Analysis:
You must visualize this situation to think this through. "C" could not add carbon. Oxidizing iron does not involve carbon– so "A" is out. Carbon dioxide is a product of burning and does not release carbon (not "B"). As gas is burned, some carbon is released without being completed combined with oxygen. "D" is the correct answer.

3. Which is an example of a physical change in this situation?

    A. carbon sticking to the pan

    B. gas burning to heat the food in the pan

    C. oxygen combining with some heated carbon to become carbon dioxide

    D. some iron rusting during the process

Analysis:
There is only one of the choices which could be easily reversed. This is choice "A." Burning, rusting and combining to make a new substance are all chemical changes.

Tip! On the proficiency test, the length of the answer does not relate to whether or not the answer is correct. Notice that in the case of the question above, "C" is the longest – and it is wrong!

Strand IV – Life Sciences

13. Trace the flow of energy and/or interrelationships of organisms in an ecosystem.

Identify the food chain in a lake

You should be familiar with the concept of ecosystems. You should be able to account for energy illustrating that it is always conserved. This includes food pyramids, food webs and food chains; the different types of interactions between organisms; and how energy and matter are transferred through an ecosystem. For example, you should be able to illustrate energy gain directly or indirectly from the sun; energy stored in chemical bonds in food; energy transformed as organisms consume food; and energy diminishing in usefulness when lost as heat.

Examples:

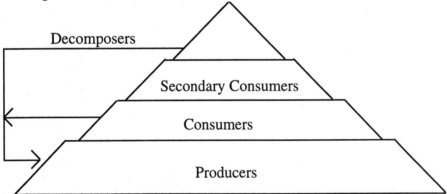

The following three questions relate to the above diagram.

1. At which level, is there the most mass (organisms)?

   A. decomposers
   B. consumers
   C. producers
   D. secondary consumers

Analysis:
You must be very careful that you look at the energy relationships in these questions and not just the height of the diagram. In nature, the most mass is in the producers. This question is a simple case of looking at the diagram – choice "C" is correct.

2. In this food pyramid, between which two levels is the least proportion of the energy converted into new biomass?

A. producers to consumers

B. consumers to secondary consumers

C. secondary consumers to decomposers

D. consumers to decomposers

Analysis:
As hinted by the diagram, energy stored in one level is passed to another level through nutrition. It makes the most sense that energy captured from the sun is likely not completely passed to the consumers. More energy is released from The largest amount of energy is in the producers, so the correct choice is "A."

3. Since energy is never lost, where does it go if it is not passed on to the next level?

A. electricity

B. heat

C. potential

D. kinetic

Analysis:
All four choices are types of energy. However, most energy that leaves systems does so as heat. Answer choice "B" is the correct answer.

14. Compare and contrast the characteristics of plants and animals.

Tell how plants and animals are alike and different

You should be familiar with the similarities and differences between plants and animals at various levels of organization. At the cellular level, the emphasis will be on those characteristics that may be seen with the light microscope. At the organism level, you should be able to explain how plants and animals use distinctly different strategies for survival.

Examples:

As winter approaches, animals and plants do different things to get ready for drastic changes in atmospheric conditions. This can be observed easily. In general, animals move and change their activities. Plants, on the other hand, stay in place and change their activities. The main problem in surviving this change is to conserve energy for better times in the spring. Use this idea to answer the next three questions.

1. Which might you observe specifically ?

   A. animals moving more to keep warm
   B. trees storing more water
   C. trees losing organs
   D. birds making warm nests.

Analysis:
Conservation of energy is not going on in "A," "B," and "D." Trees losing their leaves (one of the trees organs) conserves energy for the tree. The correct choice is "C."

2. Many birds in the northern hemisphere fly south in the late fall. How does this strategy help the birds survive?

   A. They move to an area with more available energy.
   B. They move more to get warm.
   C. They get their energy from the sun.
   D. They take stored energy with them.

Analysis:
Bird migration is not an example of energy conservation. It is a survival strategy available to them because they are animals and can move. Simple reasoning will let you know that "A" is reasonable and the others are not. It does require that birds be light (cannot store extra energy) and use energy efficiently (not extra heat). "A" is correct.

3. Evergreen trees do not lose their leaves (needles) like other trees. Instead, which do they likely do to increase their chance for survival in the winter?

    A. speed up their metabolism

    B. close their stomates to conserve water

    C. cluster together

    D. grow thicker needles

Analysis:
For evergreens to survive, they must conserve energy. "A," "C," and "D" are not conservation methods. The correct answer choice is "B."

15. Explain biological diversity in terms of the transmission of genetic characteristics.

Explain why there are different breeds of dogs or kinds of plants

You should be familiar with concepts related to population biology, including adaptation and offspring variability, and how different modes of reproduction affect genetic variability within a population or generation. Beyond the contrast of differences, many strategies for passing along genetic traits can be found among living things. You should be able to explain similarities and differences within and between species using simulations and models. Concepts covered include Mendelian genetics and natural selection.

Examples:

A large shrub is home to a population of insects. These insects feed on berries that grow on the shrub. Some of this species of insect are white and the some are black. The insects are preyed upon by a weaver bird. Answer the following questions based on this scenario.

1. The berries of this plant are white. Which insect is likely to be able to survive and leave more offspring to populate the tree?

    A. The black insects

    B. The white insects

    C. Neither the black or the white insects

    D. Both have an equal chance

Analysis:
This is a typical acquiring-type question. The insect that is less visible (more camouflaged) is more likely to escape the bird in the scenario. The correct choice is "B."

2. Over a period of years, industrial progress changed the quality of the air so that black soot covered the berries. Which insect will grow in population following this change?

   A. The black insects

   B. The white insects

   C. Neither the black or the white insects

   D. Both have an equal chance

Analysis:
Same as the previous question with a change in the surroundings. Now the black insect is less visible. Choice "A" is correct.

3. In the process of the change in the environment, the white insects were also covered in soot and many survived. What color would their offspring be most likely?

   A. All Black

   B. All White

   C. Some of each

   D. A different color altogether.

Analysis:
The characteristics of offspring are determined by the genetics of the parent. Adaptations to the environment are not inherited. The soot covering the insects will not affect the offsprings' color. The best answer is "B".

16. Describe how organisms accomplish basic life functions at various levels of organization and structure.

Describe a life function like digestion complete with the appropriate anatomy

You should be familiar with how plants and animals accomplish basic life functions, such as respiration, reproduction, growth and development, energy use, circulation, digestion, excretion, and photosynthesis at various levels of organization. The association or lack of association between anatomy and life activity is included in this concept. You should be able to describe and predict behavior and functions of organisms, using models and analogies to draw comparisons and illustrate similarities. For example, populations of organisms may exhibit group behavior to accomplish life functions that can be explored (e.g., herding, migration); and for a single organism, cells, tissues, organs, and systems (e.g., circulatory, nervous) contribute individually and collectively to life functions for that organism.

Examples:

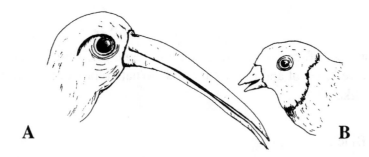

A   B

Shown above are the heads of two different birds. Their beaks are different and help the bird survive in their habitat. Use this idea to answer the questions below.

1. Which life function are these beak shapes most likely related to?

   A. Reproduction
   B. Communication
   C. Locomotion
   D. Feeding

Analysis:
This is an acquiring type question which asks your familiarity with the basic life functions of living things. Beaks are most related to feeding – choice "D."

2. Refer to the same illustration of two birds to determine what is the most likely use for the beak in picture B.

   A. Cracking seeds

   B. Eating flesh

   C. Opening pine cones

   D. Sipping nectar

Analysis:
Since structure often mirrors function, the beak should look like its probable function. In this case, beak B is thick and is probably more useful for cracking seeds. The correct answer is "A."

✍ 20. Describe how a given environmental change affects an ecosystem.

Describe how a flood or drought affects plant and animal life

You should understand how environmental changes, both living and non-living, may affect an ecosystem. This may include species introductions, extinction, pollution, biological magnification, and changes in abiotic factors, such as rainfall, temperature, and light availability. Examples may be taken from natural influences such as weather catastrophes on the local or global scale, or human influences such as pollution over a period of years.

Examples:

   In the spring of 1996, greater than normal amounts of rainfall occurred in southern Ohio. In a normal year, rainfall is associated with animal and plant populations and their abilities to survive in this environment. Think about this situation to answer the following questions.

1. The mosquito population is expected to be greater in 1996. Why might this be true?

   A. Mosquitoes live in the water

   B. Mosquitoes breed in the water

   C. Mosquito predators are killed by rain

   D. Mosquitoes feed on fish

Analysis:
An increase in population is related to breeding. Choice "B" is the correct answer.

2. It is predicted that the population of cattails and other low-water plants will be affected by the flooding. What is the likely impact?

   A. fewer plants because of flooding
   B. more plants because of more water
   C. about the same as years before
   D. can't predict form this information.

Analysis:
It is almost impossible to predict with so little information. Be very careful of these types of questions. This is a processing type question with only one hint – low-water plants. It is still not enough to make a judgment. Choice "D" is correct.

3. In general, temporary catastrophes like flooding can have an impact across the flood plain that is affected by the flood. Humans can contribute to this catastrophe as well. Which is an example of a possible negative impact of human intervention with a flood which would contribute to local habitat destruction?

   A. Storage of oil on the flood plain
   B. Controlling floods with dams
   C. Diverting water with flood walls
   D. Using flood water for irrigation

Analysis:
It is important to remember that some questions may ask for a value judgment on your part. You must be careful to read the question for its meaning instead of putting in too much of your own opinion. In the question, an oil spill caused by flooding would be the biggest problem created. The other impacts are debatable whether they are positive or negative. The correct answer is "A."

Now go on and try the Science Practice Items on your own. Check your answers with the answer key on the last page of the Science Practice Items section of your book.

Science Practice Items

About The Practice Items: Science

The science proficiency test is a thinking test. Most often, if you can think logically, you can reason your way through the test and do very well. In order for you to get plenty of practice on this kind of test, we've provided 77 sample questions. Some of these questions will seem very hard, some really easy – just like on the real test! The state did not put questions on the test to trip you up. All of the questions are fair, straight forward, and reasonable. And, some can be very challenging. The practice items are simulated to be as close as possible to the same style as the proficiency test. Although some questions will be separate, many of the questions are grouped following something to read or some data to analyze. An answer key is provided at the end of the practice items section. The questions are identified in the answer key by learning outcome, so you can see what learning outcome you miss questions in and then go back and review the material again, or ask a teacher or parent for help. Read carefully and Good Luck!

Three students have collected data on the hardness of some minerals in their science lab. They used several types of materials to scratch the minerals. Their observations are shown in the chart below.

Mineral	Scratched by
shale	nail
talc	fingernail
quartz	none
feldspar	quartz

Use this chart to answer questions 1-3.

1. Which is the hardest mineral on the chart?

    A. shale
    B. talc
    C. quartz
    D. feldspar

2. Which is the softest mineral on the chart?

    A. shale
    B. talc
    C. quartz
    D. feldspar

3. Which of the minerals on the chart would be a good material for a cutting tool?

    A. shale
    B. talc
    C. quartz
    D. feldspar

Around 350 BC, Aristotle and his contemporaries made observations of the sun and stars. This information was used to construct a model of the universe in which the Earth was at the center. By 1512, the observations of Copernicus and others led to another model in which the sun was at the center of our solar system.

Use this idea to answer questions 4-5.

4. Which of the following is probably a reason for the new model of the solar system in 1512?

    A. Copernicus traveled in space.
    B. Aristotle was a careless observer.
    C. Aristotle relied on non-standard methods of observation.
    D. Copernicus had the observations of more to work with.

5. Copernicus also relied on a new technology to make his observations instead of using only his eyes. What had been invented by 1512 to look at the stars?

    A. Telescope
    B. Computer
    C. Microscope
    D. Sextant

Go on to the next page.

6. In the science lab, a number of safety items can be used to protect yourself from dangerous situations. Which of the following safety items would you expect to use every time you work in your science lab?

    A. Fire extinguisher

    B. Safety goggles

    C. Plastic gloves

    D. Rubber apron

7. Which of the following statements is an inference and not an observation?

    A. It is rough.

    B. It is white.

    C. It is wax.

    D. It floats.

8. When we unplug an appliance from the wall, we sometimes see a spark. This is an example of which of the following energy transformations?

    A. Electrical to light.

    B. Electrical to heat.

    C. Heat to light.

    D. Sound to light.

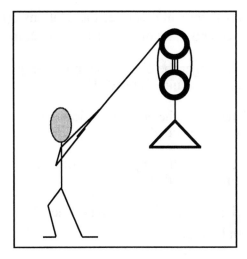

In the drawing shown above, the person is attempting to move a heavy object using a block and tackle. Using the block and tackle makes this job easier.

Answer questions 9-11 using this situation.

9. If the effort is less to move the object, what must also be true?

    A. Friction does not exist.

    B. Energy is multiplied by the machine.

    C. The rope is pulled the same distance that the object moves.

    D. The rope must be pulled further than the object moves.

10. How could the effort required be reduced even more?

    A. Take one of the pulleys out of the block and tackle.

    B. Add another pulley turn to the block and tackle.

    C. Move the pulleys closer together.

    D. Lengthen the rope.

Go on to the next page.

11. Which statement describes the relationship of force and mass in a mechanical system?

    A. The larger the object, the more complicated machine is needed.

    B. The larger the person, the less effort force is needed.

    C. The larger the object, the more effort force is needed.

    D. There is no relationship between force and mass.

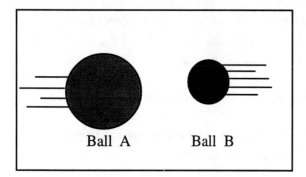

Ball A   Ball B

Shown above are two balls traveling toward each other. Questions 12-13 are related to this situation.

12. If the balls are traveling at the same speed before the collision, what is their speed after the collision?

    A. A faster than B
    B. B faster than A
    C. Both travel at the original speed
    D. Both travel slower

13. If one of the balls was to break into pieces, this would be an example of a:

    A. Chemical change
    B. Position change
    C. Physical change
    D. Kinetic change

Go on to the next page.

Consider the following food chain to answer questions 14-16.

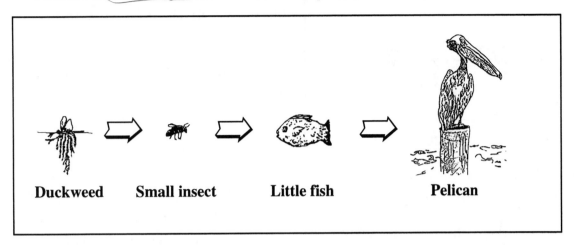

Duckweed   Small insect   Little fish   Pelican

14. In the picture above, which is the producer?

   A. Duckweed
   B. Small insect
   C. Little fish
   D. Pelican

15. Which ecological role is not represented in this food chain?

   A. Producer
   B. Consumer
   C. Secondary consumer
   D. Decomposer

16. If the lake was drained, which is most likely to be the first to disappear from the food chain at this lake?

   A. Duckweed
   B. Small insect
   C. Little fish
   D. Pelican

17. Which of the following is an observation and not an inference?

   A. 28 degrees
   B. Comfortable
   C. Good weather
   D. Too hot

18. Which of the following is the first thing to do in the case of an unknown material spilled in the lab?

   A. Get the spill kit
   B. Call the teacher
   C. Find out who is responsible
   D. Observe the substance and identify it before cleaning up

Go on to the next page.

The key below is related to questions 19-20.

A   B

A Key to Common Fasteners

1. Has a sharp end.............................go to 2.
   Blunt on both ends ....a bar.

2. Has a spiral ridge..........................go to 3.
   Is smooth the full length.................a nail.

3. Has slot on one end........a standard screw.
   Has + on one end....a phillips-head screw.

19. What is object A?

    A. bar
    B. nail
    C. standard screw
    D. phillips-head screw

20. What is object B?

    A. bar
    B. nail
    C. standard screw
    D. phillips-head screw

While walking on a city street, you notice that one side of a brick building (west) is rougher than the other (east).

Think about this situation to answer questions 21-23.

21. What is a possible explanation for this observation?

    A. The wind blows more from the east.
    B. The wind blows more from the west.
    C. The wind blows the same from all directions.
    D. The wind is not related to this observation.

22. Which could be an inference and NOT an observation.

    A. The bricks are red.
    B. The mass of each brick is about 1Kg.
    C. More weathering is occurring in the summer.
    D. Each brick is 25cm long.

23. Which of the following would NOT contribute to the weathering of the bricks?

    A. The height of the building.
    B. Acid in the rain.
    C. Amount of sunshine on the bricks.
    D. Ice build-up in the winter.

Go on to the next page.

Use the information from the following paragraph to answer questions 24-26.

A forest fire strikes an old stand of timber. Over 80% of the trees are destroyed.

24. Which of the following will probably NOT be changed?

    A. The numbers of nesting birds.
    B. The chemistry of the soil.
    C. The amount of rainfall runoff.
    D. The average rainfall.

25. What effect would the fire have on areas NOT burned?

    A. More trees growing.
    B. Greater competition for food.
    C. More rainfall runoff.
    D. More food available.

26. As time goes on, what is likely to happen to the area that was burned?

    A. It will return exactly as before.
    B. It will never grow back.
    C. The habitat will develop through competition.
    D. Everything will be extinct

27. Eventually, batteries tend to run out of energy over time. Where did the energy go?

    A. It was converted to another form.
    B. It leaks out into the air.
    C. It disappears with time
    D. The battery corroded.

Go on to the next page.

Use the following diagram to answer questions 28-30.

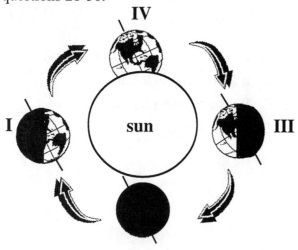

28. At which position would the Earth experience summer in the northern hemisphere?

    A. I
    B. II
    C. III
    D. IV

29. When the northern hemisphere is experiencing summer, what season is the southern hemisphere experiencing?

    A. Spring
    B. Summer
    C. Fall
    D. Winter

30. As the Earth is moving around the sun from summer to winter, what is happening to the angle of the sunlight striking the surface of the Earth in the northern hemisphere?

    A. The angle is increasing.
    B. The angle is decreasing.
    C. The angle is staying the same.
    D. There is no relationship between the angle of the sun and the earth's rotation.

Use the following chart to answer questions 31-32.

Wavelengths of Light in a Vacuum	
Color	Wavelength
Red	greater than 6.1×10^{-7}m
Orange	5.9 to 6.1×10^{-7}m
Yellow	5.7 to 5.9×10^{-7}m
Green	5.0 to 5.7×10^{-7}m
Blue	4.5 to 5.0×10^{-7}m
Violet	less than 4.5×10^{-7}m

31. Which wavelength of light has the shortest wavelength?

    A. Red
    B. Green
    C. Blue
    D. Violet

32. Human eyes are capable of seeing these colors in balance. We see the sky in the absence of clouds as blue. Which is a possible reason?

    A. Blue light travels further.
    B. The atmosphere absorbs more of the other wavelengths.
    C. Human eyes see blue first.
    D. The sun produces mostly blue light.

Go on to the next page.

Think about the following situation to answer questions 33-35.

Two species of insect live on a tree. Insect A is a diverse population genetically. Insect B is a population of genetically identical individuals.

33. Which population is the result of sexual reproduction?

    A. Insect A
    B. Insect B
    C. Both Insects
    D. Neither Insect

34. If the environment were to remain the same for a long period of time, which insect population would probably dominate the habitat?

    A. A
    B. B
    C. Neither A or B
    D. Not enough information is given

35. If the habitat changed suddenly, which population of insects would be best prepared, genetically speaking, to survive the change?

    A. A
    B. B
    C. Neither
    D. Not enough information.

Use the passage to answer questions 36-38.

For many years, before refrigeration, people noticed that fly larvae (maggots) would appear from inside meats in the marketplace. They believed that the flies spontaneously generated from the meat. In 1668, an Italian physician Francesco Redi performed an experiment to test this. He used a jar open to the air and another covered with a fine screen. No flies appeared on the meat in the second jar.

36. Which might he have concluded from this experiment?

    A. Flies lay eggs on meat.
    B. Maggots do not come directly from meat.
    C. Maggots come from meat.
    D. Flies eat meat.

37. He also observed that flies were visiting the meat in the open jar. What could he infer from this?

    A. Flies lay eggs on the meat.
    B. Maggots do not come directly from meat.
    C. Maggots come from meat.
    D. Flies do not eat meat.

38. Redi's work along with many others has helped us in our understanding of nature. Which of the following is supported by Redi's work?

    A. Energy is conserved.
    B. Genes are passed from parent to offspring.
    C. Fermentation is caused by microorganisms.
    D. Maggots spontaneously generated from rotting meat.

Use the following information to answer questions 39-41.

Since energy is required to power machines, change our environment, etc., it is an important resource. Oil has become one of the most prized of these resources. It is highly toxic and is created by thousands of years of decay. Coal is another such resource. Trees stored up the energy that eventually were made into coal. Much of the world uses wood for heating their homes, and to cook. The choice to use these energy resources is a risk-benefit situation.

39. Which is not one of the risks of using oil or coal for energy?

A. It is toxic

B. Getting it disturbs the environment

C. It gives a great amount of energy per gram

D. Accidental spills are destructive to the environment

40. Which is not a benefit of using oil.

A. Many of our vehicles use oil

B. Once gone, there is no way to renew the resource

C. It is cheaper than solar power

D. Oil does not depend on the weather like wind power

41. Harvesting trees for energy can be done

many ways. Why is the management of forests important?

A. Trees are cheap and grow on their own

B. There are enough trees to last forever

C. Trees are not really good for anything else

D. Wood is only a renewable resource if it includes replanting

42. Plant and animal cells are different. Which is not a difference between animals and plants?

A. Both plants and animals have a nucleus

B. Plant cells have a cell wall

C. Animals move to adjust to changing conditions

D. Plants have chlorophyll

43. Which of the following devices could be used to measure the volume of a container?

A. A stopwatch

B. A compass

C. A meter stick

D. A thermometer

Use the following information to answer

Go on to the next page.

questions 44-46.

Technology can be defined as any invention or process which makes it easier to do something. Examples could be machines, scientific methods, or tools. Often, these technologies lead to even more technologies in later years.

44. The metric or SI system of measurement is based on which number?

  A. 5
  B. 8
  C. 10
  D. 12

45. Which of the following technologies began with Leonardo DaVinci's fascination with bird's wings?

  A. The airfoil
  B. Helicopters
  C. Submarines
  D. Jet engines

46. The most important technology in history was the:

  A. Airplane
  B. Car
  C. Plow
  D. Corn

47. A scientist returned from the rain forest.

Which of the following is one of his inferences and not an observation?

  A. The average rainfall was 12 cm/ month.
  B. Rainfall is directly related to mold amount.
  C. Mold count was 4312 on May 22.
  D. Pollen was seen on many tropical leaves in mid-afternoon.

48. Which statement is not true about the relationship between the Earth and the moon?

  A. The moon is related to the tides.
  B. The moon occasionally passes its shadow across the Earth in a solar eclipse.
  C. The moon revolves around the Earth in 28 days.
  D. The phases of the moon are caused by the shadow of the Earth.

Use the following information to answer

Go on to the next page.

Use the following information to answer questions 49-51.

Organism	Legs	Habitat	Body Covering	Wings
Butterfly	6	Deciduous Forest	scales	yes
Hummingbird	2	Deciduous Forest	feathers	yes
Deer	4	Deciduous Forest	hair	no
Maple Tree	0	Deciduous Forest	bark	yes (on seed)
Ferns	0	Deciduous Forest	cuticle	no

49. Which of the above characteristics of woodland organisms could not be used in a key?

   A. Legs
   B. Habitat
   C. Body Covering
   D. Wings

50. Which is the best characteristic to use in a key?

   A. Legs
   B. Habitat
   C. Body Covering
   D. Wings

51. Which characteristic could be added to this chart to tell plants from animals?

   A. Presence of chlorophyll.
   B. Ability to reproduce.
   C. Uses Oxygen.
   D. Produces wastes.

Use the following diagrams of pendulums to answer questions 52-54.

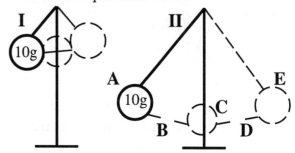

52. At which position is the potential energy (energy of position) the greatest?
   A. A
   B. B
   C. C
   D. D

53. As the balls swing, which one will make it back to its original position (A) first?
   A. I
   B. II
   C. Same time
   D. Not enough information.

54. Eventually, both pendulums will stop. Where did all of the energy go?
   A. Chemical energy
   B. Kinetic Energy
   C. Heat energy
   D. Gravity

Go on to the next page.

55. In any mechanical system, such as a simple machine, if you are able to make the effort easier, what will you usually give up?

    A. Friction

    B. Speed

    C. Distance

    D. You don't give up anything

56. Which of the following is an example of a nonrenewable resource?

    A. Trees

    B. Water

    C. Sunlight

    D. Iron

Use the information from the following paragraph to answer questions 57-59.

    Since the middle part of this century, scientists have been studying the plates that make up the crust of the Earth. These explorations have given us answers about volcanoes, earthquakes, and deep sea trenches.

57. Where, relative to a plate, would you expect to see a volcano?

    A. In the middle of a plate.

    B. Near the edge of a plate.

    C. On the edge of a plate.

    D. These are not related.

58. Earthquakes occur when:

    A. Plates slip past each other.

    B. Plates build up energy.

    C. Plates stay still.

    D. Only when volcanoes erupt.

59. Which is an observation and not an inference?

    A. Plates may be several miles thick.

    B. Plate deformation caused mountains.

    C. There was once one supercontinent.

    D. Quakes measuring between 1 and 3 are frequent in California.

60. Standing on ice, a person's feet go one way and their body goes the other way when a person falls. Which statement explains this?

    A. The mass is directly related to the force needed to move an object.

    B. An object at rest remains unless acted on by an unbalanced force.

    C. The reaction force is equal to the action force.

    D. The closer are two objects, the greater the gravity between them.

Go on to the next page.

For questions 61-62, consider the following situation swinging a baseball bat.

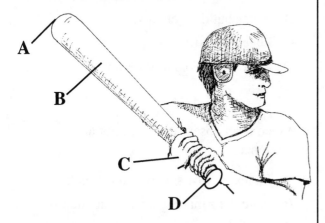

61. Where is the fulcrum of this lever?

    A. D
    B. C
    C. B
    D. A

62. Using this lever, the batter gains speed. What does the batter have to give or sacrifice to gain the speed?

    A. Quickness
    B. Distance
    C. Time
    D. Effort

Use the information from the following situation to answer questions 63-64.

   In tight corners on roads and streets, a mirror is frequently mounted so that it is visible from both directions. Sometimes the mirror is flat and sometimes it is curved.

63. Which property of light makes this mirror so helpful?

    A. Light speed changes slightly when it moves through glass.
    B. Light reflects at the same angle that it hits a reflective surface.
    C. Light moves at 3.00 x 10m/s.
    D. Different colors have different wave-lengths.

64. Often, the message printed on a mirror is "Objects may be closer than they appear". What do you expect this mirror to look like to produce this distortion?

    A. The mirror is curved.
    B. The mirror is small.
    C. The mirror is large.
    D. The mirror is placed high on a wall.

Go on to the next page.

Use the following food web to answer questions 63-65.

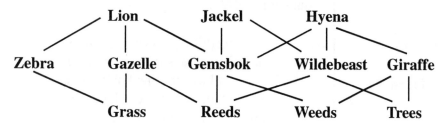

65. Which organism receives energy from gazelles?

    A. Grasses

    B. Giraffes

    C. Lions

    D. Zebras

66. Which organism probably has the smallest population?

    A. Grasses

    B. Giraffes

    C. Zebras

    D. Lions

67. In a drought year, the grasses may not be as plentiful in the area. Which population is at the greatest risk for survival?

    A. Grasses

    B. Giraffes

    C. Zebras

    D. Lions

Use the following Punnett Square to answer questions 68-69.

Possible Genotypes for Pea Plants

T=tall   t=short

	T	t
T	TT	Tt
t	Tt	tt

68. What is the genotype of a short plant?

    I. TT
    II. Tt
    III. tt

    A. I only

    B. I and II only

    C. III only

    D. II and III only

69. What percentage of the offspring in this cross for pea plants will be short?

    A. 25%

    B. 50%

    C. 75%

    D. 100%

Go on to the next page.

70. Which of the following is an inference and not an observation?

    A. The science proficiency test has 45 questions.
    B. About 50% of the students failed the test in 1996.
    C. Proficiency test questions have four choices.
    D. Schools only teach students half of the science they need.

71. Some plant eaters, such as cows have extra stomachs in which to hold microorganisms. From this observation, which might be concluded?

    A. Only microorganisms can digest plants.
    B. Microorganisms can aid digestion.
    C. Microorganisms absorb nutrients for the cow.
    D. Cows have shorter digestive tracts.

72. The dissolving of sugar in a cup of hot water is an example of which kind of change?

    A. Physical change
    B. Chemical change
    C. Heat exchange
    D. None of the above

73. Which of the following use sugar for cellular energy?

    A. Plants only
    B. Animals only
    C. Both Plants and Animals
    D. Neither Plants or Animals

Use the following situation to answer questions 74-75.

> The oil spill in Prince William Sound added hundreds of barrels of toxic crude oil to a marine habitat inhabited by many types of plants and animals. Sea birds, fish, whales, otters and others were effected by the spill.

74. In addition to the animals listed in the paragraph, what else was effected?

    A. Sea weed
    B. Algae
    C. Turtles
    D. Everything in the ecosystem was effected

75. How long will it be before the Sound returns to its state before the spill?

    A. 10 Years
    B. 50 Years
    C. 100 Years
    D. It will never be exactly the same.

76. As sunlight is captured by a solar cell, it is converted from radiant energy to:

    A. Electrical energy
    B. Chemical energy
    C. Potential energy
    D. It could be converted into A, B, or C.

Go on to the next page.

77. Which of the following is not a benefit of the invention of the computer?

   A. More people have access to advanced calculating methods.

   B. More homework is expected to be typed.

   C. Communication methods use many types of information.

   D. Design graphics can be more standardized.

STOP.

Answer Key

	Answer	Learning Outcome		Answer	Learning Outcome
1.	C	(7)	42.	A	(14)
2.	B	(7)	43.	C	(4)
3.	C	(12)	44.	C	(4)
4.	D	(17)	45.	A	(19)
5.	A	(19)	46.	C	(19)
6.	B	(3)	47.	B	(2)
7.	C	(2)	48.	D	(6)
8.	A	(10)	49.	B	(1)
9.	D	(8)	50.	C	(1)
10.	B	(8)	51.	A	(14)
11.	C	(9)	52.	A	(10)
12.	B	(9)	53.	A	(9)
13.	C	(12)	54.	C	(10)
14.	A	(13)	55.	C	(8)
15.	D	(13)	56.	D	(18)
16.	D	(20)	57.	B	(5)
17.	A	(2)	58.	A	(5)
18.	B	(3)	59.	D	(2)
19.	C	(1)	60.	C	(9)
20.	D	(1)	61.	A	(8)
21.	A	(5)	62.	D	(8)
22.	C	(2)	63.	B	(11)
23.	A	(5)	64.	A	(11)
24.	D	(20)	65.	C	(13)
25.	B	(20)	66.	C	(13)
26.	C	(20)	67.	C	(13)
27.	A	(10)	68.	C	(15)
28.	C	(6)	69.	A	(15)
29.	D	(6)	70.	D	(2)
30.	B	(6)	71.	B	(16)
31.	D	(11)	72.	A	(12)
32.	B	(11)	73.	C	(14)
33.	A	(16)	74.	D	(20)
34.	B	(15)	75.	D	(20)
35.	A	(15)	76.	D	(10)
36.	B	(17)	77.	B	(19)
37.	A	(17)			
38.	C	(17)			
39.	C	(18)			
40.	B	(18)			
41.	D	(18)			

Englefield & Arnold Publishing • P.O. Box 341348 • 6344 Nicholas Drive • Columbus, OH 43234-1348

Phone: (614) 764-1211 • 1-877-PASSING (727-7464) • **Fax:** (614) 764-1311 • **Internet:** www.eapublishing.com

Ship To ATTN:	Bill To ATTN:
School/Business:	School/Business:
Address:	Address:
City: State: Zip:	City: State: Zip:
Phone: ( )	Phone: ( )

Grades K-1 (Available January, 2000)

Qty	Item	Description	Price	Total
	102	Teacher Edition	16.95	
	103	Student Workbook	10.95	
	199	Classroom Set	275.00*	

4th Grade Products

Qty	Item	Description	Price	Total
	404	Teacher Edition	16.95	
	405	Student Workbook	10.95	
	406	Answer Key Booklet	3.00	
	407	Classroom Set	275.00*	
	412	Mathematics Flash Cards	10.95	
	413	Citizenship Flash Cards	10.95	
	414	Science Flash Cards	10.95	
	415	Reading/Writing Flash Cards	10.95	
	426	Software - Version 2.0	39.95	
	426L	Software/Lab Pack (5 CDs)	149.95*	
	426S	Software/Site License (30 CDs)	599.95*	

6th Grade Products

Qty	Item	Description	Price	Total
	601	Teacher Edition	16.95	
	602	Student Workbook	10.95	
	603	Answer Key Booklet	3.00	
	699	Classroom Set	275.00*	
	604	Math Masters	29.95	
	612	Mathematics Flash Cards	10.95	
	613	Citizenship Flash Cards	10.95	
	614	Science Flash Cards	10.95	
	615	Reading/Writing Flash Cards	10.95	
	626	Software - Version 2.0	39.95	
	626L	Software/Lab Pack (5 CDs)	149.95*	
	626S	Software/Site License (30 CDs)	599.95*	

9th Grade Products

Qty	Item	Description	Price	Total
	900	Student Book	16.95	
	912	Mathematics Flash Cards	10.95	
	913	Citizenship Flash Cards	10.95	
	914	Science Flash Cards	10.95	
	915	Reading/Writing Flash Cards	10.95	
	926	Software - Version 2.0	39.95	
	926L	Software/Lab Pack (5 CDs)	149.95*	
	926S	Software/Site License (30 CDs)	599.95*	

12th Grade Product (Available January, 2000)

Qty	Item	Description	Price	Total
	1200	Passing with Honors	24.95	

The Ohio Proficiency Press™ Newsletter (4 issues per year)

Qty	Item	Description	Price	Total
	100	Newsletter subscription	14.00*	

Method of Payment:

___ Check/money order   Ck # _____

___ Purchase Order   P.O. # _____

___ Tax Exempt   Tax I.D.# _____

___ Credit card: ___ Visa ___ M/C ___ Discover

Card #: _____

Expiration Date: _____ / _____

Signature: _____

Quantity Discounts

Qty	Discount
1 – 29	0%
30 – 49	10%
50 – 199	15%
200 or more	20%

Shipping

Qty	Rate	Qty	Rate
1-2	$4.00	11-15	$8.00
3-5	4.50	16-20	10.00
6-8	5.00	21-29	14.00
9-10	6.00	30 +	4%

Total Ordered	
Quantity Discount*	
Tax (5.75%)	
Shipping	
Total Due	

* Discount does not apply to already discounted classroom sets, lab packs, site licenses, and the newsletter.

Prices Subject to Change